Tokyo to Tokyo

A Cycling Adventure Around
Japan

Daniel Doughty

DSD UK Publishing

Tokyo to Tokyo

First Published in Great Britain - 2016

Copyright© Daniel Doughty, 2016

Published by DSD UK Publishing
www.tokyo-to-tokyo.com
dsd_uk@yahoo.co.uk

Copy-edited by In-Scribe
Cover by Gillian Hibbs
Map by Daniel Doughty

ISBN: 978-0-9955534-0-8

In loving memory of Grandad Ben,
may the happiness you shone never fade.

PROLOGUE

Being a farm hand in the splendour of rural England wasn't all it was cracked up to be... having said that, a face full of dog excrement can change a man's life in so many ways. Coming home from work every day soaked in cow shit wasn't strange for me, it was just a way of life. But *dog* shit? There was a definite line... and that line had just been well and truly crossed.

Whilst strimming the side of a river bank, the fluorescent nylon blades cut into something dark, devious and calculating that was rooted deep within the grass's hidden depths. Mere milliseconds later and my life would be changed forever. The smell was an unholy one; born of sin. The taste? Just plain treacherous.

That night I went home and thought long and hard. I needed to do something different with my life; some form of sabbatical, maybe? The kind preferably from which there was little chance of return.

I'd recently hit 30 years of age and it was becoming apparent that my life was all but over. I cast my mind back to my alcohol-fuelled, backpacking twenties. Still a blurry time, to this day, but from what I can just about recall, it was one of the greatest periods of my life. Yet, the allure of backpacking had long since waned; getting drunk and jumping on a bus from one town to the next was all too easy. If I was to ever travel again it would need to be with some sort of purpose. It need not necessarily be to my *own* advantage and it sure as hell needed to be a challenge.

Maybe I could walk around Ireland with a wheelie bin? No, too quirky.

How about walking the Appalachian Trail with a man called Dogz? No, too many bears.

Go to Bury St. Edmunds for a drug binge? No, I'm 33 - too old for drugs now.

How about I travel the entirety of the Welsh coast on a giraffe? No, too original.

But I did like the idea of travelling upon some sort of vessel, that much was certain. *Well ok, that's a step*, I thought.

I could cycle to Siberia? No, I hate the cold… but… I *do* like bicycles.

Now I was getting somewhere. A bicycle trip would be delightful… probably.

So I would cycle somewhere… *but where?*

I chucked Takashi Miike's *Ichi the Killer* into the DVD player and watched the blood flow. I sometimes find that watching violent Japanese cinema helps me to think; films that for the most part contradict the very character of your everyday Japanese. For they are a humble folk, courteous and kind - with an etiquette like no other I had ever stumbled across upon my travels. In fact, Japan was a country that I'd always had a bit of an affinity towards: cutting edge technology, exquisite cuisine, eclectic cinema, zany game shows, Anime and, of course, *Final Fantasy VII*.

I was lucky enough to have spent several months there in 2009, a couple of them living the fast life in Tokyo - whilst working in a hostel - and the rest of the time I spent rice farming. That's right, I was once a rice farmer! In the wilds of Ibaraki Prefecture, just a few hours north of Tokyo, I lived and worked alongside a Japanese family, as I learned the rice farming ropes. The hours were long and the work arduous. The heat of the Japanese summer months were far from forgiving. It was a long way from home and a long way from family and friends, but thankfully I was made to feel like one of the family. The kindness that I encountered was amazing.

Yet, during my time there I still felt like I'd barely scratched the surface of a country that although not girthy, is almost as long as the United States of America. There was still so much to explore, I hadn't even seen Mt. Fuji… now who goes to Japan and manages to avoid Mt. Fuji? Well, I did. It's a bit like going to Paris and not seeing the Eiffel Towel or going to Cairo and knocking the Pyramids on the head.

Meanwhile... in *Ichi the Killer*, Kakihara had just finished lopping off his tongue in front of his Yakuza bosses... and it was at this point that I'd come to a firm decision: I should cycle around Japan. I really should.

During the following days, weeks and months - whilst not feasting upon dog muck - I conjured up a plan of attack. It would appear that the most popular route for cycling Japan was tip-to-toe, from its northernmost point in Cape Sōya on the island of Hokkaidō, to Cape Sata some 1,700 miles to the south on the island of Kyūshū... or vice versa. This is said to take between 2-3 months and whilst this all sounded very lavish, it had already been done a thousand times over. I wanted to at least spice up my journey somehow and do something a little different; perhaps more engaging.

I popped Kinji Fukasaku's *Battle Royale* into the DVD player. Maybe a little mindless violence would help me out at a time when I craved some much needed inspiration. The film is about a bunch of high school students who are sent to an island by an authoritarian Japanese government to fight one another; after a series of brutal and merciless deaths, the sole survivor is crowned as supreme student.

Japan has many islands, 6,852 to be precise. Maybe I could cycle to every single one? *A teacher knives his student.* No, that would be far too spicy. Each island however is part of a prefecture; the equivalent to a county, state, territory or a province. Japan has 47 of these said prefectures that span a total land mass of 145,925 square miles. *A child's head explodes in front of his classmates.* Eureka! I'll cycle to every prefecture! Every single one.

I praised Fukasaku for his kind inspiration, God rest his soul.

I conducted some research but couldn't find details - in English - on anyone that had attempted what I was intending to do. Not one. I then asked my Japanese friend to check to see if any Japanese people had done it. Many, apparently, but no Westerners, especially no silly Englishman. None that had lived to tell the tale, anyway.

Somebody once said 'live every day like it's your last,' personally I find that thought vulgar, much preferring to 'live every *year* like it's your last.' So, in that sense, maybe my life wasn't over just yet. Perhaps what the other thing they say is correct though, 'life begins at 30.' Or was it 40? Fuck it, it doesn't matter, I'm going to Tokyo and my pushbike is coming with me. From there I will cycle, Tokyo to Tokyo.

TOKYO TO TOKYO
ROUTE AND PREFECTURE GUIDE

KEY

━ : ROUTE TAKEN
● : OVERNIGHTED

100 MILES

TABLE OF CONTENTS

PROLOGUE, iv

1. Tokyo, Page 11
2. Saitama, Page 16
3. Chiba, Page 25
4. Ibaraki, Page 39
5. Tochigi, Page 44
6. Fukushima, Page 54
7. Miyagi, Page 62
8. Iwate, Page 73
9.1 Aomori, Page 93
10. Hokkaido, Page 99
9.2 Aomori, Page 143
11. Akita, Page 154
12. Yamagata, Page 162
13. Niigata, Page 173
14.1 Nagano, Page 181
15. Gunma, Page 186
14.2 Nagano, Page 192
16. Gifu, Page 202
17. Toyama, Page 207
18. Ishikawa, Page 210
19. Fukui, Page 216
20. Shiga, Page 220
21.1 Kyoto, Page 224
22.1 Hyogo, Page 229
23. Okayama, Page 234
24. Kagawa, Page 238
25. Tokushima, Page 244
26. Kochi, Page 248

27. Ehime, Page 260

28. Hiroshima, Page 265

29. Oita, Page 272

30. Miyazaki, Page 277

31. Kagoshima, Page 282

32. Okinawa, Page 291

33. Kumamoto, Page 302

34. Nagasaki, Page 309

35. Saga, Page 315

36. Fukuoka, Page 316

37. Yamaguchi, Page 321

38. Shimane, Page 324

39. Tottori, Page 328

22.2 Hyogo & 21.2 Kyoto, Page 331

40. Osaka, Page 335

41. Nara, Page 340

42. Wakayama, Page 345

43. Mie, Page 353

44. Aichi, Page 358

45. Shizuoka, Page 366

46. Yamanashi, Page 373

47. Kanagawa, Page 376

EPILOGUE, 380

ACKNOWLEDGEMENTS, 382

1. TOKYO
東京

The expressway into Tokyo was like a race course as the bus driver weaved around hairpin bends into a series of dimly lit tunnels from the suburbs; deep into the beating heart of the city. He was pedal to the metal like Schumacher... Ralf Schumacher. Below deck in storage, I began to fear for my bike's general well-being as I heard things sliding and rattling about. To get it this far and for it to get battered now would be a major blow.

The driver had been hesitant about putting my bike in the stowaway compartment, so maybe he was going out of his way now to prove a point, as he swerved around another hell-raising bend at about 70mph. My bike had been padded down with foam and wrapped in a plastic bag - I hoped I'd taken enough precautions to prevent any knocks. *Maybe I should have just cycled from the airport?* But I'd had a sleepless 38-hour transition from Heathrow to Narita, and to cycle another 50 miles on top of that, all the way into central Tokyo during rush hour would have been asking for trouble.

Or maybe you're just being lazy, Daniel? Well it was too late now anyway... the damage was done. I'd just have to bite the bullet and face whatever consequences would be due at the other end.

Or more than likely, just weep.

My stop was in Shinjuku, one of the busiest districts of Tokyo, if not the world. To stress that fact, its train station sees an average of 3.5 million people pass through its turnstiles every day: to work, shop, learn, dine, drink, love... and live.

As I stepped off the bus and onto the sidewalk, I felt like an ant amongst the sprawling skyscrapers that patterned my surrounds. People flustered past and I was given no time to breathe as my bike was pulled out from under the bus's storage compartment and hoisted onto the sidewalk. I muscled through the crowd desperately towards my prized possession, like a man who had just had his winning Lotto ticket swept away by the wind. As I scooped up my steed, a woman stepped out from the crowd and asked me a question in Japanese, looking into my eyes with some concern. I had no idea what she said, though. Despite having spent time in the country six years ago, I had picked up only a little of the lingo. I could only hope that the language would eventually return to me.

I surmised that she was asking me if I was all right, yet instead of giving any concrete answer, I shamefully blushed. She in turn did the same, before bowing politely, apologising in English and disappearing back into the masses. I was going to have to sharpen up if I was to succeed in this game, that much was certain.

Away from the hoards, I propped up my bike against the wall, as the moment of truth had finally arrived. I began to unsheathe it from its packaging and noticed that everything looked intact. I straightened the handlebars, popped the peddles on and inflated the tyres, then took a step back; bumping into a business man in the process. No knives were drawn as we both instinctively apologised to one another, the man telling me that I had a nice bike. I thanked him, before returning to give it the once over. *Had it really just survived a 6,000 mile journey across the globe?* It was almost emotional, I didn't know whether to laugh, cry or jizz - or a little of each simultaneously. I chose none of the above, a wry smile being more than enough to cater for the moment in hand.

I then attached the handlebar and rear panniers, and loaded my bike up with the only possessions I could take for the whole journey: a puncture repair kit, a bicycle pump, spare inner tubes, combi spanners, a sleeping bag, waterproofs, a hyperthermia blanket, tent, t-shirts, slacks, pants, socks, a first aid kit, a map book, a Japanese dictionary, water bottles and - most importantly - extra pants for the typhoon season.

Effectively, I was good to go, and I began to cycle towards my hostel, hugging the sidewalks like a scared pup. I moved slowly yet wistfully through one of the most bustling metropolises in the world; everything for a moment just felt so right. The build up to this point had played upon my mind for many, many months. I was at the beginning of something and to finally be in Tokyo was nothing short of bliss. For in Tokyo, every day was a new adventure.

It was hard to believe that this massively vibrant city, positively choking with life, was once just a tiny fishing village - Edo - that sat sleepily on the edge of the Pacific. This village would in time rise to prominence in the 16th Century with the arrival of Tokugawa Ieyasu, the ruler of the Tokugawa Shogunate. It was here that the Shogun would claim Edo as his base and thus it became the political and cultural centre of the country. Later, in 1868, following in the Shogunates footsteps, Emperor Meiji would move from Kyoto to Edo where the rapidly expanding city would become the nation's current capital: Tokyo. Ruling from here would put Tokyo firmly on the path to becoming the hive of activity that it is today. It is a city that houses some 13.35 million citizens, but the Greater Tokyo Area brings the grand total to a staggering 37.8 million inhabitants: the highest concentration of people on Earth.

In Tokyo there is something for everyone: in Shibuya, millions flood its famed and manic Shibuya Crossing every day in the name of shopping and entertainment. At night, the streets are dressed to the nines as the latest victims of fashion enjoy a top-end range of nightclubs, karaoke joints and izakayas (Japanese pubs) - amongst the constant glare of neon. A stone's throw north and Harajuku attracts an equally cumbersome crowd of adolescent fashion seekers desperate for something that they haven't got. Next door is Yoyogi Park, one of Tokyo's finest; in spring you'll witness the marvel of the cherry blossoms where thousands congregate to toast

Nature's splendour. Venture north and you'll reach the vibrant and glitzy Shinjuku – it houses the largest red light district in Japan with the predominantly Yakuza-run Kabukichō. Here you'll find a number of entwining alleys lined with host and hostess bars where one can pay for the exclusive company of the opposite sex - to engage in a night of false camaraderie. Sex is absolutely and 100% off the table, though - unless you happen to find your way to one of the area's numerous love hotels where horned-up couples can spend a few hours - or the whole night - getting their rocks off.

Head farther east and you'll stumble across all manner of attractions such as Akihabara, a.k.a. Electric Town, here even the most anal of geeks can become fully nerded-up as every shop offers the latest and even most prehistoric of gadgets, gizmos and video games. Close by is Ginza; for the plush and dapper: a business district dominated by salarymen and women with a few added designer stores for upper-class measure.

A little closer to the mighty Arakawa River - which spews diligently into the Tokyo Bay - one will find Tsukiji Fish Market: the biggest of its kind, it processes over 2,000 tonnes of fish product every day. Arrive early enough and you'll see the auctions, where for a mere £25,000 you can get yourself a bluefin tuna for breakfast. And if that's too much for the moth-lined wallet, then you'll have to just settle for the freshest sushi in town.

Meandering north, along the Arakawa, you'll arrive in a familiar haunt of mine: Asakusa. It was here that I once worked in a hostel for a couple of months. One of the oldest parts of the city, it houses the much visited Sensō-ji Buddhist Temple. Yet away from the clickity fingers and broad daylight camera flashes of the tourist droves, one will happen across the quietest and most laid back of areas in the city. A decadence of a bygone age still heavily encapsulated, one that beguiles and removes any traces of the hasty 'live fast, die young' lifestyle of many a Tokyoite. Here I have always found sanctuary, and here I will always return.

For close to two weeks I would indulge in the delights of Tokyo, quite easily managing to spunk a fifth of my savings. After discovering this heinous fact, I realised that I couldn't delay the core of my journey any longer; my immediate departure would now become inevitable. I needed to get my spokes in motion or the city would swallow me up whole and spit me out. I wouldn't be the first and certainly wouldn't be the last. The flamboyant lifestyle of the Tokyoite is a far from enriching one for a simple man such as myself, but then I was in the most expensive city in the world, *what did I expect?*

I pulled on my socks, 'Daniel' they read. *That's me* I noted, before staring out into space with a sudden loss of agenda. *Could I really pull this off? Who was I trying to kid?* Well I guess there was only one way to find out.

2. SAITAMA
埼玉県

Asakusa – Kawagoe
63 miles

Saitama Prefecture sits northwest of Tokyo, a prefecture commonly referred to by folk as *'dasaitama'* (uncooltama), due to its apparent lack of attractions. It made sense to tackle Saitama first, as I planned to end my journey on a high by visiting the likes of Shizuoka (Mt.Fuji) and Kanagawa (Yokohama). And so, after such gratuitous eye candy, it seemed like somewhat of a drag to venture all the way over to a prefecture that boasted a vast array of sweet fuck all. But Saitama would certainly be able to act as an early trial to test my metal, before the real fun and games began. *Little did I know that they were just about to begin, effective immediately.*

The night before I was going to scale an attack upon Saitama, the weather forecasts were telling me that the wind was going to be completely off its tits. I'd already fallen down a flight of stairs during the past week and that was without the aid of wind. I must confess, I was a little nervous from the outset.

There was also a reluctance to leave Tokyo, it is a place in which I feel very comfortable. It is diverse, vast, unique and inviting with streets that you could spend a lifetime exploring. A city in which there is truly something around every corner. Not to mention the fact that I had already made a few good friends, something that is always welcome when usually my communication skills are about as useful as a dead hedgehog's. But…. I had an agenda and something of a plan – so I had to forge on.

I would start my journey from Asakusa along the banks of the Arakawa River, one of the main rivers running through

Tokyo. The source of the river begins its journey in my current destination - the mountains of Chichibu - from there the river flows for some 107 miles through Saitama and into Tokyo, before emptying its load into the Tokyo Bay.

I hated it instantly. The wind howled off the face of the water and made my first day on the road a pure, soul destroying misery. An impaling 30mph north-westerly gale tackled me head-on for a bulk of the day; its compassion remorseless. This was obviously a concern for me the night before and I had actually enquired into staying an extra night at the hostel, but unfortunately they were fully booked. Hence it was a 'tough shit, eat shit' scenario.

Averaging some 6mph into the wind, I found myself going nowhere slowly. Ball bags to say I was quite unhappy with life. *Was this all really going to be worth it?* But I couldn't always blame the elements, there was a whole contingent of possibilities every step of the way that could mess-up one's plans. In Urawa, for example, I had initially planned to spend the evening watching the most heavily supported football team in Japan: the Urawa Red Diamonds. But I discovered the game was to be played behind closed doors, as they were being punished by the J-League, due to the fact that the fans of the Diamonds had just recently been labelled as racists. They had been protesting against the club's Serbian manager by brandishing banners that read 'Japanese Only.' This was after a string of poor results, and they were understandably irked. This kind of incident though is not something that sits so comfortably on an International sporting scale, and therefore - quite rightly - a red card was dealt to the club's supporters.

With my sporting plans dashed, I had to continue along the Arakawa. Tokyo's urban sprawl made me wonder if the city actually had an ending at all or if it was just some kind of mythical concrete beast that grew ever larger by the day.

As dusk crept along, the chances of my making it to Chichibu before sundown became nothing more than a marred vision.

Yet, if I continued to hack away at the wind, I should eventually end up in an old settlement called Kawagoe. En route I would run into some troublesome roads; narrow and absent of any pavement or hard shoulder, dimly lit with traffic flowing heavily in both directions. Thinking of this scenario, a mushy version of myself suddenly became a strong possibility. I countered this scene by closing my eyes and thinking about lesbians for a while - before sometime later coming across my first Japanese expressway. An intimidating sight by the light of day, at nighttime they could quite easily be deemed: Highways to Hell! Thankfully there was a sidewalk for cyclists and a protective barrier, to try and convince the motorists not to murder the cyclists.

Seeing a sign for Kawagoe brought a sigh of relief though, and upon arriving there, I would have to find somewhere to make camp. This is not always an easy task, but in a perverse sense I do kind of enjoy it. However, the last thing I wanted whilst trying to get my head down for the night is a shovel to the head or to wake up missing a few toes, due to some hungry rodents... or fellow hobos!

I scouted around for a bit and then found a car park with a big tree and bit of greenery underneath it. It had my name metaphorically written all over it: 'BUM'.

It was a cold, cold night and I slept uneasy in my one-man tent, thinking how, the night before, I was in a nice warm and cosy bar in Tokyo, chatting up beautiful Japanese ladies with the unsuccessful ease of a third-tier Macedonian football club taking on a Premier League giant. Yet, regardless of my errorneous charms it was warm and comfortable there, something that should never be taken for granted when one is freezing one's bollocks off in a parking lot.

Yet this was my choice... I had to keep reminding myself of that.

Kawagoe – Chichibu
50 miles

Towards the end of my second day on the road, I found myself winding down in the cafeteria of a modestly-sized supermarket. A hot coffee from the vending machine should have perked me up, however having pressed the wrong button on the machine's display panel, I had to settle for a very unseasonal and uninspiring iced coffee. I'd had very little sleep the night before in Kawagoe, due to the cold, and tonight would be no exception. I was also under the shadow of a boisterous looking Mt. Buko. As soon as the sun had submerged beyond the horizon, a spell would be cast across the land turning it into what felt like an ice planet. My marbles clung together tighter than ever before; like a pair of long lost North Korean relatives reunited for the first time in a countless number of years.

Yet the day would start off pleasantly enough, daylight allowing me to have a cycle tour around Kawagoe. It almost seemed quaint for a city, but still boasted a population of some 340,000 or so.

The city was traditionally known as 'Little Edo,' meaning Little Tokyo and it's renowned for its *kurazukuri* style wooden warehouses and sweet potato candy stores. I was up and about too early to sample the goods, so had settle for a traditional 7-Eleven egg muffin and a packet of donuts. I know, I'm terrible, I truly am.

Heading out of the city and back in the direction of Chichibu saw me encroach upon a tremendously terrible highway. I noticed that the general rule of thumb between motorist and cyclist is a mutual agreement that there is *no* mutual agreement between motorist and cyclist. I also saw that many a sidewalk was encumbered with a mass of bumps and holes, exposed storm drains, broken glass and all sorts of puncture-orientated material. This makes for a nerve-racking cycling experience. My brand-new, virginal bike, had been purchased from sunny Swansea, but only after a day of heavy workout, it was already showing signs of wear and tear: brake pads sticking, an anonymous knocking noise and clunky gears as soon as I hit a slope. This was a bad start for the Ridgeback: I felt a love/hate relationship setting in.

Away from the highway and onward towards the small rural town of Ogawa, I was accompanied by clear skies and a prevalent sun; the wind having died down somewhat since yesterday. Ogawa was a sleepy sort of a place: locals tended to their smallholdings, an elderly man walked his limping dog, an archaic petrol station sat lifeless whilst independent traders sold their wares at their own pace; opening and closing their stores as they pleased.

Beyond the assortment of farming plots, a coniferous woodland range took hold, merging up into mountains that raucously dominated the surrounding landscape.

My climb up to Chichibu would be my first bout of real physical and demanding exercise. Prior to the expedition I'd bone idly committed to no actual training, deciding that I'd find my own pace on the road. And so it came as no surprise to me that just a few minutes into my ascent I'd already broken into a burdensome sweat. I would go on to climb several hundred metres around a multitude of bends - over the space of a couple of hours. The roads themselves weren't overly busy for a weekend, probably because nobody likes Saitama. There were a few other cyclists however and the occasional knob-head motorbike driver or two that would race each other without caution around hairpin bends... to probably prove to one another that they both had equally tiny penises.

Reaching the top of the range was the payoff. This is where the proceeding hour's hard graft was put to some positive use. In my mind, descending a mountain exemplifies fun to its fullest. Obviously, like most thrills, bar making fun of Millwall supporters - the adrenalin rush is short - yet sweet. Flying down the mountainside toward Chichibu at some 30mph with all my gear, I felt like I was going to turn into a flaming ball of fire; a menacingly unstoppable force. Only a lorry pulling out in front of me now could have possibly ruined my day, or a… no, I must stop here, I am being too negative.

As the pines peeled away and the land levelled, I would roll steadily into downtown Chichibu with just mere remnants of daylight remaining. I was tiring fast by this point. A supermarket's cafeteria enticed me over from the side of the road; the idea of a nice hot coffee seeming more alluring than anything else in the world at that moment.

One iced coffee later and I found myself looking despondently at my reflection in the mirror of the supermarket restroom. A zombie glared back at me, red veins in its eyes that looked like a sadistic game of Spirograph. My muscles ached and my mind was barely able to formulate any constructive train of thought. After the previous night's conditions in the car park at Kawagoe, the desire to be someplace warm and cosy was again humongous. I was quite simply dreading the night ahead on the doorstep of Mt. Buko; every thought about my predicament was cold, so very, very cold.

Inevitably, the night would turn into one of the coldest experiences of my life. At around 11pm, I found myself on a baseball pitch in the city's suburbs. I set up my tent and the weather seemed mild enough before I snuggled into my sleeping bag. The fact of the matter was I'd worked up such a profound sweat setting up camp, and at the time I was content, the fact that I was also wearing eight layers of clothing also made me feel that the chill couldn't possibly antagonise me.

Fast forward two hours from my initial naivety and my water bottle had ice crystals in it. My body had spent the best part of 20 minutes trying to convince itself to get up, pack everything away and get moving - or die. But my half-sharp mind was telling me otherwise, trying to slyly persuade me that it was too cold for that now. *Nah stay where you are mate, it be way too cold outside of this 'ere tent, there could be nonces out there!*

My body and mind fought for some time before I was able to take a hold of my senses. My subconscious shunned my crooked mind, for the bastard was quite simply trying to murder me in my dormant and dreary state. I feared that the onset of hyperthermia was drifting dangerously close... this was to be a learning curve! Warmth was now my only goal. Leaping into life, I did a couple of quick laps, running the perimeter of the baseball pitch before chucking in a few star jumps and a half-arsed press-up at the end for good measure. I was then pumped enough to be able to pack up camp.

I still had some four hours or so to kill before day break. Traversing the mountains during the dark not being an option, I sought out a 24-hour Sukiya, a sort of fast food noodle outlet that supports drunks and English idiots that nearly freeze to death within the local vicinity. I sat down and ordered myself a beastly bowl of ramen; the hot broth instantly hitting the spot. Across the way from me were three drunk, noisy Japanese girls. They tried to converse with me, using a mixture of Japanese and slurred English, their Japanese perhaps slurred as well but considering how awful my Japanese skills were, that was a difficult one to wager. I could smell the booze in the air; they reeked. Even when I can understand the language, a drunk person conversing with a sober person is a near on impossible conversation, the wave lengths just being that far apart as to render the situation annoying and unwarranted. I slurped my noodles with haste and equalled the bill.

The remaining couple of hours or so were spent abusing free Wi-Fi in a 7-Eleven and browsing through the jazz mags.

At around 5:45am, the dark shadow formerly cast upon Mt. Buko - that towers up 1,304m above the city to the south - began to lift. The sun was beginning to wake and the formidable looking mountain before me looked scarred and mistreated; a row of terraces cut into its sides from years of limestone excavation sat as shelves blanketed in snow.

The mountain looked vengeful, I just prayed that She would pardon my exit gracefully.

It was still ice cold outside, but with chattering teeth I was able to now begin my journey out of the Chichibu mountain range.

Chichibu – Asakusa
63 miles

The alternate route south-easterly out of the mountains of Chichibu wasn't as strenuous as the previous day's ascent coming in from the north-east. This would come in part from an 1800m tunnel that ran directly through the mountains; the first of many gruelling cyclist death traps that I would encounter throughout my time in Japan. With the amount of traffic heading in both directions, I deemed the tunnel too dangerous to cycle through. There was a minuscule sidewalk available that I could just about walk along with my bike. With my body pushed up tight against the tunnel wall, I began the long trudge. The walls were thick with grime and the path slippery, the thrumming of approaching traffic would build up the closer that vehicles got to me, adding a morbid intensity to the situation. In time, I hoped to deal with tunnels with more confidence; Japan is one of the most tectonically active countries in the world, so mountains and therefore tunnels as a go between are simply a way of life.

From the other side, a descent began. I eased off the peddling and let the gradient take me along the winding road. My adrenaline failed to gather momentum though and I almost nodded off at the handlebars on several occasions. I was glad when a 7-Eleven eventually cropped up. I plied my body with coffee and chocolate which seemed to bring me back from the dead.

23

When the gradient levelled again this would end my little test run to and from Saitama; as I began to creep slowly back towards the northern suburbs of Tokyo. My legs were a little achy, but this was to be expected. And with this merely being the beginning of the biggest project I have ever attempted, they still had a lot more to prove, but by now I felt more confident that they would be able to prove their worth. My initiation into the world of tour cycling had begun… and my pants swelled with delight.

As dusk breached, the neon lights of the city began to flicker into life, as the pulse of traffic surged to and fro, like the veins of a colossal monster's beating heart. Without this bolshie vibrancy, the great beast would be drained, but alas with so much to give and so much desire - just like my lust for the road - it could only grow stronger.

STATS

Dates: 21/03/2014 – 23/03/2014
Total miles traversed: 176 miles
Total time in the saddle: 21 hours and 30 minutes

3. CHIBA
千葉県

Asakusa – Ichihara
55 miles

Chiba boasts one of the largest industrial areas in Japan, specialising in steel, petroleum, chemical and machinery production. The Keiyō Industrial Zone, situated northeast of Tokyo Bay, is positioned on a vast area of reclaimed land that amalgamates some 8 cities across Chiba. For productivity and economic wealth, the area sets a shining example for both growth and prosperity, yet for a cyclist it makes for a complete and utter nightmare.

The air was foul, as factories spewed pollutants up into the canopy of the Gods and articulated lorries chugged about relentlessly, in and around a confusion of expressways that themselves scaled up high into the stratosphere. Cycling through the area was like trying to find one's way out of a giant bowl of oil-stained spaghetti.

It was difficult to believe that one can traverse through an area for some 6 hours and still not even get the faintest glimpse of the countryside. The sight of a rice paddy would have no doubt given me an instant arousal after such a time. But the closest I got to the country's agricultural heartland in the Keiyō Industrial Zone was a half-eaten rice ball tossed from a window by a passing trucker.

Away from the industrial whorehouse of Tokyo Bay, I entered the city of Chiba where I would pay a fleeting visit to the Chiba Port Tower, a 125.1 m lozenge-shaped structure thrown together in 1986, to commemorate the population of the prefecture surpassing the five-million mark. It poked the sky vigorously amongst a well preserved park that as dusk set in would have made for a suitable stealth camping habitat. Yet an eagerness to keep my wheels rolling prevailed.

I pressed on towards Kimitsu, a city I'd initially intended to be at by sundown. Again I would let my optimism get the better of me as the elements disabled my plan of action. I only reached the suburb of Anesaki in Ichihara before the heavens opened upon me. If it was warm piss raining down, I more than likely would've been willing to continue, even during the dark hours. Alas, it was cold, calculating and heavier than a Christmas carol performed by Cradle of Filth. I found an underpass in which to shelter from the wet stuff; a place where I could sit and reminiscence upon the day's events. I noticed that I'd already begun to soliloquize. Thankfully, I didn't give a shit.

Ichihara – Kimitsu
29 miles

When the previous evening's rain had simmered down, I found myself a small park to hold fort in for the night. It was a mild enough night, yet I still slept uneasily.

As I was packing my gear away at dawn I was greeted by an old man and his poodle. I couldn't claim to understand everything he was asking me, so I told the old man the story of my trip in hideously broken Japanese - and he seemed to enjoy my yarn. So much so that he disappeared around the corner for a couple of minutes and came back with the biggest can of Pepsi I had ever seen. Seriously, it was the size of a newborn calf, the thing must've been decommissioned in the late 80's and come from a batch of very elusive stock. I felt privileged as he offered me the can, along with some smokes. I accepted the Pepsi and declined the smokes. He then squatted with his pooch in his arms and watched curiously as I sweated over packing all my gear away.

The exterior of my tent was saturated by the night's rain, luckily for my Japanese audience, traditional British slapstick comedy is a big hit around these parts. The stranger wouldn't be seeing an idiot like me again for a very long time, so if I could put a smile on the old chap's face, in exchange for a ginormous Pepsi, well then naturally I was only more than happy to oblige. I set about attempting to pack away a slippery tent; to almost a round of applause.

After everything was in order, I said my farewells to Yoshimitsu-san and Poopoo-chan and set forth in the direction of Kimitsu, in order to take on the Boso Skyline. In roughly the 3 hours or so that it would take me to get to Kimitsu, the rain would gradually get heavier and heavier. So, on this day, I would not be traversing the Boso Skyline; any attempt would have been nothing short of sheer tomfoolery. The day was essentially a dead duck, and with clearer skies due tomorrow across the peninsula I sought out a place in which to wait it out.

I ashamedly found a McDonald's, but at 10am they were only serving breakfast. I wouldn't wish a McDonald's breakfast upon my worst enemies, so I would have to go on a hot drink binge until such a sentence was passed and it became Big Mac 'O' Clock. '*Hotto chokorēto onegai shimasu,*' I asked. 'Hot chocolate, please.' The young lady behind the counter looked at me as if I had just done a shit in her hair. Remembering another version of the word 'Hot' I rephrased my order for my next instalment of terrible Japanese. '*Atsui chokorēto onegai shimasu.*' Her face shifted awkwardly as she searched for some sort of resolve. Then, she blushed and began pointing at the menu on the counter before me. As she began to speak, some old crow popped up, her bushy eyebrows frowning at me. She appeared to come from under the counter, from some place very cold, I should imagine.

'*Nai.*' No, she abruptly told me. Her attitude almost communist in nature, she looked disgusted to make my acquaintance. A McDonald's with no hot chocolate, was this really a McDonalds? I smelt a conspiracy. 'Hmm....*kōhī onegai shimasu,*' coffee please. I changed my order. The old crow's face swiftly changed its tune, converting into a scene of sheer delight as a sudden warmth seemed to ricochet throughout her person. She was no longer an old crow, she was an elegant and gentle dove... just like that! Her younger colleague would also find her voice as she named her price. I paid my dues and retreated to a quiet corner, mildly confused as to what had just taken place. Whipping out my laptop, I urged myself to find out why McDonald's in Japan doesn't do hot chocolate, only to find out that McDonalds in Japan doesn't do Wi-Fi either! My life was in turmoil.

Kimitsu – Togane
87 miles

The park I had found to make my nest in for the night was ideal, but again the climate was not. By 4am I couldn't bear the cold any longer and was up and about looking for a fast food outlet to bide some time in, until sunrise. Again, like in Chichibu, I found myself a 24-hour Sukiya, however this time a very closed 24-hour Sukiya. I huffed in disgust. 7-Eleven of course wasn't closed, so I treated myself to a mighty fine microwavable ramen and dumplings. Convenience stores in Japan really do surpass themselves in the array of consumables that they have on offer. Back in Blighty a rather bland ham sandwich and a packet of pickled onion Monster Munch would be about the most one could generally wish for. Yet here convenience is more of a big deal – and it was a concept I would come to rely heavily upon over the coming months.

As dawn began to take hold, the sun sat shyly behind a thick blanket of fog. Undeterred, I began to ascend the Boso Skyline; a toll road set up in 1979 that allowed the road users to traverse from west to east across the Boso Peninsula. However, due to a tunnel caving in somewhere close by, the government of Chiba had declared the toll extinct. Bonus.

As I ascended, my body slowly began to feel the strain, and, with each passing mile, I had to remove a layer of clothing; six layers quite simply being overdramatic for the task in hand. As I approached the top of the range at just over 400 metres in elevation, the thick mist that governed the start of the day was beginning to lift and streams of light began to seep through, illuminating the road before me. It was difficult for me to see the surrounding landscape, as the tree line to the sides of the road obscured the view. It wasn't until the descent that I got more of a pronounced observation across the peninsula. Pronounced yet by no means intricate, as when one is cruising downhill at 31.8mph there can be no mucking about and slamming on the brakes in order to take a selfie - for that would be a sin and the adrenaline rush would become forsaken.

Heading down the skyline and continuing eastward toward Kamogawa, rice paddies glistened under the sun as an orchestra of frogs staked their claim for territory. The area is affluently abundant in agriculture, in fact Chiba's agricultural output is only second to Hokkaidō's. Yet, when it comes to vegetables, Chiba leads the pack, growing: carrots, cabbages, radishes, pears, spinach, tomatoes and the local speciality, peanuts. The prefecture producing 78% of all of Japan's peanuts.

Nearing the coast of Kamogawa, I almost became overwhelmed by the sight of a beach; its obligatory salty sea breeze enticing me closer. With the weather being a complete polar opposite to yesterday's tragedy, the whole idea of a beach on a hot sunny day was an exceptionally appealing one, so much so that I even purchased myself an ice cream to commemorate the said moment. A silly grin spread across my face, and I was unable to prise it off for the remainder of the afternoon. I was feeling smug, and there was nothing I could do about it.

The beach in reality was not the most idyllic when you compare beaches on the grand scale of things; the sand having that darker ash-like tinge to it and not the dreamy yellow stuff that makes for that all-important picturesque postcard. Still, at least it wasn't shale. I hate to sound like a beach racist but shale beaches are just shit, nobody likes them, apart from geologists, but everyone knows that geologists are biased. Yet, despite the weather carrying with it the grace of a hot summer's day, the sea's temperature was far from suitable for a quick dip; it was after all still March. A selection of die-hard surfers were out in force though, along with families, couples and singletons, all strolling along the black stuff, making the most of a perfect day. A Shiba Inu then lowered the tone somewhat by pissing in the sand. True story.

I followed a quaint coastal road north for the greater part of the day through a selection of fishing villages. I wound around coastal paths and through mysterious looking mountain tunnels, reminiscent of Miyazaki's animated classic 'Spirited Away.' As I coerced upward alongside a cliff face, I peeked over the edge to a cacophony of waves crashing against the base of the cliffs. Seagulls rode the thermals and a desolately blood red torii gate sat upon a craggy rock some 500 metres out to sea, itself being suppressed by an endless crescendo of waves. It was easy to see how much inspiration can be sought from the wilds of this country. I was truly captivated.

When nightfall beckoned, I still had some 20 or so miles to cover before reaching my destination of Togane. For tonight I had a date... with a Couchsurfer. Couchsurfing for those of you that are not in the know is an Internet service that connects travellers across the world; a form of hospitality exchange.

A host will welcome a weary traveller into his or her respective home, in order to rest up for the night, and in return one would hope that the said weary traveller would do the exact same for another like-minded traveller, someday. So, for me, considering I had a hell of long road ahead of me and that I'd be stopping in well out of the way random towns, it would prove an extremely beneficial asset to my trip. One could only hope that I wouldn't get raped, for that would be exceedingly rubbish.

I rode like a bastard to get to Togane, I'd covered close to 90 miles and my right kneecap felt like it was getting ready to burst out of its joint. But knowing how much it would mean to me to have a roof over my head for the night - and to finally get a hot shower after close to a week of not having a wash, made the strain all the more worthwhile. That's right, you read correctly, a week of not washing, what's the point of being a hobo if you're going to have a wash every day? Jesus Christ never bathed, not that I'm comparing myself to the son of God of course. I just hoped that I wouldn't get turned away by my Couchsurfing host for smelling like a dead bear. Or if that's her thing, then game on!

Togane - Narita
27 miles

The morning would present me with a flurry of pubes. Not something I was entirely expecting, yet if one is going to parade around the house with a short nightshirt on, stretching and yawning with an absence of undergarments, then I guess vagina's will accidentally happen. I mean, I can only presume that my Couchsurfing host's vagina escaped by accident, unless of course I'd mistakenly waltzed onto the set of a baldy 1970's sex comedy.

Her name was Sofiya and she was a 21-year-old student from Ukraine. She was tall, thin with shaggy brown hair and cutesy dimples. Downstairs, she was sporting the regional look, which I respected. 'When in Rome, do as the Romans

31

do!' Or in this instance, Togane of course. I have no idea if she was aware about the presence of her vagina over breakfast, but what could one really say? And I didn't want to offend her through ignorance, just in case it happened to be some sort of cultural Ukrainian thing. And so, Sofiya's hairy vagina remained present over breakfast. She was a sweet girl though, enthusiastic about life and full of ambition, finding her way to Japan to study the lingo at the University of Togane. When I arrived last night I was absolutely shattered after an exhaustive day and found myself almost punch drunk when trying to formulate a sentence. Not to mention the fact that I hadn't needed to speak for the best part of a week to anyone, bar myself. I must have passed the test though, as the following morning she showed me her bush, so from my first Couchsurfing perspective I couldn't help but take away an eyeful of positives. Although there is no denying, muff aside, it was a slightly weird experience to have gotten to know somebody for just a mere few hours - abusing their home for your own personal gain and then pissing off. But having no real personal sense of shame, I was more than willing to Couchsurf again.

As I left Sofiya and her vagina in Togane, I felt an ample sense of loneliness. It felt surreal to be cared for and nurtured by a stranger, knowing that, come the following night, I would be alone and out in the cold again - like a stray.

Narita was a short 20 mile ride from Togane, predominantly along a vicious Route 409. Narita, is famed for its International airport, situated just some 50 miles away from downtown Tokyo. It handles roughly 20,000 flights every month - that's around 3 million travellers every thirty days. So with a heavy bulk of tourism flowing through the region, compacted with heavy commercial and industrial factions, the roads around Narita City were a bit like cycling through a mosh pit of motor vehicles. My guard would have to be up.

Apart from just being a gateway to Japan, central Narita does hold an ambience of touristic antiquities. It's a place to while away a bit of time before a flight. Narita-san Temple is the big draw, the grounds within encompassing a vast area with numerous buildings, monuments, gardens and lakes. It all sits prominently at the end of Omotesando Street, a 1 km stretch of restaurants and traditional handicraft and souvenir shops. The temple itself was originally established in 940AD by a disciple of Kōbō-Daishi, the grandmaster of Japanese Buddhist teachings, a.k.a. Shingon. The site is dedicated to the fire God Acala, one of the five wisdom kings of the womb realm. Now I scarcely now what any of that means - as I'm not really much of a religious buff, but I'm sure you'll agree, it certainly sounds important!

Heavy rain was on the cards for the next day, and with all hostels and hotels within the vicinity of my price range booked up - including the 365-day-a-year Christmas themed love hotel - I would have an interesting 48-hours ahead of me. I'd located a park bench on a hill – which was situated in a sheltered enclosure. I guess in reality that would make me a genuine hobo, but if I was to complete this journey with my limited funds, then living rough would just have to be part and parcel of the journey. As long as nobody got hurt and I didn't have to blow anyone, there was no real reason that I wouldn't succeed in my mission.

I killed time before the inevitable by devouring a curry in the dry warmth of a CoCo's curry house. The curry was so large that I was almost convinced I'd ordered a portion to share between eight sumos. I knew though that I'd burn off a portion the size of my slightly smaller left bollock just cycling the hill towards my 'homeless' shelter in the park, and so it was all necessary fuel for my greedy pistons.

En route to my hobo lair, I'd found an outdoor shop where I was able to get myself an inner fleece for my sleeping bag. This made sleeping as a homeless person all the more exciting.

It's nice having new things, especially when you've got next to nothing, perhaps all I needed now was a well-fed dog to complete the picture.

Upon arrival - as I'd hoped - my shelter was void of life. I was mildly fearful that other hobo's or junkies might have had their eyes on my spot or still did. A bridge I'd just have to cross - if it came to it.

Narita

The rain fell earlier than expected, and it really wanted me. I'd read it was due to kick off at around 8am, but come 2am I was already drenched. I'd not set up my tent as it wasn't really a viable option and I thought I'd be fine under the picnic table. However, water encroached from the northern side of the shelter, so I etched closer to the opposite side where it was nowhere near as dramatic, and closed my eyes.

Somehow, I actually managed to sleep for a further 3 hours; a record since I'd been on the road. A road that today would not see me streamlining into Ibaraki Prefecture as initially envisioned. For this early in the expedition the cold, wet wilderness still appeared to me as virgin and slightly daunting territory. I'd need to man up at some point though, especially with a rainy season on the horizon. But not today, for it was a Sunday and just for a little longer I was more than happy to play the part of the innocently dry cycle touring virgin.

So I waited.

And I waited.

And then I... waited.

When there was a break in the elements, I proceeded to a nearby Aeon Mall: a humongous shopping centre comprising of more shops than any one human could possibly count in a lifetime.

I spent the day there, walking from shop to shop with the soul intention of buying absolutely nothing. I was bored, so very, very bored. In the dry comfort of the ever popular donut franchise Mister Donut, I gorged fiendishly upon a vast swathe of doughy goodness, and then I waited.

And I waited.

And then I waited some more.

The rain would was still thrashing down when I left for my hobo shelter upon the hill. But I couldn't take the mall anymore, the constant high pitched hollering of *'irrashaimase'* echoing out in repetition across the mall from every female shop assistant would finally take its toll upon me.

If you walk into any shop in Japan you will catch hold of this phrase, pretty much a welcome gesture, usually stretched out over a number of seconds converging into what feels like minutes - all in order to get the desired effect of really, really welcoming one to the said establishment. It's something that will perhaps strike you as odd when you first set foot in the country, but soon enough it becomes a customary trait of the culture. However, after about the 13,209th time, I'd had enough of *'irrashaimase'* for one day - and so it was time for bed.

My shelter was again desolate and not a creature stirred. And, as was tradition, I bunkered down for the night. Homeless, damp, alone, but not hungry, and for Mister Donut I thank thee. I fell asleep quickly.

Narita – Tsuchiura
60 miles

I awoke suddenly, normally being a light sleeper I'm able to account for any abstract noises within my general proximity, yet not in the presence of the Ninja who was watching me sleep. The scenario was significantly weird. Obviously the guy had the right to be there, it was a public shelter, but why *would* he be there? Just… looking at me. I felt that I was being closely examined by that of a 'hobosexual': someone who loves the homeless and thinks that they are dead sexy. And ideally for me, not dead and sexy.

I got my phone out and pretended to be doing stuff, I wasn't, it was just merely a guise whilst I thought about the scenario in place. It was 2am in the morning and it had now finally stopped raining, so the guy wasn't here to seek shelter from the rain, and he didn't look homeless - he didn't have a shopping trolley with him or any material possessions that I could see. He also didn't smell of sour piss... like me.

I stood, letting my sleeping bag drop to the floor in the process... thanking the Gods that I was sleeping in my trousers and not sporting the ol' John Thomas look. I let out a big masculine yawn, this to me represented a sign of confidence, that I wasn't being outdone by the surrealism of the situation. I pointed at the sky, 'Ah, *Ima wa ame owarimashita ne?*' Ah, the rain has finished now, huh? He had no response. He just looked some more. 'Right, well fuck this then!' I concluded, as I began to roll up my sleeping bag and pack some of my gear away, keeping a close eye on my curious new friend. And on that note he left, just upped and left, walking off into the darkness of the park.

Was he just curious? Was he a psycho? Did he want a blowy?

In the end, it appears he wanted nothing more than a seat and to watch me sleep. Makes my skin crawl as I write this, thinking about a world of possibilities of what could have happened that night. But I was in Japan, famed for its safety and it's all-round congenial levels of discipline. Yet it still does harbour criminals and the insane. Just one comfortable night's sleep in the shelter allowed me to get instantly comfortable with my surroundings for the second night. I'd let down my guard - assuming my safety, whether or not I was ever seriously in jeopardy I guess I'll never know.

I relocated across town, behind a row of vending machines, adjacent to a Shintō shrine. There I would sleep surprisingly well until dawn, undisturbed… and unbummed. My favourite kind of sleep.

With clear skies, I made my way to Sawara, a 16 mile ride from Narita and my last port of call in Chiba. I had an awkward side wind for most of the journey, along with a few technical defects. My gears started slipping and my chain came off, as patience in my front mud guard was all but lost. The tips of my feet constantly contacted with the inner rim of the guard whenever I turned a corner; a hindrance as well as an annoyance. I would rip it off in a fit of rage and launch it across a rice paddy.

It appeared that I'd woken up on the wrong side of the tent. Barely had the day begun and it was already beginning to feel like a long day. I'm a truly terrible person to be around when I'm in a foul mood. Luckily for the world I was cycling on my lonesome and I could only make my own life a misery. What made it all so much more painfully terrible was that I'd had 'Call Me Baby' by Carly Rae Jepson stuck in my head for the past 9 days. Pure torture.

My stay in Sawara was brief, the old centre being an aged merchant town with several souvenir shops offering ancient crafts and artwork.

A canal meanders through the centre with an accompaniment of cherry blossomed trees. It was a quaint and novel place – and just a couple of hundred metres away a big grisly main road tore its way right through the hub of modern day Sawara. Streets were lined with every manner of industrial and commercial convenience known to man: 7-Elevens, drug stores, mechanics, DIY shops, gas stations, McDonalds, sex shops, pachinko parlours etc., etc. This grisly road I would have to visit just briefly to ease my transition into Ibaraki.

STATS

Dates: 26/03/2014 – 30/03/2014
Total miles traversed: 434 miles
Total time in the saddle: 47 hours and 10 minutes

4. IBARAKI
茨城県

With the aid of Google Maps, I thought that I'd found myself a quiet little road to lead me to Lake Kasumigaura. Yet, despite the road not even having a name, I couldn't have been more wrong. The road, unassuming to begin with, was narrow and devoid of any traffic; I thought that it was just a farmer's country path through the rice paddies. However, my thinking was quite wrong, as the road would soon become about as abrasive as a rabid penis in a whorehouse. Articulated lorries were the order of the day, veering so close to me that I was forced to come to a halt and practically throw myself to the ditch on the side of the road every time one passed. It was either this or the road would be getting a brand-new claret paint job at my expense. At some point, out of sight, there must have been traffic lights as every now and then there would be a break from the heavy flow of traffic, allowing me to peddle like crazy, before becoming inundated again by the next batch of monstrous vessels. It was a slow if not meticulous process, but a necessary one all the same.

I eventually caught sight of the lake and found myself a more peaceful and accommodating road, which trailed around the lakeside's perimeter. Bar a few wide-boy farmers zipping about in their obligatory white micro machine-esque trucks that all farmers appear to possess around Japan, the route was a virtually a motor vehicle free zone.

Kasumigaura Lake has a surface area of 85 mi² and as well as supporting the local fishing industry, it is used for irrigating the region's rice crop and the local delicacy, lotus root. I stopped for a while by the lake's edge. Water lapped up gently against its shore as a cluster of reeds rustled together under the tenaciously growing western wind; seed heads breaking off and dispersing across the lake. Through the gaps in the silence a number of widgeon advertised their presence upon the lake with their shrilly call.

The place had a soothing tranquillity to it. That was until I began to pedal north-westerly towards Tsuchiura, where the wind again would become my enemy. For some 10 miles I traversed into the prevailing gale at an average speed of 5 mph. Before long I would become sick of the sight of what seemed like an infinite void of water; the wind's wrath little by little eating away at my very soul in an attempt to leave it in tatters. I cut away from the water's edge from time to time and navigated through a small series of fishing hamlets that I used as a temporary wind break. Yet inevitably, all roads led back to the lake.

As the sun dropped and hung low in the sky, an amber glow was cast across the lake and its surrounding rice paddies. Tsuchiura beckoned; I would reach it by dusk. There I sought out my second Couchsurfing host, Ron - from Nebraska.

Ron had found his way to Japan some 13 years previously in the form of an English teacher, a guise he still wore. During that time he developed a great bond with the country and its people and was adamant that he would never leave. This was all a very understandable and a stereotypically familiar yarn, yet Ron's appearance on the other hand, due to my self-propelled shallowness, was a marginally ominous one. Yes, I like to judge a book by its cover sometimes, and that makes me a wanker, this much I know. Figuratively speaking though, everything about Ron did strike me as relatively normal, yet there was just one main offending feature... his moustache. Its style was highly pornographic with a slight hint of sex pest. It was waxed to the tips - tips which pointed aggressively away from either side of his jovial and strangely likeable head. But could I trust a guy that sported such a look? Was there a hidden agenda behind such an outlandish moustache? Perhaps I just didn't know enough about moustaches to fully comprehend the situation. The few times I'd sported one myself, I looked like a transsexual in a passport photo. Ron seemed friendly enough though, but we only bantered for some 20 minutes or so before he made his apologies and headed out for the night to see friends, leaving me to my own devices with a fridge full of beer. He told me to help myself. Me! An Englishman being offered a free fridge full of beer! Again, was this normal? Leaving your home to a complete stranger after knowing them for just 20 minutes? Was it a trap? Were there hidden cameras about watching my every move? Was it acceptable to masturbate when the host wasn't home? Or should I just play it safe and order a couple of prostitutes and a gram of coke? *Or was that what Ron wanted?*

Scepticism would keep my sins at bay. But in all seriousness I'd just inherited an apartment for the night... was Couchsurfing really meant to be this awesome? Or was I destined to become undone by associating myself with so much trust and free goodwill. As I stepped into the bathroom to wash away the day's grime, I noticed a tub of moustache wax beside the sink. I thought briefly about what happened to Ned Beatty's character in *Deliverance*, then shuddered, removing my clothes gingerly before stepping into the shower.

Tsuchiura - Utsunomiya
55 miles

When I write down each day's notes in my diary, I often try to convince myself that when it comes to looking back over them, I will most definitely be able to decipher my rushed and squiggled handwriting. Unfortunately, this is not always the case. For example, as I sit down some several months later in order to read the events of, 1st April 2014, I can only see the words: 'Pigeon Dick.' Nothing more, nothing less. To this day, I still have absolutely no idea what it means. Pigeon's, like most birds don't even have penises, they have cloaca's. Pigeon

Dick is code for something obviously, but what? I just cannot seem to fathom it out - and I don't think I ever will.

Well, anyhoo, back to the story in hand. Luckily, for me the day in question was memorable enough that I didn't need to crack any of my own pigeon dick codes. At around 9am, Ron tumbled back into his apartment after a heavy night out. Heading straight to the fridge, he grabbed himself a carton of milk and drank directly from it. He was a thirsty boy, and as he finished chugging and pulled the carton away from his lips, a milky white residue lined the bottom half of his gross, still holistically waxed to the tips moustache. I quickly averted my eyes, pretending that I'd seen nothing. I only wished I hadn't.

'So what's the plan today, Dan?' Ron asked.

'The Rinrin Road, and then on to Utsunomiya,' I confirmed.

'Great, I think I'll join ya.'

Gladly I accepted his company, it meant that I wouldn't have to talk to myself for a while like a crazy person. Instead, I could just talk to Ron like a perfectly normal crazy person. And with that, we saddled up.

The Rinrin Road is a derelict railroad/designated cycle route that stretches some 25 miles or so from Tsuchiura to Iwase Town. The path for the majority runs through a vast plain of agricultural land at the feet of Mt. Tsukuba, situated to the north.

There was still a strong north-westerly wind slowing us down at times, but the air was warm and the scenery agreeable. Cherry blossoms lined a multitude of the route as we passed a series of defunct station platforms, that would inform us of our steady progress.

As we cycled, I got to know Ron some more. We chatted about everything and nothing and I would soon learn that despite his vindictive tash – he really wasn't a rapist after all. He was just a bloody nice bloke. I like it when that happens, it's always a pleasure to meet a fellow non-rapist. Initially, he had only intended to travel a few miles of the route with me but would end up traversing the entire section all the way to the end of its course in Iwase!

Upon arrival there, he insisted upon treating me to lunch. I told him that it would be my shout - for the inconvenience of hosting me at his gaff for the night. Ron replied that he had an actual job, a good job, and that I did not. He had a point. Ron treated me to lunch.

Over lunch he cleared the air with me, revealing the story behind 'That Moustache.' Whilst on a trip to Tokyo one weekend - sporting a beard - he was approached by a moustache wax agency. They offered him a moustache modelling role in exchange for a small fee. Ron, just like any good prostitute, accepted the advance and never looked back. Apparently, his vibrant tash can be found in several fashion magazines around Japan. It is a tash that he must wear by contract, and also I can tell, for fun. He was proud of it, for he had fathered it all by himself and what anyone else thought about it, I got the notion, he really didn't give a rat's arse.

With the truth out in the open it was time to part ways. Ron returned to Tsuchiura along the Rinrin Road from whence he'd came, the wind in his sails. I rode forth in the opposite direction, leaving Ibaraki and entering Tochigi, a reasonably straightforward affair where I was able to cut through a number of back roads through an ever-present body of rice paddies. I kept the main roads at bay and filtered out any heavy traffic that was bustling its way towards the prefectural capital, Utsunomiya.

STATS

Dates: 31/03/2014 – 1/04/2014
Total miles traversed: 489 miles
Total time in the saddle: 52 hours and 46 minutes

5. TOCHIGI
栃木県

Utsunomiya is vibrant, sensual and quite simply just rammed full of *gyōza*! Embedded between a number of swanky cafés and bars dotted around town, you'll find a number of *gyōza* joints offering up various adaptations of the familiar Chinese dumpling.

Legend has it that some Japanese soldiers - during WWII - obtained Chinese dumpling recipes whilst occupying Manchuria. Upon returning home to Utsunomiya, a handful of these soldiers set about putting these recipes into commercial effect. One thing led to another and there were all sorts of recipes flying about the city; a *gyōza* boom was born. This has essentially typecast Utsunomiya as the best place in Japan for *gyōza*! People come from all corners of the country to smash these regional delicacies into their faces. Oh, and the things they do to a *gyōza* in Utsunomiya: you can get your pork enshrouded goodness boiled, steamed, sautéed, fried or battered and served up with an assortment of dips such as: soy sauce, chilli sauce, tomato sauce, curry sauce and miso. What if you don't like pork? Well then that's just fine and dandy too, you can get your dumpling stuffed with beef, veg, cheese, nuts, liver, heart, you name it and the Utsunomiyan's will dumplify it for you! And for those of you with a sweet tooth, you'll also be able to find a selection of dessert orientated *gyōza*, with such ingredients as: ice cream, yoghurt, bean paste, fruit, chocolate plus tea or coffee flavour. So, I think you'll agree there's quite the selection up for grabs. I personally opted for battered pork *gyōza* served with a sour curry sauce dip. Divine.

As evening etched into existence I went to meet Ryu, he would be my first Japanese Couchsurfing host. Ryu was 31 and doing one of those proper city office jobs that quite frankly I would just never understand, possibly because it had something to do with maths. I hate maths, its shit, just give me a cow to milk and then I'm happy enough.

Ryu lived in a refurbished hotel, it looked raw and urban with exposed brickwork and ceiling joists; the building itself spanning across 5 floors, which he shared with nine other tenants, male and female, all of a similar age and all seemingly good friends. They had a huge downstairs communal room with an *onsen* that had been converted into a snug, a couple of huge widescreen TV's on the wall, a dining table like something off the set of Game Of Thrones and a kitchen that Jamie Oliver would be able to get lost in for days on end.

In between meeting and greeting a stream of Ryu's housemates and friends of housemates, Ryu would crack open a bottle of sake and a small group of us would rattle our glasses together to a toast of '*Kanpai,*' cheers. It seemed to me that these boys and girls were living the life: they had their careers, they had each other, they had their slice of inner city freedom and, as a passing straggler, I almost felt a little awkward and out of place. But I had sake, we all did, and we also had a common friend.

We drained the sake whilst discussing the finer things in life, travel and… errr… travel. Our experiences, our adventures, days that seemed to have long passed, but memories that will never perish. It's in the blood and talking about it only fuels the desire for wanderlust; it unites people of similar purpose, and this was why I was allowed to be here, doing what I was doing.

It was refreshing to have met Ryu and his housemates, and as I left the next day for Nikko, I felt like I had an edge; I was more committed, more determined. I felt that this little project of mine was ripe for the taking and that I could probably pull it off. Probably.

Utsunomiya - Nikko
29 miles

En route to Nikko, I happened across a curious thing that boggled my mind. Maybe sometimes I just think too much, but when I came across a magazine of pornographic content on the side of the road, directly adjacent to an odd shoe, my imagination wandered. Could someone really do that? And... in a shoe? Why would they do that? WHY??? I mean I know people as a whole, especially men, can be sexual deviants, but was such a person so desperate to relieve himself of his demon seed that he had no other choice but to do it in his own shoe?

People will never stop amazing me, they're mental, the sexual innovation and the heights of self-depravation can quite simply startle me at times.

The ascent up to Nikko was a steady one, yet despite all the training over the past week or so I found it surprisingly draining. All the physical exertion was obviously taking its toll and upon arrival in Nikko my body was due a recharge.

I'd actually been to Nikko some 7 years previously as part of a 6 month tour of Eastern Asia, and as I pulled into town, it still seemed all so very familiar. There was the central bus station in the town square, its perimeter lined with souvenir shops and an Indian restaurant where a friend and I once dived into one evening to escape a sudden downpour. A succession of side streets led away from the town square and up a steepish hill that ventures up towards the temple district. This is where I found my hostel.

The Nikkorissou: a rickety looking building from the outside, yet a prudently charming one from within. It was a traditional little Japanese house, very homely, especially the living room with its *tatami* flooring, a *kotatsu*, *shoji* sliding paper doors and a log burner. This stereotypical Japanese themed house was fused together with the stereotypical hostel theme: writing on the walls from the travelling community, world flags, a guitar and a compulsory set of Uno, an excellent requisite to any hostel. If any game was going to bring a pack of travellers together then it surely has to be Uno. Some smooth revellers have probably got themselves laid due to the gift of Uno, God bless them. The only negative I could possibly find was that in the toilets it encouraged everyone to sit down to pee. Well, to comply, I just sat down to pee like a good girl. I'm a firm rule abider, especially under someone else's roof.

I nestled here cosily for the next few days, sharing my room with a self-centred American chap with very little travel etiquette. A consistently smug grin addressed his face as he refused to answer any questions from his fellow travellers, as is generally common courtesy. He obviously knew something that no one else did, and that made him special. One awful person aside, my other two roommates - unlike myself and the American gent - were respectable travellers: one chatty Romanian fella and his Hungarian counterpart. I almost got excited by the fact that his girlfriend was Hungarian. I'd seen Hungarian girls before in Budapest; they have a curious tendency to look a lot like porn stars. Unfortunately, this Hungarian girl did not have such a look. Yet still, regardless of appearance, it's nice to shoot the breeze mindlessly and have a couple of drinking partners at the end of a long day. It makes one feel more human and less alone in the world.

Nikko

I awoke the following rainy day having had an odd dream. To clean my bicycle chain I used a toothbrush, a very oily toothbrush, I might add. In the ethereal realm and against the science of hygiene, it appeared to be perfectly acceptable for me to use this said very oily toothbrush in order to clean my teeth. Most would consider this to be a nightmare of sorts, yet in my dream I seemed to be perfectly content. I do worry about my sub-conscience sometimes… and upon waking up I instinctively checked my teeth. As a British standard, horrible, yet not oily. It was after all just a dream, and for that I was thankful.

As it was chucking it down, I re-created a scene from 7 years previously by having a stroll down to Kanmangafuchi Abyss. An eerie, secluded gorge just outside of town, it was formed many years ago by the eruption of nearby Mt. Nantai. A mood lingered in the air here as a row of stone carved Bodhisattva's known as Jizo align a pathway along the gorge. The Jizo, often referred to as 'Bake Jizo,' meaning Ghost Jizo, sit upon a short stone tablet in the lotus position. They wear red bibs and a hat - and are said to be the guardians for the souls of dead and unborn children in the underworld. Local lore tells of how the number of Jizo in Kamangafuchi Abyss is unknown as they are ever-changing, hence the name 'Ghost Jizo.' But, for sake of argument, there are about 70!

They exist in various states, some well-defined and a little weathered, others merely piles of rubble and some just completely absent. As I walked past them, my footsteps felt heavy upon the loose gravel, seemingly much louder than the rapids of the nearby gorge. Despite being the only human stupid enough to come here in the heavy rain, I felt as if I was being watched, not in an unsettling way. It's just that the Jizo have a certain presence about them, as does the forest that contains them; an aura of mystery that when combined with the day's elements created a somewhat soothing, yet mystical ethos. One can really feel at peace here; it's one of just a few places in the world where I have ever felt like this. I believe this is what drew me back.

Towards the back-end of the afternoon, the rain began to peter out and I proceeded to the temple district. One of the tourist Mecca's of Japan, designated a UNESCO World Heritage site in 1999, Nikko consists of around 103 buildings and structures, some dating back as early as 766. Most notable is the Tōshō-gū Shrine, the final resting place for the founder and first Shogun of the Tokugawa Shogunate, Tokugawa Ieyasu. It is here that the tourist droves sportingly participate in taking pictures of people taking pictures of people... taking pictures. And just when you think you may have found a classic photo opportunity it will be marred by a big white 'No Smoking' sign. However, the lack of good photographic opportunities cannot void the craftsmanship on display. Many buildings are intricately decorated and highly detailed, Tōshō-gū Shrine alone consisting of some 5,173 sculptures. Unfortunately, one of the big draws - the Yomeimon Gate - was currently being refurbished and was smothered in scaffolding, the results which wouldn't be seen until sometime in 2019.

Walking further around the complex, soaking it all in, I strolled along a small internal wooden walkway just about fit enough for a kitten to do some break-dancing upon. Before long, I encountered a group of rather solemn and angry looking individuals; their ferocious voices echoing from the front of the brigade. Russians. Were they issuing death threats? Or was it just casual banter amongst close friends and loved ones? I couldn't tell. Either way this was not where I wanted to be. I turned to retreat but found myself caged in by the remainder of the tour group that came flooding in behind me. I tried to ease past, but got scorned at by a middle-aged lady with hilarious hair. The Russian flashmob were not going to let me pass, and this is why inevitably that the Russian's are always the baddies in films.

I was now part of the tour group. Agreeing and nodding my head from time to time, I was mostly trying my best to look like an angry person too, until I could slip away undetected and unscathed. For, away from all the unsolicited anger and hate, the mountains beckoned me on.

Nikko - Nasu
56 miles

Approaching Nasu should have been a straightforward affair. I made sure it wasn't though and spiced things up by taking a country road that would essentially lead on for an eternity and further into oblivion. Things always get a little nervy when you haven't seen a road sign for a town, for at least an hour. The only sign I did come across was a 'BEWARE BEARS' sign and a picture of an angry bear revealing his flesh-rippingly spiteful gnashers, just to emphasize the fact that bears have the integral power to be nasty bastards. Statistically, however, it is most commonly old ladies that get eaten by bears in Japan when they're out in the woods pottering about, looking for mountain veg for their supper. I should imagine that they taste a little over-ripe, but then I'm no granny-munching connoisseur like the big bad brown bear.

The road continued to twist and turn, leading off on a tangent to nowhere in particular. I was so far down the road that I couldn't possibly backtrack, so I was a little reckless and kept pushing forward, in the hope that at some point I would be thrown a bone. These country roads at times were hard work; with no passion for common sense, they were more keen to meander on and on like a winding river and do as they so pleased, where exactly they ended up no doubt being the stuff of legends.

Eventually, I stumbled across a sign for 'Nasu' and became endowed with a brief burst of excitement; I was at least heading in the right direction after hours of uncertainly. I even decided to peddle a little faster, not too fast mind, but just enough to feel a little extra pain.

I made it to Nasu just a little before dusk and noticed how significantly colder it was, the more northerly into the mountains that I proceeded. Thankfully, I was staying in a cosy cabin for the next couple of nights, for to camp would've been to compel myself to a certain death.

There were just a few other guests staying at the Ittan Guesthouse, and the two young chaps working there - Heihachi and Toru - invited me over to the lounge area for some food and drink. Toru cooked up a mean feast - for a meagre fee - which I was glad to wolf down. His partner in crime, Heihachi - who was dressed in snowboarding gear - tried his best to engage me in conversation, but alas after feasting and the all-important compulsory beer, my Japanese was about as impressive as a plate of cold baked beans on toast. Besides which, my cabin bed was calling me over with the promise of its snugness.

I said my farewells for the night and retreated. As I walked back to my room, it was freezing outside and snowflakes were beginning to gently fall. It appeared that Tochigi's winter was still in full swing. Yet, inside my room, the gas heater was raging: warm and cosy. I slept like a corpse.

Nasu
16 miles

A thin layer of snow had settled overnight, giving me the perfect excuse to build some snowmen. I hated how cold it was in the mountains, yet the sight of my snowmen over breakfast gave me some warmth and encouragement.

The 5-mile climb up to Yumoto Park from my guesthouse was a relatively gruelling uphill ascent. I was gratefully travelling light though; my luggage remaining in my room.

My uphill monologue normally went a little something like this: '*Fucking, shitty wank, piss, cunt, bollock, muff... why the fuck am I doing this? What kind of mug am I? Stupid twat, fuck, piss.*' And that's even a toned down version, so as not to offend anyone's Mum. But it also has to be said that I quite often offend myself with the physical assault of words that spew forth from my wretched tongue, to the point that I often want to kick my own head in. Clearly physical exertion more often than not brings out the worst in me at times.

It would take me roughly an hour to reach Yumoto Park and my arrival saw my attitude switch remarkably. 'Ah wow, this is brilliant, life is great, I love you world, you have nice hair...' etc., etc.

In Yumoto Park itself one can find Sesshoseki, a.k.a. 'The Murder Stone.' The stone is shrouded in legend, and is the subject of a lot of speculation. Back before you dear Reader and I were born, some 800 years ago in fact, it is said that a 9-tailed fox roamed the lands; a fox that traversed through both India and China bringing havoc and mayhem to anyone that should cross its path. The fox would eventually make landfall in Japan. Here it would disguise itself as a beautiful young maiden and try to seduce the emperor. But the evil fox's plan was foiled by a wise old fortune teller and it was chased into the mountain of Nasu-Dake by 80,000 troops, where it was eventually slain. Here its soul turned to stone. The stone was full of anger and rage - and monks would often pray to the stone to try and calm the evil spirit within; a spirit so hate-fuelled that the stone cracked, releasing poisonous gases. Anyone that ventured too close to the stone would instantly be struck dead by its deadly vapours.

Today the stone is cordoned off and it is said that the gases emitted are only strong enough to kill small mammals and birds that venture too close to it. The pale grey stone and surrounding ground is strewn yellow with sulphur. In the air, the egg-like sulphur stench was present from surrounding vents and hot springs. In my presence the fox lay dormant, today death would not be on the agenda... always a pleasure to know.

Whilst observing The Murder Stone, an ice cold wind straight out of the depths of a harsh, unforgiving winter swept through the valley, making me shiver. Snow fell and I looked up past a forest of leafless trees toward Sanbonyari Peak, the highest point of Nasu-Dake (1,917m). Its once snow-covered peak was now gloomy and smothered in a dark and ominous cloud cover. On this day I had no need to be up there, no need at all. The cold wind was a selling point for me to descend the mountain back to my guesthouse, a journey with its uncomfortable bumpy descent, saw me take only a mere 17 minutes - as opposed to the previous hour-long uphill trudge. If only when life is metaphorically going downhill it could be as much fun as a cyclist's downhill descent. But it just isn't… is it?

Sadly, back at my guesthouse, my snowmen were dead.

STATS

Dates: 2/04/2014 – 6/04/2014
Total miles traversed: 590 miles
Total time in the saddle: 62 hours and 3 minutes

6. FUKUSHIMA
福島県

Nasu - Aizuwakamatsu
75 miles

I spent a vast bulk of the day ascending into headwind through the mountains and into Fukushima Prefecture; the cold crisp air numbing my cheeks. It was a tiring affair, but I was passing through some serene landscapes: small villages snuggled deep in the mountains, snow littered rice paddies, fresh running water served directly from the surrounding mountains and a collection of curious but friendly eyes greeting me as I passed.

I'd exhausted my food rations relatively early on and by the time I'd found my old friend 7-Eleven, I swear I was burning up vital organs as body fuel. I gorged on carbs until I felt like a bloated marmot and ascended further up a small narrow mountain road to the former trading post station of Ōuchijuku. During the Edo Period, the village was used to connect Aizu with Nikko along a road known as the Aizu-Nishi Kaido trade route. The village with its dirt roads and thatched roof houses has been completely restored to how it would have looked during those early Edo Period days. The shops offer up local produce, food and handicrafts; the only thing out of place being the automobiles and chirping iPhones.

The sun was sitting low in the sky and I could feel it getting rapidly colder as I neared the end of the small main street of Ōuchijuku. I still had some 16 miles of ground to cover before nightfall, so with haste I climbed up further into the mountains and away from Ōuchijuku. I was treated to a beautifully appeasing ascent, with captivating views across this snow entrenched landscape, twice stopping to marvel at the surroundings and more importantly to ply on extra layers of clothing. The cold was slowly creeping into my bones and I would be happy when I made it to the city of Aizuwakamatsu mere moments before sundown.

On this night I would decide against the cold, for it was my 31st birthday and I thought that I'd treat myself like a little prince. For the first and only time during my entire journey, I checked into a lush hotel; flash-packing, some might call it. Situated on the 8th floor with mind-numbing views of a brick wall from my window, I, for one night only, acquired my own double bed, television, central heating, bathroom, curtains and a carpet. I opened a can of beer and stared at the wall for bit, my birthday having the potential to be an incredibly lonesome and desolate one, until I made a wonderful discovery. Now, I'm normally not a very nosey person (what??), but I decided to open the bedside table drawer. Inside the drawer was a magazine, a pictographic magazine to be precise, filled with little, far from cutesy stories about sweet and innocent Japanese ladies that just so happened to keep accidentally losing all their clothes. Instantly, this eased any notions of the birthday blues, for lonesome I was no longer. And 10 minutes later I was asleep. Warm, content, snug and... drained!

Aizuwakamatsu - Fukushima
67 miles

I awoke early from my slumber, knowing that a formidable task lay ahead of me; one that had been lingering at the back of my mind for some time. For today, I was to attempt to tackle the Bandai-Azuma Skyline; my greatest feat thus far. The road traverses for some 18 miles through the Azuma Mountain Range at an average height of 1,350 metres above sea level. At its highest point the road reaches 1,622 metres, just a short depreciation from the peak of Azuma-kofuji, an active strato-volcano that sits at 1,707 metres.

Down upon the deck it was apparent that I was in for quite the challenge. And as I sat outside 7-Eleven bracing myself and supping on a preliminary coffee, I was being curiously eyed by a local who was sitting in his vehicle. I eyed him back with suspicion, *'What the hell is this guy's problem?'* The next time I'd look back over at him he would be stood before me smiling brightly. It would turn out that he wasn't the enemy after all, just a mere ally interested in my being.

'Doko ni ikimasu ka?' Where are you going? He asked.

I pointed to the mountains of Azuma, *'asoko,'* over there.

A grin began to glisten upon his face. *'Hontou ni?'* Seriously? He then patted me on the leg. *'Daijoubu?'* Ok? Wondering if my legs were fit for the job.

'Ah tabun daijobu desu.' Ah, yeah, maybe, ok. I replied. He nodded approvingly before whipping out a carton of boiled eggs. He offered me one, which I gladly accepted.

'Samukatta nai?' Won't you be cold? He said, before tucking into his egg.

'Tabun.' Probably, I replied, with my mouth full.

'Hmm...sou nan da' that's probably right. *'Ok, oki wo tsukete!'* Ok, take care! Before pushing the rest of the carton of eggs upon me and returning to his vehicle. His hospitality was stamped with kindness, something that is no rarity in Japan.

The mountain range surrounding me rose and fell, before distantly fading into a light-blue haze; everywhere dotted with a procession of trees stripped by the indignities of winter. The snow in some places was stacked at some 12ft high along the sides of the road - which is closed for the bulk of winter due to such heavy snowfall in the area. Yet today however as luck would have it, the roads had been cleared of snow and it was the first day of the year that the skyline was open to the public – a.k.a. me!

The ascent of the skyline was naturally a long, hard trudge, as expected. Yet, I felt that my legs were now becoming more and more accustomed to the daily abuse, and allowed me to traverse the mountains all day without any aches or pains at the end of it. A pleasing note for the amount of strain I had been putting my body through.

With the altitude, came the inevitable drop in temperature, accompanied by a bitterly cold and biting wind. The scenery though was spellbinding and addictive; some of the most spectacular I would encounter - beauty that fuelled my urge to proceed further.

After a couple of hours, I made it to a snow corridor along the highest section of the road, at the end of which I caught sight of a floss like plume of sulphuric gas being emitted from the craggy, snow-splashed mountainside.

At around 5pm, I was starting to lose light fast, but finding myself in relative proximity to the conical peak of Azuma-kofuji, temptation struck me. I began to tussle with the idea of trekking to its summit. Whilst doing so, a sudden and pressing wind swiped through the mountains, chilling the cold sweat upon my spine. 'Nah, fuck that,' I immediately murmured. To linger now would have been a mistake. And so I ventured directly into the skyline's descent.

The road, lacking in traffic, allowed for a rapid descent as I weaved with ease around the skyline's winding bends, hitting a personal record high speed of 32.6 mph; I was in an adrenaline junkie's paradise. However, the more I gained speed the more the wind seemed to howl back at me, exposing the critical error I had made of not having bought any gloves with me. Within minutes I could barely feel my digits; the freezing conditions making them look like a collection of very raw looking and slightly weird penises. I had to stop, I was getting frost bite. I would have to Bear Grylls it, or risk losing a pinky. And… I needed my pinky!

Unzipping my fly, I ushered my pork sword forth out into the open, a task which in itself, considering the climes, was a trifle tricky. I felt like I had to wave something sexy in front of it just to get it to come out of the grotto. Yet, once this was achieved, I was able to bring life back into my frozen fingers by dousing them in what felt like molten piss. I could feel the blood warming from within, allowing me to gain back the sensation of actually possessing fingers. This was a good sign. I gratefully clenched my hands together with all the sensation I could muster, and looked out in the direction of Fukushima City. At such an altitude, the city looked a lot like Legoland - the sky, for now, still bright, but it was beginning to fade a little at the edges.

Breaking away from the city, the vegetation took on various shades of green, yellow and orange, filling the beautiful landscape with a contrast of colours all the way up to my current snowy white surrounds. I was beginning to feel like I was trapped in a massive freezer, but to see the mountain in its wintery state, added an immeasurable charm to my whole adventure.

I rifled through my bag and plucked out a couple of pairs of Family Guy socks, placing them over my hands. Stewie and Quagmire acted as my digit defence system as I set forth, rallying down the remainder of this cold and exciting mountain range.

The skies eventually darkened the closer I got to suburbia, but the bright lights of the city guided me towards its colourful core.

Fukushima

History dictates that Japan is no stranger to Mother Nature's wrath: earthquakes, tsunami's, volcanoes, torrential rain, landslides and typhoons have blighted Japan's islands for millennia. Situated precariously along the so called Pacific Rim of Fire, a number of the Earth's tectonic plates converge, enabling islands, mountain chains and volcanoes to formulate. It is here that trouble is often birthed as the Pacific plate moves westward towards Japan and collides with the Okhotsk plate, forming a subduction zone; the former is forced under the later, causing great friction and unrest amongst the earth's fault lines, which inevitably leads to earthquakes. And on March 11th 2011 the world was to bear witness to the cruel and cantankerous ways of this highly volatile area.

At 14:46 in the afternoon, 45 miles east off the Sanriku coastline, a magnitude 9.0 earthquake struck; an earthquake that would come to be known as the Great East Japan Earthquake. It triggered one of the most fearsome tsunami's man has ever borne witness to, bringing relentless death and destruction to all in its path. The tsunami reached the coast of Japan some 50 minutes after the earth was jolted by the gigantic earthquake. It unleashed waves of 20 metres, ventured some 6 miles inland and flooded an area of approximately 217 square miles. The results were devastating, but this word seems massively tame when compared to the scale of carnage caused. 15, 853 people lost their lives and over 300,000 lost their homes and possessions.

Yet, amongst this already completely disastrous event, would rise another catastrophic monstrosity that would plague Fukushima for years to come. Along the coast, just 40 miles south-east of Fukushima City, is the Daiichi Nuclear Power Plant. The Plant was not spared during the tsunami and its cooling systems were disabled when inundated with vast swathes of the Pacific Ocean. The back-up generators, which pumped the water into the reactors to keep them cool, failed, which led the reactors to overheat and caused three of the six reactors at the plant to merge into a full scale nuclear meltdown. This would be the biggest nuclear disaster since Chernobyl, back in 1986. The meltdown led to some 50,000 people being evacuated locally and a 12-mile exclusion zone being set up, amidst fears of high levels of radiation. At one stage, evacuation plans for Tokyo were even being considered.

So, when I came rolling down into Fukushima, it was only natural to feel some sort of trepidation. Yet, as far as I could tell, no one looked significantly altered by the effects of radiation – which was a relief. This city of some 290,000 people looked as any other big Japanese city would: salarymen stumbled around drunkenly after work, shouting at vending machines; people passed me on the bus, burying their heads into the world of their mobile phones; young girls paraded out of department stores cluttered with bags of expensive designer clobber; old ladies terrorised the sidewalks on their bicycles - colloquially known as *mamachari*. Life, continued on as normal.

My Couchsurfing host for the night was Nina, an English teacher from Wisconsin. She confirmed that she wouldn't be living here if she didn't feel safe, as she poured me a glass of tap water. I drunk hesitantly, but the water tasted as pure as any other water I'd drank in Japan. Needless to say, I wasn't as nervous as Japanese MP Yasuhiro Sonoda would've been when he shakily sampled some decontaminated water directly from a puddle inside one of the nuclear reactors, in an effort to boost trust in the government. And who could blame the public when stories were breaking about botched jobs by TEPCO (Tokyo Electric Power Company) at the plant - where approximately 300 tonnes of contaminated water was said to have been leaking into the Pacific Ocean every day for at least 2 years, post nuclear meltdown. This killed the local fishing industry and with soil and groundwater also affected, it was hard to persuade the local residents of the area's overall safety.

The World Health Organisation stated that there would be no discernible long-term health effects in Fukushima, which in theory should give warmth to those that rely on the land for a living.

Hopefully, in time, people will be able to gain back the trust lost in their government. But for something so truly devastating, is time really the answer?

Fukushima - Sendai
68 miles

In grand parallel to yesterday's climbing bonanza, I felt somewhat spared. Straddling a path alongside Japan's 6th longest river the Abukuma, I was able to traverse a stress-free 30 miles uninterrupted, along the clear water's edge. The weather was warm with a gentle breeze. To the west, the mountains jutted with their snowy peaks; a constant reminder of the past week's hard graft. As I ventured closer to the coast, the river broadened, rapids formed and the waters became more opaque with churned up sediment, as the Abukuma gained momentum; becoming livelier in its quest to reach the Pacific.

Filtering away from the course of the river, I joined the rather vulgar Route 4 to Sendai. Heavy traffic plied back and forth hurriedly along a soulless road lined with an array of commerce that would repeat itself over and over - like the background of a chase scene in a Tom & Jerry cartoon; outlets eagerly enticing the passers-by. For some 20 miles I would be oppressed, confined to the sidewalks through fear of becoming human tripe. It was slow and monotonous, and then I found Sendai.

STATS

Dates: 7/04/2014 – 9/04/2014
Total miles traversed: 800 miles
Total time in the saddle: 84 hours

7. MIYAGI
宮城県

Sendai

In the 17th Century there lived a Daimyo with balls of steel; a guy so hard that when he came face to face with the smallpox as a juvenile, he plucked his own eyeball out - giving him the nickname of 'The One-eyed Dragon.' That Daimyo's name was Date Masamune, and as he grew, he became more dastardly and baleful as he raped and pillaged local lands. Inevitably, he became a prominent power recognised by the great Tokugawa Ieyasu who would gift the local brute further land – plus the title of 'Lord of the Domain.' On this land a sleepy little fishing village was to be transformed into one of the most profitable powerhouses in the country, that city was Sendai.

To this day, the city continues to flourish as its population punches in at just over a million, making it the largest city in Miyagi Prefecture and the whole of the Tōhoku region.

Its downtown encompasses a number of shopping arcades and long boulevards lined by a multitude of trees and green spaces, giving the city the nickname of 'The City of Trees.' It is also the home of *Gyūtan*, the local specialty of grilled cow tongue, the non-professional Sony Sendai F.C, and one of the largest Tanabata Matsuri Festivals in Japan. In August, the city is bedecked with a series of multi-coloured decorations crafted by local shops, schools and community centres; each item intrinsically detailed with its own symbolic meaning. Unfortunately, I wouldn't be here for the Tanabata festival; but arrived just in time to get stuck behind a big, stinking, dumpster truck. It was a very vocal truck, as it blasted out a sad, almost broken rendition of 'Happy Birthday'. The oddity of the situation almost distracted me from the bad odours being emitted, but not quite, for the truck truly hummed.

It didn't take me long to find myself a small mountain to contend with; Mt. Aoba being the base of Sendai's very first castle, constructed by bad balls Date Masamune himself, back in 1601. A castle that throughout history has been destroyed continuously by earthquakes and fires, its ultimate demise coming at the hands of an American carpet-bombing session in 1945.

Little remains of the castle today, just the earth and stonework of the wall, yet from there one is able to observe contrasting views across the city.

Scattered across Mt. Aoba one can also find various campuses belonging to the Tōhoku University; a university that I must confess I just couldn't imagine attending. Asking a student to battle a hangover with a mountain each and every day is quite simply begging for disaster. The only possible approach that I could conjure would be to remain drunk on a constant basis, but then that would come at the risk of vomiting upon ones shoes or a fellow student's notebook; a very impractical situation yet, thankfully, due to the gift of being an imbecile, one that I would never have to likely encounter.

With hunger taking a stranglehold upon my guts, I raced back down the mountain, gormandized on a curry and then swiftly checked into my hostel for the night.

The moment I walked into my dorm room, I knew that I was heading for a sleepless night when I clapped eyes on the fattest Japanese man I had ever seen. A guy so fat that I swear I could actually see him getting fatter in real-time - before my very eyes. He made a sumo wrestler look like a stick insect. There was no possible way that he was ever going to sleep quietly. Just looking at him I knew that he was going to snore like a complete bastard. And do you know what? He *did* snore like a complete bastard, all night long... the bastard.

What made matters worse was that he was on the top bunk, so not only was I not sleeping due to the noise pollution of persistent snoring and someone potentially choking upon their own blubber, but I was also lying in fear of being destroyed outright. For, if the top bunk should fall, I would never be found.

Every movement from above saw me holding my breath in anticipation of ultimate decimation. I consider myself to be a bit of dorm veteran now and have over the years mustered up a few ways of disabling the designated room snorer: the scrunching of a plastic bottle or rustling of a bag, a deep and heavy cough, a high pitched screech, the slamming of a door, a boisterous fart or a cheeky jab to the ribs. However, in this instance, all of my dirtiest tricks would be to no avail. The guy was an impenetrable fortress and would not be broken.

I'd lay awake, seething through till dawn where I would - without any other choice - rise early.

Sendai - Ishinomaki
37 miles

As soon as I was back on the road, muscling my way through the inner city traffic and back out towards the coast, I was feeling decisively calm.

My morning saw me take in one of Japan's three most scenic sights, Matsushima. During the Edo Period of the 17th Century, a Confucian scholar by the name of Shunsai Hayashi traversed Japan by foot and listed three sights which he felt were the epiphany of the nation's scenic beauty: Amanohashidate of Kyoto, Miyajima of Hiroshima and my current locale - Matsushima in Miyagi Prefecture.

'Matsu' means 'Pine' and 'Shima' means 'Island'. These equate to the perfect name for this idyllic bay dotted with some 260 small alpine coveted islands and islets. The arrangement of the islands had geographically enabled the area to succumb to very little damage from the tsunami.

Planting my bike amongst a small gathering of pines, I walked over to the small island of Oshima. A small red bridge connects the mainland to the island and upon the bridge were four noisy young Chinese girls taking selfies with their hideous selfie sticks. I courteously said *hello* as I passed and the squabble abruptly came to a halt as the four girls eyed me with suspicion. I was dismissed by silence and upon reaching the other side of the bridge to Oshima the squabble was back up to peak levels again. I'd blatantly interrupted selfie time; I felt like a prize boob with donkey manure on top.

Oshima contains a couple of short walks. The island was once a retreat for monks and houses a number of caves that were used for meditating in, along with stone scriptured tablets with cunning crows perched atop of them that appeared to be stalking my every move. I sat on a large stone and cast my eyes out to sea, it radiated tranquillity and I could see why Mr Hayashi had favoured this place. Taking a rice ball from my coat pocket, I instantly gained two new little black 'cawwing' friends.

Upon my exit of Oshima, the Chinese girls were still hard at work, trying their best to take at least 9.4 million selfies. I obeyed the rules of non-acknowledgement and in return it made the crossing a considerably smoother transition.

As I continued to cycle, I wondered if a world without the Oxford Dictionary approved "Selfie" would be a better place, but I also wondered if there will ever be a goat born that can make spaghetti. Both thoughts led to an unsustainable quagmire, but kept my mind copiously busy all the same. And then… something depressing happened.

Just a short ride north-easterly of Matsushima was Higashi-Matsushima, here I was suddenly hit by the consequences of the March 11th 2011 Tsunami. The change sudden and without warning, a world unlike any I have ever encountered would unravel before me.

I cycled passed the now defunct Nobiru train station, with its faded information signs and wilted wooden platform chairs. Nature had destroyed this station and it was now overcome by vegetation. Across from the station, toward the coast, were miles and miles of flattened open land. It was desolate and empty - bar the myriad of trucks, diggers and graders now plummeting back and forth reshaping the land; a land people once called home. A flurry of topsoil kicked up, tearing a reckless path across what was now a quarry. I felt uneasy about being here, a place where 1,039 souls had been cruelly taken. This would be my first snippet of the effects of the tsunami and from here on in, my journey along the devastated Sanriku coastline would not get any easier. A sturdy wind was taking hold as I pressed on along some testing roads. Construction vehicles passed with just centimetres to spare as dust and fetid wet sludge from the roads surface plastered me, it was a struggle to keep balance and my full attention was needed if I was to avoid an imminent nobbling.

A post-apocalyptic-esque wasteland continued to unfold as a real sense of the damage caused was becoming horrifically evident. Although all the tsunami debris had since been cleared (some 25 million tonnes of it!) the occasional abandoned house - once part of suburbia – stood eerily secluded amongst the open plains, destined to ruin.

By late afternoon, I made it to Ishinomaki, one of the most heavily affected areas. Waves here in places would reach as high as 20 metres, destroying some 50,000 buildings and taking 3,162 lives; even now some 400 people are still unaccounted for. Amongst the baron and flat unkempt land adjacent to the coast, were a number of grave sites dictating the horrors of that fateful day back in 2011.

I cycled through what felt like a void in reality, before straying inland away from the coast to find a smaller rendition of Ishinomaki that was in the process of finding its feet. Amongst a concoction of shabby buildings and cracked roads, were signs of innovation. A number of quirky little back street coffee houses and restaurants were dotted about, along with the all-important snack bars. A 'Happy Recovery Centre' had also been established, essentially a series of small containers converted into shops, bars and eateries - in an effort to draw back the crowds.

Sprinkled about the city were a number of statues of cartoon characters designed by local manga artist Shotaro Ishinomori, who also has a spaceship shaped museum dedicated to him close by. A vibe of sorts had been etched into the city and life went on. It had to.

After a bite to eat and a coffee, the town had sunk into darkness; accommodation was thin on the ground, so I needed to find a place to stealth camp for the night. Instinct brought me to the top of a hill, the same hill that some three years previously would have saved countless lives. Unfortunately, not the lives of 70 of Okawa elementary school's 108 students, for when the earthquake initially struck there was great debate amongst the school's teachers as to where they should evacuate their students. One teacher suggested that all students and teachers should evacuate to the hill directly behind the school - where I stood - the majority of staff disagreed with this common sense suggestion. The teacher stuck to his guns, but only managed to persuade one other student to accompany him up the hill. Both survived. The rest of the teachers would lead the students across a bridge towards a hill much farther away. They in turn would all be swept away by the tidal wave, very few surviving.

One of the surviving teachers was condemned by parents after the disaster; he was later to end his own life.

I apologise Reader if I am bumming you out somewhat, but there was little light on this section of my journey. The events witnessed from distant lands via YouTube or the News offer a terrifying perspective, but just being here in person during the aftermath gave me such a real insight into one of Mother Nature's cruellest hours. But rest assured, when there was light, it shined bright and beautiful. There is something truly heart-warming about communities coming together during times of tragedy and overcoming the differences that have turned their worlds upside down. Like war or any catastrophe, a great number of stories unfold, some we learn by - some we don't. Everyone who has experienced the likes of the tsunami will have a story burnt on their memory; such is the power of a catastrophe. And, as I lay camping on a tennis court atop a hill - out of the reach of the sea's cruel potential - I felt safe. I prayed for the dead and the future safety of the people who had lost everything. It's all I could do.

Ishinomaki - Minamisanriku
79 miles

Traipsing the Oshiku Peninsula was a regrettable decision, for situated just 45 miles off the coast of the peninsula was where the 2011 earthquake began. This would make the peninsula the closest part of Honshū to the quake's epicenter.

It was becoming easier to see why Miyagi was one of the most devastated prefectures. All around me new roads, bridges, tunnels, sea walls and *debatable* new housing were being pieced together on a grand scale. Inside just a couple of miles, I found myself inundated with hoards of construction vehicles, some 20 to 30 passing by the minute. My presence was an obvious hindrance; with no sidewalks or hard shoulders I would give way frequently to allow for safe passage.

The terrain was formidable; a bulk of the roads consisted of loose gravel and this made for an uncomfortable ride along a succession of rollercoaster-like hills; occasionally revealing battered, heavy depopulated fishing coves. A staple part of the local economy that for years has survived on its fishing industry now faced a stiff challenge to reclaim its former years of glory.

By early afternoon, I was famished; my general all-round lack of brain matter meant that I'd scoffed all of my food during the early part of the morning... and it doesn't take too much trudging up and down hills for one to burn up the calories. Of course, this region being heavily stricken by a gigantic natural disaster - almost beyond human comprehension - hasn't allowed for too many convenience stores. Normally, all one has to do is whistle and a 7-Eleven will pop-up from out of nowhere like a cheeky gigolo.

I now longed for a hideous 30-mile sprawl of convenience stores and fast food joints that I would traditionally grumble about. Consumerism suddenly had sex appeal; surprising how an empty stomach can bring about such a change of heart. This is when I decided to form a mostly nonsensical game in my head, whereby I question what depraving acts I would be willing to torment myself with, in order to obtain an all-important food fix. It went a little something like this:

Q1: Would you kiss a rabid badger on the lips for a Mars Bar?
A: Hmm... yeah go on then.
Q2: Would you play naked Twister with a sumo wrestler in exchange for a packet of Fizzy Chewitts?
A: はい.
Q3: Would you devour your own flesh trumpet in an attempt to relinquish your very own starvation?
A: What??? No!!!...What??
Q4: Would you be willing to admit to anyone that reads this garble that you're a crazy person... for one single, yet decadent, Twiglet?
A: Definitely.

And so on and so forth. Needless to say I was a pretty hungry lad and with every hill I climbed and every corner I rounded, I nuzzled with this slight notion that I might just catch sight of a shop. Every time though my hopes would be consequently dashed; hopes that I felt were melding into far-off dreams that might possibly never come true.

The sight of Onagawa Town, or lack of perhaps being the more appropriate description, would direct my mind away from my hunger for a while, and in turn saw my heart plummet. An omnipresent cartel of construction vehicles were decorating the land, with dirt being bought in from the surrounding mountains, raising the ground level to above what it had been before the earthquake. The wind tormenting in nature would try its very best to be repulsive, kicking up swathes of loose dirt and sending it in the direction of a flock of tourists that had just turned up on a tsunami tour bus. The bulk of them headed over to one solitary capsized four-storey building; all that now remained of a town centre completely obliterated, again hundreds of precious lives lost.

I pressed on further, still as hungry as ever, around copious bends, through dark, claustrophobic and dingy tunnels and then finally up my last ascent of the day - before light became my saviour. Just as I was coming around to the idea of eating my own flesh trumpet, I happened across something quite miraculous. From some 80 metres or so above sea level, it was at first like a mirage, a radiant glow of green, red and white. I squinted ever so slightly to try and focus upon what felt like some sort of unheralded epiphany. A 7-Eleven! It was indeed an epiphany!

I raised my hands to the air jubilantly and looked around for others to share my joy with. Yet there was no one. I was cold and alone – which had become a standard. I journeyed down the hill, my mind racing with thoughts of what I was going to gorge upon. My surroundings got ever darker by the second, but the exuberant glow emitting from the 7-Eleven would only get brighter the closer I neared. Upon arrival, the store itself looked as if it had only been slung together some 4 minutes previously. *Please note that this was certainly no complaint, merely an observation.* I parked my bike and quite literally ran into the store as if I had only minutes left in which to consume food - or I would die instantly. I filled my basket with all manner of supplies: noodles, burgers, tinned fish, chocolate, crisps, cream cakes, corndogs, more chocolate, boiled eggs, fried chicken and, for good measure, more chocolate.

I promptly paid for the goods and then scuttled outside excitedly into the cold of night. The proceeding moments however I have to say were somewhat hazy. Everything that I could get my hands on became harvested – until: piles of wrappers, cartons, crisp packets, chicken bones and plastic bags lay discarded around me in a heathen fashion. Food first, environment later was my motto of the moment! Passers-by looked at me in amazement - or perhaps confusion - as the feeding frenzy continued. And then, suddenly, my stomach began to ache and I felt a little dizzy; I'd had my fill.

I sat down amongst my own squalor, feeling content, and let my food digest. After which, I picked up my litter and then sought out a place to spend the night.

The odds of a tsunami actually hitting during my brief stint along the coast were vastly slim, but for a thin sliver of self-harmony - and peace of mind - I would again seek out higher ground.

Back on the road, it was now eerily quiet and not a motor vehicle stirred. I could see very little of my current surrounds, bar a row of dim red lights and a small, illuminated shrine upon a hill... a steep yet short climb away from the main road would lead me to its summit.

At the foot of some steps leading up to the shrine was a small park; a designated evacuation point should a tsunami strike. I set up camp under a climbing frame and, soon after, lost consciousness.

Minamisanriku - Ofunato
57 miles

Daylight bought little change to my eyes. A vast nothingness of baron land would greet me in what was once a place known as Minamisanriku, a town that was 95% wiped out during the tsunami. My thoughts dismally led out to each and every place that I would encounter along this devastated section of coast: Kesennuma, Rikuzentakata and Ofunato, all equally decimated towns and each a stark reminder of that fateful day that saw nearly 16,000 people perish.

The wind again was ice cold and biting; a constant burden. It was a Sunday and there was no construction work going on, which meant that I stood a lesser chance of getting mashed by 70 tonnes of solid truck. I was more fortunate on the food front today as well, stumbling across a number of recovery markets. Buying local food and produce, in some small way, allowed money to seep back into the dwindling local economy. With very few options post-tsunami or even homes to live in, many residents had no choice but to move away from the area or into bigger cities. But it is these small up and coming enterprises - like the recovery markets - that are allowing the local economy to slowly claw its way back. Through the importance of a little faith and courage - which I have most definitely witnessed - Miyagi's battered coast will strive again.

STATS

Dates: 10/04/2014 – 13/04/2014
Total miles traversed: 973 miles
Total time in the saddle: 103 hours and 50 minutes

8. IWATE
岩手県

Ofunato - Kamaishi
35 miles

I spent a cold and unrewarding night under a bridge in true hobo fashion. Even with multiple layers of clothing - inclusive of waterproofs - the cold still had a way of chilling me to the bone. I lay in silence, occasionally shivering, whilst watching the darkness of night slowly peel away; it was in no rush. My tent was already showing signs of wear and tear: a split seam some 3 inches directly above my head, a foot-long tear at the bottom of the tent where the support poles were too long - and one trapped zipper. I guess this was to be expected, for when you buy cheap, you pay twice.

When light became more of a prominent factor, I crawled out of my sleeping bag; struggling tirelessly with the cursed zipper in the process. It was going to be one of those days.

It had snowed during the night; the mountain peaks to the north tipped with a fresh layer of white. I headed in their general direction, a stiff climb leading me away from Ofunato. My legs felt unstrained and unfazed, it was as if I'd gained their trust; mountain hurdles were now part of my daily ritual. It was when I had to go between the hurdles, that concern would grip me. Being a Monday, the roads were laden with construction vehicles again, making the tunnels along Route 45 nothing more than a cyclist's death trap. As I reached the mouth of one such tunnel, I could see no end through the conglomeration of traffic. There was no hard shoulder for me to straddle and to venture further would have been suicide. I had to look for a different way around.

To the side of the tunnel, a small road sloped away down toward the coast. From here an even smaller mountain path intersected and led back up into the mountains. Only assumption dictated that this battered old path with fallen trees strewn across it would lead me to the other side. It was either this or take a chance on imminent death back toward the tunnel. The path looked as if it hadn't been journeyed upon for years; one of many ancient and seemingly lost mountain paths that I would transcend during my time in Japan.

Before long, the path would narrow further and eventually become devoid of any bitumen; condemning itself to a collection of loose rocks and huge boulders that in places blocked the majority of the path - due to past landslides. This was no place to be cycling. I dismounted and began to push my ride up the mountain. I would sweat and curse every moment of the way, creeping slowly upwards for what seemed like an eternity. My footing occasionally slipped upon the loose rubble, my shins hammering frustratingly into the teeth of my bicycle pedals, sweat stinging my eyes. I sought brief refuge under a small canopy of trees where I took a break to eat a couple of gigantic oranges that a kindly farmer had given me on the outskirts of Ofunato. It was inspiring to see that in such harsh times, people were still willing to give, it was such acts of kindness that urged me forward.

After an arduous hour or so, the path began to level out and then inevitably fall, giving way to the bitumen. I then returned to my saddle. Racing down, I exited close to the other side of the tunnel of death, still clogged with a filthy number of trucks, their flashlights barely visible amongst the tunnel's haze. I shuddered at the thought of what might have become of me if I'd have entered, as I continued on with my journey away from the light-less tunnel. Verging left around a long winding bend though, I would be greeted by another dauntingly life-sapping tunnel. Shit!

I had neither the time nor the energy to find an alternate means around this one. A tunnel just as formidable looking as its predecessor, but the fact that I had to venture inside it made the whole scenario all the more appalling. I stopped outside the entrance and counted seven trucks before there was a break in the flow of traffic. Again with no hard shoulder or sidewalk, I could almost sense the musk of my own death before forcefully cajoling myself forward.

From the moment I was inside the tunnel, there was no turning back, I had to commit. It was dark and I choked on the traffic fumes. A dreary set of oncoming lights emerged from the blanket of murk before me. From behind, the traffic would soon return. What began as a distant hum would soon grow in intensity to a heavy monotonous drone; the closer the drone got, the faster my heart would beat. With every truck that approached from behind, I stopped to give way; my heart was in my mouth as the trucks passed within a fraction of my body. And, with every passing, I would restart the process and begin to pedal again. It would be a gradual affair and a mentally draining 600 or so metres, yet concentration was pivotal, to think of tits for a mere shadow of a second would've lead to my own undoing.

As I etched closer to the end of the tunnel, the light got suddenly clearer, I found myself drawn to it like a moth; a sudden rush of adrenaline seeing me out victoriously. Ecstatic at my survival, I gasped for fresh air, never once looking back at the tunnel. A tunnel that would scar me for some time, but such gruelling tunnels were now forcibly becoming a part of the cycle touring life for me.

Approaching Kamaishi, I hit the 1000 mile mark. To my right, overlooking the Pacific, was the Kamaishi Dai-kannon: a 48.5 metre tall Goddess of Mercy statue; untouched by the 2011 tsunami. Yet, as I drew closer, unfortunately the same could not be said for central Kamaishi. From a vantage point upon a hill, I had haunting flashbacks of a YouTube video I once saw of the port area of this city getting completely engulfed in water and consequently swept away; houses and cars being tossed about as if they were toys. The city lost around one thousand of its inhabitants. Even now, the place looks significantly gutted.

This was not the first time that Kamaishi had been severely affected either, just over a century earlier, in 1896, the Meiji-Sanriku earthquake hit, causing widespread damage to the Sanriku coastline and completely destroying Kamaishi. In 2011, the local people again were left to pick up the pieces - just as their ancestors had done.

In the darkness, I found an angel, her name was Junko Miyashita: petite and bubbly, armed with a sinister smile that declared a voracious attitude that appeared to be constantly ready to take on the world. There was nothing not to like about her, she was laying down the foundations of a positive future for many a Kamaishi locals. Her role as part of a tsunami recovery project was to engage the public by arranging community events; putting some cheer and hope back into the broken hearts of a broken community.

She offered me the most unique of Couchsurfing experiences, inviting me to her home in a tsunami refugee shelter. Essentially this was a sports park upon a hill that, post-tsunami, had been decked out with a series of mobile shelters to provide accommodation for hundreds of locals. Junko informed me that in 3 years only 2% of the population had been re-homed locally, so many were still forced to live in these makeshift shelters. City planning and the difficult and compulsory Japanese red-tape was making redevelopment frustratingly slow. Around the camp, many elderly women strolled about, some tending to potted plants outside their shelters, some staring at the wall, whilst others huddled in small groups, nattering. To have everything taken by the sea: your home, your possessions, your life - was explicitly daunting. Yet they still managed to afford me a smile when I passed them; greeting me like I was an old friend. Their spirit admirable, their spirit strong.

Kamaishi

The following day, Junko showed me around downtown Kamaishi. It is a city once famed for its steel production, yet now like many a coastal communities, it relied heavily on its commercial fishing industry. The port area had been invariably stripped, but showed small signs of resurgence. New cafes and recovery markets, along with a monstrously huge Aeon Mall, were all present. However, reminders of the tsunami were always constant: the surrounding hills dotted with gravestones, void plots of land and deteriorating buildings; some structures bearing a red cross with a circle around it. Junko informed me that, post-tsunami a red cross was placed on a building when dead bodies were found inside the premises. When the bodies were collected and taken away, a circle would then be placed around the red cross to let everyone know the bodies inside had been removed. A chilling thought.

Closer to the water's edge, a building bore a marker some 15-metres up, pinpointing the exact height to which the deadly wave had reached; everything in the area had been decimated. It was then that I really began to appreciate the work of Junko, like the elderly ladies back at the refugee shelter, she too was able to pull a brave smile out of the bag every day in the face of tragedy; this was certainly no easy feat, but she did it well.

As evening approached, Junko took me to a friend's house for dinner. Along a mutilated street we approached a house of recent structure. The condensed muffle of a television set blazed from within the house as we approached the front door. After Junko knocked, the door slid open within seconds, and an elderly man appeared, stout and greying, seemingly surprised by my presence.

'*Oh! Gaijin desu!*' Oh! It's a foreigner!

Junko introduced me and told the man about my trip. A kind warmth coaxed his face as he introduced himself as Hiro and swiftly invited us out of the cold night and into his home. He gave me a guided tour of his traditional Japanese dwelling. A home once destroyed, yet, post-tsunami, the 76-year-old Hiro-san would find himself re-building it with his own bare hands; his neighbours either dead or re-homed, hence the reason why his house was the only solitary structure in the area. The government recently requested that he re-locate, as they wished to once again demolish his property and use the land for other means. But Hiro-san stood proud in his home and defiant against a government he had lost faith in. If he and his wife Naoki-san could live the remainder of their days on the land - where they had spent the past 50 years of their lives - then they would leave this Earth a happy couple.

Hiro-san ushered us both to sit down around the *kotatsu*; a low table covered with a futon which one can slide one's legs under. The big surprise came from underneath the futon, heat! I was consequently treated to some remarkable Japanese hospitality. Naoki-san was equally surprised by the sight of a *gaijin* within her home, but like her husband she instantly warmed to me and fussed over Junko and I, supplying us with enough home-made food and drink to sink a battleship. And by drink I mean sake, and there appeared to be plenty of that flowing. Every time a sentence was conquered that would equate to the refilling of a glass. I liked Hiro-san's style, him and his wife were truly honourable hosts. Despite the age difference, after a few sakes, Hiro-san and I were pretty much long lost brothers; arms clasped around one another and talking about the good old days in a confused mishmash of both English and Japanese - and also some kind of language that doesn't even exist... yet.

After deer heart sashimi, things took a spontaneous turn. A knock at the door revealed that a taxi had been ordered. It was time to hit the devastated streets of downtown Kamaishi for a karaoke binge, which was probably just about the last thing I was expecting. And so, in an empty bar guided by a few beers, several sakes and some dodgy Beatles duets later, Hiro-san and I found ourselves proverbially shit-faced. Junko was the only one of us to maintain any kind of modesty, sitting silently either in awe or utter embarrassment that two fully grown men could commit to singing so very, very badly.

As was the norm with the fuzz of vast quantities of alcohol consumption (for me, anyway) the memory would slowly begin to ease before taking on a cognitive stand-off, to the point that when I woke up slightly confused the next morning, my embarrassment for the best part had been forgotten. Beneficial for me, not so much for those that happened to be in my exclusive company.

'You were drunk!' said Junko over breakfast, shaking her head and grinning cheekily.

'Me? No not me, I'm English, we don't get drunk,' I contended.

'Yes, very drunk, but Hiro-san more, we had to carry him to taxi,' she replied.

Which I had actually forgotten about, like a piece of the jigsaw puzzle that somehow gets knocked underneath the dresser; once found it could allow you to piece things together with a little more significance. In this instance, when it involved my singing, I really had no intention of completing the said puzzle, so let the pieces remain missing.

'What will you do today?' Junko asked.

I sighed aloud at the thought of cycling, my head throbbing.

'Please stay, and rest,' she affirmed.

I gratefully accepted.

I felt slightly reckless that I wasn't continuing on with my journey today, but I was also enjoying Junko's company - and her friends' too, so was glad to stay another day.

I rested, but not for too long, as Junko had big plans for me. After lunch, driving like a maniac, she took me to a place just north of the city. We parked on the foundations of where a building had once stood. Junko told me that this is where a tsunami evacuation building used to be situated, a building that being designated as a refuge for an oncoming tsunami was considered a safe haven in such an event. The tsunami however would inundate the building, drowning everyone inside. Junko was very teary eyed when she told me the story and I didn't feel the urge to press her, but this was no isolated story, a great number of designated evacuation points were overwhelmed when the tsunami hit; blame again being cast towards the ill-prepared government. Close to the site was a small shrine dedicated to those that died there. We went inside and paid our respects, then lit incense to purify the surrounds. A condolence book lay upon a side table; I left a message.

Outside of the shrine, Junko's car was now accompanied by two other vehicles, containing her two work colleagues, Masaya and Kenta; both equally as charismatic as Junko. The newcomers introduced themselves to me in excitable and slightly hyper English. Then they all joked amongst themselves amiably and it was obvious as to why they were responsible for engaging the public and bringing light back to an area that had fallen upon such dark times. Kenta asked me if I was ready for work. I nodded curiously *'Hai... tabun!'* yes... maybe! They all chuckled at my response.

'Ok, let's go,' said Kenta jovially, before hastily running to his vehicle and whizzing off like a wacky racer towards the coast.

Masaya soon followed, screeching after him in a car that looked as if it had been flung together over breakfast. I jumped into Junko's car with her, before she gamely put her pedal to the metal. Her tongue peaked out of the corner of her mouth slightly in a concentrative effort, she was genuinely racing her work colleagues. I gingerly gave my seat belt a tug, it seemed secure. I'd probably be all right... probably.

Moments later and we were all rejoined at the fishing docks, greeting a local fisherman, Kazuhiko. He too was jolly and infused with life, but like many a folk of these parts he too had a sad story to tell. Kazuhiko, his wife and child all survived the tsunami, but his wife then came to fear for her family and the Sanriku coastline. She moved away from the area, taking Kazuhiko's only child with her. Kazuhiko grew up in Kamaishi and had been fishing these waters all his life, so had no choice but to remain. He still tried valiantly to make his marriage work, but some two weeks previously he had received divorce papers from his wife. He ended his tale by telling us all that it's okay as he has plenty of beer. We all laughed off his misery.

Kazuhiko then put us to work. Donning Wellington boots, disposable aprons and latex gloves, we all certainly looked the part as we were introduced to a big white trough packed full of seaweed. Our job was to throttle the seaweed, making sure as much salt, and what I can only describe as sea gunk, was removed from the plant, before draining it of water and placing it into little blue crates to be stacked on palates. These palates would then be whisked off to market. It was repetitive work, but as the jokes flowed, the team soon hammered out the contents of the trough - surprising Kazuhiko as he praised us for our dexterous pace.

Upon waking up that morning, I never pictured I'd be working as a fisherman, neither did I imagine that I would become a kick-boxer. Spontaneity, was seemingly Junko's middle name, and after saying our farewells to my new work colleagues for the day, she decided to drag me along to a kick-boxing class. Here my strength and cognitive responses were truly put to the test; the teacher using me as a focus point for the small class of about eight students. In fact, it was here that I discovered that I had no strength or cognitive responses at all, and at this point of the evening my Japanese language ability was almost as equally non-existent. I was unable to comprehend even the simplest of instructions. I sweated, dribbled and clawed my way through an intense hour of torment, naturally providing the class with some light Mr Bean-esque entertainment; every muscle-stretching minute of the way. No matter what my own failings may be, especially in regards to the kick-boxing world, as a stooge I shine.

'Wow, you terrible,' Junko said, making the knowledge official.

'*Arigatou*,' thanks. I concluded, slightly out of breath.

'Hungry?'

'Fuck, yeah!'

Back at Junko's refugee centre, after oyster pizza and sharing a beer that I wasn't prepared to demolish myself, I was feeling decisively spent. Junko then pulled out an ominous looking DVD in a transparent plastic wallet. 'You want to watch?' she asked.

'Err…what is it? It's nothing too kinky is it?' I questioned

'No you *hentai*,' *hentai* meaning pervert. 'It's tsunami DVD.'

'Hmm… have you got anything kinky?'

'No, we watch this, my friend make when tsunami come, I never watch before.'

At the time I could think of no worse way to wind down for the evening than to watch tsunami footage. It actually felt a little bit sick, but I would soon learn that Junko just didn't want to be alone when she watched the film. It was a harrowing account from a small fishing village just a short way south of Kamaishi. For 40 minutes we watched as this small part of Japan was engulfed by the sea, an eerie siren repeating over and over as the water rose sharply, people screaming and crying, their lives destroyed. Misery piled upon misery. Junko clutched my arm and I held her as she wept.

Kamaishi – Settai
67 miles

I'd barely blinked and three days had passed. Junko asked me to stay the weekend but as much as I was enjoying her company, an eagerness to continue my journey was beginning to eat at me. My time with her had been an unexpected delight; an intriguing one that left me with mixed emotions. With their earnest spirit and hard work, Junko and her colleagues were helping to rebuild the bleeding hearts of this devastated region. I was sad to say goodbye and as I readied my bike early morning, the elderly lady next door to Junko was already out and about watering her potted plants. She smiled generously, accompanied by a bow, as I in turn reciprocated. I sincerely hoped that she wouldn't have to live the remainder of her life in a refugee camp, it was no place for a grandmother.

I said my farewells to Junko and took a short ride downhill towards central Kamaishi to see Hiro-san. He was up having his breakfast when I arrived, and was a little bewildered to see me. A grin soon beamed across his face, before he shouted: '*Yopparai!*' drunk!

'*Hai, demo anata mo ne?*' Yes, but you too, right? I replied.

'*Sou, sou, sou,*' that's about right.

We both laughed before shaking each other's hands firmly and going about our respective lives. I'd like to think that we'll meet again someday and maybe shame good Beatles records in the name of vocal obnoxiousness; for if anyone knew how to do that, it was certainly Hiro-san and I.

Some 6 miles northerly from Kamaishi lays Ōtsuchi, here another carcass of a town sits upon the fringes of despair. A town that in 2011 lost 10% of its 16,000 population. It was also here that a 27-meter-long sightseeing boat was marooned upon a hotel rooftop, becoming one of the iconic images of the tsunami's aftermath. As I cycled through the town's broken streets, a lonesome Caterpillar digger paraded back and forth, piling up rubble from demolished buildings. A blue pick-up truck lay wasted in a rusted, smashed up heap to the side of the road, having sustained wounds that would never be healed. I headed over to the docks. It was still early morning with the sun perched low in the sky, shimmering off of the open sea; the ever so gentle open sea. An elderly man stood close to the edge of a jetty, gazing out into the endless ocean, his hands clasped behind his back, his eyes strewn with unanswered questions.

Ōtsuchi was a town that felt truly lost. In every devastated town I encountered along my journey, I would often find myself stopping to think. To become accustomed to the realities of what actually happened along this section of coast was and still is exceedingly difficult to comprehend. I often to this day shake my head in disbelief at the tragedies that this part of the world underwent. A monumental feat lay in the hands of the Japanese and for the sake of the scattered communities along this vast section of coast one can only pray that a tragedy such as that on March 11th 2011 will never repeat itself.

Several hours later, I would again be shaking my head in disbelief as a drama besieged the city of Miyako. On the approach to the city, I could see great plumes of thick black smoke aggressively billowing up into the atmosphere. Everywhere I went, people were gathered in the streets looking ahead and discussing the source of the smoke. Fire engines darted past me, their sirens wailing as an all-round commotion set in. Being the budding tourist that I am, I felt that I had no choice but to investigate.

A small collective had formed on a hill skimming the edge of town. I parked my bike, released a banana from my pannier and took it with me to join the masses. I stood next to a group of four elderly Japanese men who were all chuntering away excitedly, in regards to Miyako's fiery new attraction; they were a bit like a Japanese version of the 'Last of the Summer Wine' boys. If there was an odd bathtub lying about somewhere I had no doubt that these boys would've been getting themselves into all sorts of capers with it. One of the gentlemen closest to me, the Compo of the posse, was half way through taking a toke upon his cigarette, when he turned to me, pausing briefly to process my features. Eventually exhaling, he laughed and told his friends about me. They also looked at me and laughed. I deduced from the laughter that it wasn't aimed directly at me, but more of an affable kind of laughter of general surprise at my very existence upon a random hill near a random Japanese town… observing a random local catastrophe.

Japanese Compo gestured to me and pointed down the hill in the direction of the carnage. It appeared that a fishing factory upon Miyako's port was ablaze. It burned gloriously as several fire crews battled maniacally to put it out. A crowd quickly built around me; it appeared that I had haphazardly stumbled across some of the best seats in the house. I would later learn that it took the fire crew some 8 hours to extinguish the blaze. Thankfully there would be no fatalities or injuries.

I devoured my banana to the further amusement of Compo and the boys and then decided to make tracks.

A short ride out of Miyako would take me to Jodogahama Beach; one of the jewels of the area. The name Jodogahama comes from Buddhism; it is said that the landscape of the area is similar to the "Pure Land" - a.k.a. Paradise. Close to the pebbled shoreline, a series of rugged, craggy islets - sparsely covered with vegetation can be found jutting up out of the ocean. The gentle surrounding waters and a perfect blue sky allowed for a placid setting. I walked alone, enjoying my own company.

When night came I always liked to be within close proximity to a town; this was generally a convenience thing: I could eat cake, have a beer, surf the net, do a poo and also not be savaged by a bear whilst I masturbate in my tent. Yet, as dusk began to clutch, I found myself a long way from anywhere, straddling a less than handsome set of mountains. With snow still sitting upon the ground and a temperature slipping by the minute, the night would be a tough one. Eventually, I came to a halt at a small train station in the rather quaint Settai, a remote hamlet buried deep amongst the mountains. The station was basic and unmanned, but had the all-important public toilets.

I climbed a small series of steps to the platform and entered the waiting room via a sliding door. A few chairs, a waste bin, a light and a train timetable awaited me. I checked the train times. There was still one final train left to come for the evening. So as not to draw attention to myself I exited the platform and sat out of sight in the darkness; waiting, shivering. The train appeared from out of a hole in the mountainside; its bright lights tearing a path into the surrounding darkness. It had a single, solitary carriage and, upon its arrival at the station, nothing happened – no embarkers and no leavers. I inquisitively etched myself a little closer. Bar the driver, the train was completely empty, and I almost got the feeling that this was probably always the case. It was all very odd, but I was in Japan and odd was expected.

The train quietly set back off into the mountains. Moments later, the platform lights phased out. I then in turn crept back into the station's waiting room and unrolled my sleeping bag upon the cold hard concrete floor. Its shelter would offer me some refuge but I found myself missing her. Over the past few days I'd become very attached to the charismatic Junko, it was only now that I regretted my decision to leave Kamaishi. I kicked myself at not having agreed to have stayed for the weekend. I'd be under her nice warm roof, beneath her nice warm bed sheets. We'd be together. But, alas, now I had made my stone cold bed, I would have to freeze in it.

Settai – Kuji
49 miles

The sudden sliding open of the train station doors saw me instantaneously jolt upright, my body knew I shouldn't be there and so did the bewildered old lady peering down at me.

'*Gomen*,' sorry, she said bowing her head apologetically at my own sin.

'*Nai, gomen nasai desu*,' No, I'm sorry, I affirmed, before quickly rising to my feet and scuffling about for all my belongings.

She then suddenly appeared to come to terms with the fact that a foreigner just so happened to be kipping on the station platform; shrugging it off, she stepped inside the miniature train station with me and, cloth in hand, began to clean the windows. I looked at my watch, it was barely 5am.

'*Koko de samuku nakatta?*' Wasn't it cold in here? She asked casually, whilst giving an already spotlessly clean section of window some serious elbow grease.

'*Chotto!*' A bit! I replied, bundling my sleeping bag under my arm. She laughed.

'*Ima doko ni ikimasu ka?*' Where will you go now? She queried.

'Kuji,' I replied.

'*Aww sou nan da?*' Aww... is that so?

'*Hai, sou desu,*' Yes, that is so. Now gradually beginning to feel like I was getting the hang of Japanese common courtesy.

'*Ganbatte ne.*' Good luck, she offered.

'*Arigatou gozaimasu, ja mata!*' Thank you, see ya!

I left her to her early morning routine, as I committed to mine. I just hoped that she took a little more time cleaning the already clean train station windows, before heading on down to the communal toilets. For an unholy aroma lingered. And, in shame, I made haste.

Up in the mountains, I passed an electronic sign board which read 1°C, this fact offering up a fine explanation as to why my face felt so numb. The cherry blossoms that bloomed some 50 miles south in Kamaishi, signalling spring, did not exist here. These trees were still void of flowers and the vegetation was sparse in a once again snow covered landscape. I had effectively gone back in time and caught up with winter again. And as I passed across a gargantuan bridge, above a roaring river, a biting cold wind brought tears to my eyes. I prayed in my head for the day that it would be hot, humid and so dirty and sweaty that it might even be deemed vulgar. Would I have been better off in Thailand? Getting smashed at the beach on Mojito and failing miserably at trying to cop off with a Norwegian stunner. Probably, yet my proverbial contract had been signed, I would stick to my guns. I had to.

Heading farther north-easterly I returned to the coast. Here I would ride on the troublesome Route 45 for just a short while before finding solace along the more scenic and docile Route 44. The Rikuchū Kaigan National Park offers up a spectacular section of coastline in the form of the Kitayamazaki Cliffs, a 5 mile stretch of coast where the cliffs in places would rise up to as high as some 200 metres. It had an abundant display of natural architecture, years in the making; its caves and small islets had been battered and manipulated into intricate shapes by centuries of abuse from the sea. As well as sometimes being a cruel mistress, it was evident that Mother Nature was also a true craftswoman.

Twenty-five miles later, I found myself in Kuji, a city which has often been cited as one of the coldest cities on the planet, this is not quite true (in fact it's a blatant lie), yet, to my mind, Kuji pretty much felt like it deserved the honour.

Kuji

Thanks to the art of Couchsurfing, I met Karin - an English teacher from Alaska. I gratefully accepted a warm futon to snuggle under for the Easter Weekend. Karin was also my guide to Kuji, home to some nearly 36,000 residents and the northern most point for 'Ama,' a.k.a. 'Sea Women.'

Ama date back roughly 2,000 years and are famous for their free-diving abilities with limited apparatus, at times venturing as deep as 30ft to harvest the ocean of its seaweed, abalone, oysters and various other shellfish.

Karin took me to a section of coast which is a popular spot for Ama and also an area often used in a recent and very popular Japanese soap opera, based on the life of a sea woman named Ama-chan. The spiteful wind rolling off of the sea was a cutting one and, as we half suspected, the popular diving pool bore no signs of Ama.

Modern times saw the divers wear wetsuits, yet, traditionally, the women dived practically butt naked, donning nothing but a meagre loincloth. The women are said to be better divers than men, as they are able to withstand the extremes of cold for a longer period of time - due to an apparent excess of body fat insulation. Some Ama even being able to stay underwater for up to two minutes at a time. It would have been nice to have seen an Ama at work (especially a naked one) but considering how horrifically cold it was, I really didn't blame them for not wanting to dive today.

After this excursion, we retreated to church, it was Easter Sunday after all. It would be my first time in 17 years at a church service; I hoped that I wouldn't burst into a ball of flames upon entering the holy compound. Alas, I did not. Karin introduced me to her boss, Kazuya, who looked like a crazy scientist! His pinstriped sweatshirt was tucked into his high rising trousers, his hair was haphazard and there was a look of eccentricity about him. Yet his manner was amiable and direct, and his English excellent.

Before entering the main church hall, he pulled Karin, myself and three other English teachers into a side-room. The agenda was that after the vicar had delivered his speech, an array of musicians would then come forth and play some tunes to appease the good honest church folk. He confirmed with the teachers what they were to play and then asked them all to do a little rehearsal. Karin then reached for a guitar that was situated close by and they all began to practice. Kazuya needed to be sure of the talent before he sent them out into the public domain; for embarrassment would not be an option. After a successful rehearsal, Kazuya turned to me - the new guy in town - and asked if I had any skills. I found myself cowering behind Karin slightly, feeling that she would somehow protect me from the Christians.

'Err... no, not today, I'm err... on hiatus,' I mustered.

His eyes scanned me sceptically, as if trying to judge my hidden attributes. Then he nodded his head in acknowledgement, to conclude that I could offer nothing. I couldn't. My voice sounds like a dying walrus... and I can only play the triangle. And, nobody likes the triangle - it's shit.

Satisfied with his students, Kazuya let us all assume positions amongst the busy congregation.

A Miss Thomasine Allen was responsible for the church's existence; a Christian missionary who settled in Kuji in the late 1930's from whence she built a steady relationship with the citizens of Kuji, appropriating a number of facilities such as hospitals, schools, kindergartens and of course a house of worship.

There was plenty of banter amongst the congregation pre-sermon and I tried to converse with Kazuya in Japanese. He understood my muddled tongue and nodded his head in agreement with my statements, before dealing me some crushingly honest blows to my standard of linguistics. He actually said that my Japanese was very poor. However, his English delivery was immaculate which allowed me to be criticised without feeling any malice. He was half way through destroying me further, when the vicar appeared and a sudden and respectful silence fell upon the congregation. I prayed I wouldn't fart.

For some 20 minutes, the vicar delivered his speech - of which I understood nothing. Then to the concert, which was a vast and diverse array of artistic output. Firstly, Karin and her brethren played a couple of well-crafted ballads for the congregation and then they were followed by a very un-Christian punk outfit. Next came some opera, a slice of A-capella, compulsory J-Pop, a bit of folk music, some genre-less mess that I never want to hear again and then finally the headliners: the Kuji Mandolin Orchestra.

It was here that the Kuji Rock Festival really carved its name into Kujian history. A collection of some 30 local school children with an assortment of mandolins, violins and cello's took to the stage to perform a number of flawless arrangements that would leave everybody in the room uplifted and in awe. Every note to perfection, these kids certainly had talent. And when they finished, a standing ovation was in order, along with shouts for an encore. The audience were full of praise; their faces jubilant. All present were completely humbled by what they were witnessing.

I spent another few days in Karin's company – she was a kind and generous host, opening up her home to me as if it were my own. Again, I got to sample a small insight into the life of a *gaijin* living and working in Japan. Far, far away from the tourist trail. I was oh so grateful for the warmth of shelter and the warmth of heart; I had again found another friend for life.

Kuji - Hachinohe
45 miles

Easter Monday saw me return to the mean spirited and far from holy Route 45, the chaos as casually end to end as ever. It would however be my last appointment with the said road, as making it to Hachinohe saw me bid a fond farewell to its ruthlessness for the very last time.

Amongst the city suburbs, I found a bleak and grainy park to set up a stealth camp, a solid night's sleep being a must, as come morning, I would have an important meeting with none other than our Lord and Saviour. However, as was tradition, I would again freeze deep into the night.

STATS

Dates: 14/04/2014 – 21/04/2014
Total miles traversed: 1,169 miles
Total time in the saddle: 125 hours and 38 minutes

9.1 AOMORI
青森県

Hachinohe – Lake Towada
57 miles

It was now a Tuesday and I was a day late for the resurrection, yet Christ's grave looked undisturbed and I had an inkling that he'd slept through his own party. Which I thought to be rather rude, considering how far I'd come to visit him; yet he is the son of God, so I guess really he can just do whatever he wants.

I found myself standing atop a small hill in the unassuming village of Shingo; a sleepy little place with seemingly little agenda, bar our Saviour. Before me lay two large earthen mounds, each spouting gigantic 12ft wooden crosses. To my right lay the body of the world famous Jesus Christ, to my left, his brother… Isukiri!

Now information on the existence of Christ in Japan is sketchy to say the least, yet a small sign-board next to the grave site dictates that when Jesus was 21 he came to foreigner-friendly Japan to seek knowledge of divinity. He would spend 12 years in Shingo before returning to Judea to spread the word of his divine knowledge. As we all know, the Romans thought that Jesus was a bit of a gob-shite and thus decided to crucify him with immediate effect. Luckily for Jesus however, his Japanese brother Isukiri was a super nice guy and casually traded places with him directly before the crucifixion and strangely nobody seemed to notice the difference. Nobody.

Jesus, thanks to his kindly and sacrificial brother, fled back to Japan where he married, had three kids and lived to the ripe old age of 106… what a guy! There's a moral to that story somewhere, a really shit one at that. Yet, it's the eccentricity of the claim that draws the tourist in, well this tourist anyway. Even as a budding atheist I still felt the need to see this place. But looking around, I gathered that not too many other folk had quite that same urge, I was alone with fake Jesus, but I didn't mind.

Veering away from the open plains of Shingo, I climbed west into the mountains towards Lake Towada. This was a rapid transformation in both terms of landscape and climes. From a flourishing agricultural plain up into the snowbound highlands, within the space of a couple of hours, the temperature fell dramatically from 23°C to a solemn 9°C. As I happened across an old mountain rest stop, a series of vending machines poked up out of the snow, as former restaurants and other miscellaneous outlets lay boarded-up and abandoned. A gentle breeze disturbed a canopy of amply clad treetops as a stern overreaching branch scratched against the corrugated roof of an old souvenir shop. I'd arrived in a Stephen King novel.

A short stretch away, lay the roughly 5 mile descent down from the mountains to Lake Towada. Unfortunately, it was at this point that I would end up throwing my toys out of the pram. The road, which would have taken me all the way down to exactly where I wanted to be, was closed; a barrier blocking my way was accompanied by a sign board caked in Kanji. I decided to test an iPhone app out on the Kanji to see if I could decipher what the problem was. The rough translation I got was 'spinning elbows happy nothing'. It sounded ominous. The other problem was that I wasn't being diverted anywhere else, the road was just quite simply closed, just like that. I was less than double digits away from where I wanted to be, yet I could do nothing about it, unless I wanted to intimidate the mountain's spinning elbows. I shouted and cursed for a couple of minutes, venting being the easiest form of release. Back in Shingo, fake Jesus would've been spinning in his grave.

I decided to backtrack slightly, eventually finding another road that seemed to run south. I couldn't find the road on my map, but geographically speaking it wasn't heading back out east towards the coast from whence I'd came. I took a gamble on it.

The road seemed to run level for a while, as I passed a few bleak and climatically challenged farmsteads, before gradually descending. The views upon my descent were the pinnacle of picturesque; somewhat belying the wind chill factor that was trying to eat me up. I gradually slipped down out of the apparent skyline and into a baron and lifeless woodland, before trailing close alongside a steady flowing river. The thrill of the descent would soon be overruled as I stumbled across a sign for Lake Towada that dictated almost double what the road blockade intimated. The road was also creeping back up into the mountains again. So, I had essentially gone back down one side of the mountain to inevitably be forced back up it on the other side. This would seriously put my body to the test as I burned up further calories that I wasn't in the position to replenish. This all forced me to utter some more bad words.

And so I huffed, puffed and cursed my way back up the mountain, before the trudge finally exacted its payment with the beauty of the great Lake Towada. Its rich blue colour highlighted its prominence amongst the serenest of landscapes. At some 28 miles in circumference, Lake Towada is the largest lake on Honshū, formed in a caldera some 40,000 years ago by the eruption of Mt. Towada. Although still considered an active volcano, its most recent mass eruption dates back some 13,000 years, so with that in mind I felt the odds were in my favour; I wouldn't be experiencing a red hot molten shower anytime soon. Always a good thing.

So, despite being led astray from my initial intended route, I was still spoilt at the climax, this was important. I stood alone, south-west of the lake, upon a viewing platform absorbing the lake's magnificence, not a tourist in site. I was humbled. Yet with sundown only 30 minutes away, I decided to descend down into the caldera where I had pre-booked a night in a hostel: a place that was encumbered with a conglomeration of Australian youths. Sadly, the aforementioned youths lacked any form of social etiquette; fighting amongst themselves, breaking objects, stomping about the place - whilst screaming and shouting at the elderly staff. They showed about as much respect as a fat man might show a honey-glazed donut. This would however in no way, shape or form dissuade my hunger though. The hostel offered a selection of over-priced pot noodles and cookies, the steep rates perhaps the reasoning behind the Aussie's impertinence. However, it was food that right there and then was most certainly ideal for the famished cyclist. I gorged into the night, like a modern day Henry VIII… but with less wives.

Lake Towada - Hachinohe
61 miles

Yesterday's physical abuse would be rewarded today with a gentle stroll east back towards the coast via Oirase Gorge. A gorge being a gorge is generally quite consistent with being beneficial to the cyclist as it essentially cuts out the middle man - the mountains. The road through the gorge meandered alongside the Oirase River for several miles through a section of virgin forest, offering up a foray of stop-off points to observe waterfalls, rapids, ancient moss laden rock formations and obligatory free Wi-Fi spots - before trailing off in the direction of Hachinohe and spilling out into the Pacific.

Yesterday, although somewhat of a grind, I'd somehow managed to find myself a quiet little back door to Lake Towada, along a road virtually devoid of traffic. However today, I found that my main challenge would be trying not to get battered by the swathes of tourist buses flooding the roads in and out of the mountains. Roads which due to the very nature of the river would snake along the gorge with a number of sharp and fraternising bends. My instincts saw me through the calamity, just by my being alert and expecting the unexpected, I'd be able to tackle a great number of formidable circumstances. So… I might just avoid being road kill.

Once through the gorge and heading in the opposite direction to the mountains, the buses would soon peter out and become replaced with other motorised and equally haphazard alternatives, i.e., more terribly shit drivers.

Now, bearing in mind, I'm only discussing my 9th prefecture traversed, I feel it best to try and evenly distribute my complaints throughout this book in regards to the general all-round level of driving standards in Japan.

Fast-forwarding several miles saw me re-enter the scuzzy, industrial port city of Hachinohe. It's tatty, weed infested and litter strewn sidewalks marked the city as a place of limited appeal. It was once known as a prosperous castle town, yet thanks to the Meiji Restoration in the late 1800's, it no longer has a castle. It does boast one of the largest cities in eastern Aomori Prefecture though, which today basks in the glory of having some of the biggest catchments of fish in the whole of Japan. Hachinohe also serves as a hub to Hokkaidō, Japan's northern most main island. Here I would embark upon my first ferry trip in Japan, the first of many. After some mild confusion of filling out an all Japanese passenger form, or just plain fun and games - depending on how you look at it, I boarded the night ferry to Tomakomai.

Leaving my bike with the ferry crew, upon a near deserted car deck, I ventured up onto the echoey main deck. I had reserved a small futon in one of many large open planned communal sleeping areas. I would be there alone and as the ferry came ever closer to embarkation only a very small number of passengers joined the other remaining rooms. I wondered how the route made any profit with such a limited amount of clientele; *perhaps with that hidden drug cache stored on the lower decks?*

I scoped out my emergency escape routes, should the ship go down during the night, and during the process got a feel for what the ferry had to offer. It was a relatively barebones affair with a small canteen area offering pot noodles and beer vending machines, compulsory shitters and of course a video game arcade. Yet, for 8 hours, it would do the job.

It was already dark outside as the ferry left Hachinohe and thus my viewing pleasures were constrained. And so, with very little choice in the matter, I took it upon myself to grab a beer and make base upon my futon which conveniently had an electricity outlet next to it. I plugged in my laptop and caught up with a brain splattering episode of Game of Thrones. Come morning, I would be in Hokkaidō.

STATS

Dates: 22/04/2014 – 23/04/2014
Total miles traversed: 1,287 miles
Total time in the saddle: 136 hours and 18 minutes

10. HOKKAIDO
北海道

Tomakomai - Sapporo
39 miles

The prospect of tackling Hokkaidō was one that excited me from the outset, it had an impression of a wild and lost place doused in a beauty that could charm even the likes of an amoeba. But it would certainly be no push over, as at 32,221.6 square miles, it is Japan's largest prefecture and second largest island. Weather would also be an integral factor to my time here, and despite my first day on the island being a mild and accessible 18°C, Hokkaidō is no stranger to its extremes, even in May.

The winter sees strong north-westerly winds from Siberia bringing cold air to the island, often issuing lows of -20°C. This then allows one to understand why this large and vast island accumulates the second highest amount of annual snowfall in the world. Some parts, most notably Niseko, had been known to receive up to as much as 15 metres of the white stuff on an annual basis; effectively plunging the island into a 7-month winter for the greater part of the year. These facts are tantalising for the snow junky, yet somewhat intimidating for the cyclist.

Further to the north, where I intended to head, snow was still to be encountered with areas plummeting below freezing at night. Now would not be the time to start getting reckless...well, any more reckless than usual, anyway. Timing my journey across this mammoth prefecture would be of the essence.

My ferry from Hachinohe had arrived in exactly the 8 hours as scheduled. Landing in Tomakomai, some 42 miles southeast off of my days target, I would follow the frisky Route 36, hugging the nobbled sidewalks as and when I could, in an effort to avoid annihilation in a real life game of Frogger.

All roads and traffic pumped towards my final destination of the day, Sapporo. With just over 1.9 million citizens, Sapporo is Japan's fourth largest city by population; home to: Miso Ramen, Soup Curry, Jingisukan (Lamb Barbecue), the Hokkaidō Nippon Ham Fighters, the Sapporo Brewery, the 1974 Winter Olympics and Susukino - one of the biggest red light districts in Japan. Situated upon the Ishikari Plains, the central part of the city has a grid plan layout encompassing a number of historical buildings, parks, shopping districts and restaurants - which cluster avenues all the way out into the foothills of several mountains to the south and west of the city.

The city hummed with the vibrancy that one would expect from Japan's fourth largest, as I took a leisurely cycle through Odori Park, in the presence of the red and white Sapporo TV Tower; genuinely considered to be the city's iconic landmark. A feel good aura lined the tree clustered boulevard: families picnicked, a young girl busked on her acoustic guitar, students danced and grannies yapped, a couple played frisbee as skater boys and girls grinded.

I found the city to be instantly accommodating. And as I sat in the park making some notes, I was accosted by an elderly gentleman who stumbled towards me, reeking of booze. This I don't have a problem with, my old man reeks of booze all the time and yet is a perfectly nice and senile old chap.

'Welcome to Sapporo!' the stranger blurted out, before handing me a Sapporo beer from his stash, which I gladly accepted.

'*Arigatou gozaimasu*,' I replied, with a bow.

He seemed to nod his head in approval.

'Have a… nice…' he paused and began to search deep, 'day!' He had found it.

I thanked him in English, as he nodded his head again and then went on his way. I pulled the ring of my beer and took a hit: cold and refreshing. I could get used this place.

I found my hostel a short ride away from Odori Park. Operating reception was Takashi, a completely bald, perfectly round-headed fellow. His straightfaced look was added to by a warm, well-mannered persona. He took a mild interest in my journey before conferring to me about how cold the north of Hokkaidō still was and that I would more than likely freeze to death there. This much I already knew, for it had been plaguing my mind for a while now. It was during this conversation that I noticed a poster on the wall, advertising help within the hostel in exchange for a bed for the night. An imaginary light bulb suddenly filled my mostly empty head. Pointing at the poster abruptly, I asked Takashi if he had any jobs going. A smile began to creep around his extremely circular face, '*hai.*'

'Great, when can I start?'

'*Ashita*?' Tomorrow?

I felt the corners of my mouth slide upwards. 'Okay, sound's good.' We shook hands and thus a deal was struck.

The cherry blossoms had not yet arrived in Sapporo, so it seemed only wise to wait for them to bloom before heading out into the wilderness. Time was still on my side, as I'd been granted a year-long visa before leaving England, and having just cycled for the best part of a month, the idea of resting up for a bit and letting my hair down, seemed a more than tolerable one.

Sapporo

For a month, I dedicated my time to drinking vast quantities of beer and exploring the delights of Sapporo. Yet, of course, amongst all the frenetic drinking, a few hours each day would be spent tidying up the realms of one of the busiest hostels in Hokkaidō. This invariably meant mopping up vomit, hoovering up pubes, rinsing away anonymous jizz from a multitude of surfaces and also putting a stranger's misplaced

101

faecal matter into the toilet for them. If I hadn't have backpacked so excessively in my twenties, then the whole ordeal might have scarred me for life, yet, thankfully, I was wise to the semi-vagabond notions of the sweaty backpacker. Although at times grimacing, it was nothing that my fine-tuned stomach couldn't handle.

My new routine went a little something like this:

> 10:50 - 10:59: Wake, vomit.
> 11:00 - 14:00: Clean up customers' spunk and pubes.
> 14:01 - 14:30: Ramen.
> 14:31 - 17:30: Go to Starbucks, write words.
> 17:31 - ??:??: Drink beer until random blackout.

I'd stick as stringently to this routine as I could, seeing a multitude of faces come and go from the hostel, some welcome, some not so much. And I would again witness the bloom of another cherry blossom season. During such time a hunger would inevitably begin to congregate from within, a hunger riddled with an eagerness for change. I had enjoyed my time in Sapporo but with the season finally mending its ways, my number in the city was up. It was time to get back into the saddle. That and a new receptionist from Belgium had just started work at the hostel – with whom I shared a sobering bond. I'd slept with his wife. Awkward? Yes! And although the account dated back to Tokyo some 6 years previously - before the happily married couple had ever even met - the whole scenario was a complete and utter mess. A coincidence so bizarre that one couldn't even dream it up... and so on that note, I felt it was definitely high time to be making tracks before things got any weirder. For, the weird ship was full to capacity and it was time to bail.

Sapporo - Takikawa
62 miles

Despite the coming of the cherry blossom, the weather the week prior to my departure from Sapporo had been a cold, wet and windy disgrace. A hostel guest, that had just recently returned from the north, would tell me that it was the coldest place he had ever been to in his life and that if I planned to camp, well then I would surely die. A small knot had begun to weave itself into my gut. So it would come as some surprise that the day that I had decided to venture north would be the day that summer arrived. It was as if by the flick of the switch, that the reverberations of winter were shut down and spring overridden - as to allow for a glorious 27°C belter. It was a perfect and unexpected start to my exploits around this huge prefecture.

Cycling out of the big smoke and farther into the Ishikari Plains, I soon found myself deep in rural Hokkaidō. In the distance, mountains drew shadows ominously, whilst in the foreground, rice paddies glistened in the early stages of development; reflecting the heavens above with drastic measure. It was good to be back on the road, almost sensual.

For the most part, the day was uneventful, but being on the flat allowed for some steady progress as I passed through a handful of downtrodden rural towns: Iwamizawa, Bibai, Sunagawa and finally, Takikawa. These towns seemed to be fraying at the edges; they'd been through some long, harsh winters. Many homes were still boarded-up and deteriorating, abandoned and/or forgotten, a far throw from the web of wealth being spun back in Sapporo. I did however find a familiar friend in Takikawa - Mister Donut being pretty much the only shop open in the high street, as I sought out a coffee and a light snack.

On the fringes of town, I found a large meadow, adjacent the Sorachi River, there I would put my new tent to the test. My

103

previous one-man affair was no longer cutting the mustard and so I had sought out an alternative back in Sapporo. I was still unwilling to commit to any form of big spending, the ¥60,000 (about £330) price tag for a North Face tent was enough to split my spleen in shock. The way I saw it, the sky was the limit in regards to the price of a tent, yet no matter how much one pays, a snagging thorn will never discriminate. Thankfully, I found a second-hand camping store where I was able to pick up a brand-less two-man tent for a fraction of the price of one of its elitist cousins. I would also purchase some masking tape from the ¥100 shop for good measure.

Removing the tent from its sheath, I laid it out upon the dry grass. It was a pop-up tent, whereby all one is supposed to do is pull a cord and the tent in effect should self-erect. I pulled the cord. One of the support poles snapped instantly. Classic. I then fumbled about with the tent pole for some time, before coming to an acceptable conclusion that it was fucked. And fucked it would remain, for the rest of my trip. I grumbled for a bit, before deciding to get over it and focus on getting some shut-eye. And so as I lay in my already fucked tent upon the soft meadow ground - surrounded by my worldly possessions, the last light of day would gently slip away as a skylark sweetly took it upon himself to sing me to sleep.

Takikawa - Furano
41 miles

I awoke to the sound of a natural cuckoo clock; the skylark's reeling also soon following suit from where he had left off the previous night. I was surprised by how well I'd slept on my first night back under the stars. Being broad daylight already, the night had quite simply flown by. I yawned raucously and felt for my watch, 3:30am. 'What!!!' I exclaimed to myself. Summer had truly arrived in the north. I decided not to be hasty, the air around me was still cool as I lay motionless in a reptilian state for at least another hour or so, to allow my being to warm up. And it wouldn't take long, as the day's climes soon rose to a sweltering 34.7°C. Just a mere few miles out of Takikawa and I would be sweating like an undercover steer in a queue at Burger King.

The weather gave me a positive outlook, really boosting my morale, knowing that the cold wintery days of the previous couple of months were finally behind me; the nights of shivering myself to sleep were over. I hoped.

Following close to the Sorachi River, I passed the towns of Ashibetsu and Akabira as the surrounding terrain began to take on a more hilly trajectory, a teaser perhaps for what was to come as I approached Hokkaidō's mountainous core.

By noon, I found myself in Furano; my arms and face burned raw from the sun's intensity. Just south of town lay the Log Yukari Guesthouse, a hidden treasure at the base of a small mountain where an aged, gracious Japanese couple would greet me. Cicada's from the surrounding forest were screaming as Shinobi-san gave me a small tour of an assortment of innovative cabins and facilities which he had mostly hand-crafted himself. It must be nice to actually be good at something. I envied him.

I also learned that I was the night's only guest in the cabin's eight-man dorm, perfect. And as soon as Shinobi-san had left, I stripped off, doused my throbbing face and forearms with Aloe Vera and settled down upon my bed in my boxers, like an idle waif. Perfect!

Furano - Asahikawa
46 miles

Furano is famed in summer for its fields of lavender, and with the season's sudden change, farm labourers were out in force, maintaining the crop in readiness for the hive of tourists that would shortly follow. Being slightly too early, I would miss out on the lavender at its peak, but did however - as the day progressed into another absolute blinder - witness Hokkaidō's agricultural splendour. Its produce includes: milk, beef, potatoes, soybeans, sugar beet, pumpkin, onions, wheat, corn and, of course, rice. These are all consistent in making the island Japan's number one producer of agricultural products. And it's really no surprise when you consider that Hokkaidō farms a fourth of Japan's arable land.

The idyllic panorama and patchwork roads just outside the small rural town of Biei offer up a fine and scenic example of the island's farming paradise. A network of narrow pathways criss-cross a hilly deluge of young crops and freshly cultivated land. A truly resplendent landscape; a photographer's Mecca in any season. Where this labyrinth of aimless pathways lead to however is any fools guess, but with a marginally less than adequate dose of common sense and an ever reliable compass, I was able to beat out a route to Asahikawa.

At -41°C, Asahikawa brags about being the coldest city in Hokkaidō, but that was in 1902, so come on, get over yourself. Today it was a crotch drenching 31°C as I sat on the curb outside a Seicomart, taking in a beer and a box of fried chicken. This far from absorbing city - the second largest in Hokkaidō - is centrally located, offering a good base for the following day's excursion into the mountains of Daisetsuzan National Park.

Rimming the outskirts of the city centre was a small English bar, run by a Couchsurfer, a portly chap named Kev. A bar at first glance which had a certain seedy curiosity about it, like it might be the kind of place to have a secret stash of hookers (dead or alive) hidden out back. But hey, that was just the look...and feel of the place, the most important vice of course was to be found at the bar itself, the key element to any a weary traveller, booze! Kev was also a keen cyclist, and with the Football World Cup looming - and us both being Englishmen - we had plenty to talk and bullshit about. And 6 pints, 2 gin and tonics and a whiskey highball later... I was more than ready for my nap.

Asahikawa - Sounkyo
50 miles

I was up and about early, not quite reeling from a hangover, as I was still drunk. But the day ahead was playing on my mind and I needed to get moving. Kev pointed me in the direction of the Ishikari River, from there I found a cycle path that would traverse for some 20 miles or so in the direction of Sounkyo Gorge; my base in the mountains of Daisetsuzan National Park. The path was quiet and appealing, diverting away from the roadside traffic and meandering alongside the river, through a small series of woodland copses. The snow-capped mountains that had been sitting formidably upon the horizon during the previous days, began to creep ever closer.

At 35°C, and in the absence of human life, I took it upon myself to expose my less than ample bosoms and ride topless. This was something generally frowned upon and not very stereotypical of the Japanese, due to cultural modesty, unlike in the West, where as soon as the dial hits 20°C we all can't wait to get our tits out. Modesty would however prevail when the cycle route rejoined traffic along Route 39, my usual fully non-nude state completely restored.

Shortly before pulling into the small village of Kamikawa I began to feel queasy. Initially I suspected it was my hangover finally kicking in, but as well as feeling dizzy, my palms were also beginning to swell, heat exhaustion striking me as a possible contender. I took a break. There was a small tourist outlet in the village offering up overly priced local novelty produce and delicacies. But they had nothing particularly nourishing on offer that would sustain my calorie burn; cheesy beef chocolate just wasn't going to cut it. Instead I sat in the shade with a cold can of Coke, until I perked up a bit, little did I know that I was sat upon a nest of angry ants!

Route 39 was for long distances completely straight and completely flat, the sides of the roads lined with tall coniferous trees, offering very little insight into my surrounds; a drab comparison to the cycle path out of Asahikawa alongside the Ishikari. I found myself feeling increasingly shitty and wanting to throw up, yet there was little I could do. Zoning out and getting on with it was my only real choice. With luck, as I was headed into the gorge from the west, the day offered very little inclines which would have no doubt only added to my discomfort.

The gorge seemed to appear suddenly as a section of the tree line rapidly began to filter away and huge limestone karst cliffs emerged, towering up high above me. A short drop to my right and the Ishikari had returned; its rapids flowing heavily now. The skies ahead lacked promise as dark clouds began to congregate. They would soon be accompanied by a dramatic light show, I would need to find shelter, and ideally not under a tree canopy. But being 5 miles from Sounkyo, my fate was already sealed, I was to clash head-on with the thunderstorm.

First it was an abrupt gust of wind, bringing with it a series of small droplets that soon increased in size and capacity; followed by the heavens which rumbled angrily as lightening cracked so loud above me that for a second I thought I was done for. Rain ricocheted off of the bitumen, causing a blanket of mist some 2 feet high; in mere seconds I was soaked to the bone. I stumbled across a perimeter fence to a golf course, and inside were a number of shelters. In one of them I would be able to escape from the sky's wrath. Yet the compound was locked tight, but being already drenched, what difference did it really make?

The hail changed perspectives though, its coldness offering very little invigoration, just sheer pain. The porch of a derelict building with a tree positioned directly through the middle of it, would soon nevertheless offer a light relief. Here I waited out the worst of the storm. The rain slammed hard against the building's broken open roof as water poured into the premises. One could only hope that the structure would stand firm for just a little longer. A series of buses splashed their way past, a number of tourists pointing and laughing at how stupid I looked. The storm was refreshing and it had certainly livened me up, but now on the opposite end of the spectrum I was beginning to feel cold. So, as soon as the bulk of the storm had passed and the rain had simmered somewhat, I surged forth towards Sounkyo.

Daisetsuzan is Hokkaidō's largest National Park and could easily be considered a place of unspoilt splendour and natural beauty, apart from say… Sounkyo! Nestled at the base of Mt. Kurodake, Sounkyo is the Park's tourist hotbed and a starting point for the majority of excursions within the park. Each year, this little speck of land within the gorge, witnesses some serious touristic abuse. But it was also a star example of Hokkaidō's failed business ventures. On the village's outskirts lay an abundance of hotels and stores completely defunct of life and now going to ruin. Businesses that had long folded, now sat un-nurtured, unloved and destined to become consumed by the very nature that surrounds them.

In the late 90's, Hokkaidō's main bank, Hokkaidō Takushoku went bust. The bank had loaned out vast swathes of money to some 60% of businesses throughout Hokkaidō. When the bank crumbled, then so did a bulk of these businesses, taking vast portions of the island with it. And, as I ventured further around this hefty prefecture, its ailing economy would day by day become increasingly apparent. Centering in on Sounkyo were a number of other seasonally and economically weathered hotels, barely hanging on to existence; the newer more lavish hotels only weighing in as further eyesores in an area that houses some limitless wilderness. But, in the name of tourism, Sounkyo was a necessity.

The main hub of Sounkyo however looked as if it had recently undergone a face lift, offering up a more aesthetic feel. A small central strip contained a collection of souvenir shops, convenience stores and restaurants. A musky vaginal like aroma lingered in the air, the world's first National Park titty bar? Alas, no, its source was a public thermal foot spa. I dipped my pinky in, and as suspected, it was hot like magma and completely pointless. Now I'm no snowman, and I'm quite privy to a nice hot bath, but I have to wonder what kind of preterhuman would enjoy the heat of some of these ridiculously hot *onsens*. I tutted rudely at the foot spa, as if to show my disappointment towards it. Nonchalantly in reply it bubbled right back at me.

Cycling up a small winding path away from central Sounkyo took me to my 1980's themed youth hostel. Woodchip walls, linoleum tablecloths and chintz sofa - unfortunately the Thundercats duvet set must have been in the wash, so I had to settle for just plain old poo brown. I dumped my belongings in my dorm and went to inspect the bathing facilities. Again I found another *onsen*. I dipped a digit. My finger didn't smoulder, so I dived right in.

Sounkyo

The 1,984 meter Mt. Kurodake can be tackled in two ways: hiking or cheating. It was my day off out of the saddle, and thus decided that it would be in my best interests to opt for the latter and cheat my way to the mountain's summit. I'd achieve this by firstly taking a gondola half way up the mountain and then jumping on a ski lift for the remainder. Taking the opportunity to cheat was a wise choice on my part, as I hovered over a guy on my ski lift that had decided to hike; a decision I feel he may well have been seriously regretting as he found himself wading through some 4 ft of snow. I tried not to look smug upon passing over him, as I swung my legs about dandily from the comfort of my seat, yet as I etched past, I couldn't help but feel the hiker's angry eyes burning into the back of my head. Jealously, is assuredly a terrible thing.

Clear skies at the summit offered up some astounding views across the Ishikari mountain range. A real impression of the canyon can be observed as a sea of contrasting green foliage clambers up Sounkyo's deep rift, before being abruptly halted by a montage of snow and dark, rugged rock. The cool, fresh air was satisfying, so I lingered, having myself a little moment.

A short way out of Sounkyo village is the area's other big draw, Ginga no Taki and Ryusei no Taki, respectively the Milky Way and Shooting Star Waterfalls. From their base the views of the falls were blotted out by waves of tourists pimping out the peace sign. So to seek a more inspiring view one must ignore the sign advertising grizzly bears and look to find a vantage point. Oh, did I just say grizzly bears? Yes, yes, I did! The Hokkaidō grizzly can only be found in…well, Hokkaidō, and at about 300kg it is much bulkier than the Asiatic black bear found in Honshū, Kyūshū and Shikoku. Although apparently less volatile than its southern counterpart, that hasn't stopped it from mauling 86 people and killing 33. This is all according to the Bear Crimes Register that has only been in existence since 1962.

Before that, one can only assume that the bears were probably having a free for all, partying all night with bellies full of human flesh.

This was something that didn't seem to faze the indigenous Ainu of Hokkaidō too much however, for they used to worship the bear as a god in a gruesome ceremony known as *Iomante*. The bear would be skinned, its blood drunk, its skull stuck on a spike and then wrapped in its own fur - the resulting relic was worshipped. Well, I for one wasn't here for any grizzly idolatry; I was mostly here to see no bears, no bears at all. But what if one does see a bear? How are you meant to react? Stand firm, and get eaten or run... and get eaten.

The whole Man meets Bear scenario still has a lot of groundwork to cover, unless of course an individual happens to be carrying an Uzi. I wasn't. Instead I trod gingerly, away from the tourist hoards, until I was truly alone, following a narrow path up a mountain opposite the falls. Despite being ridiculously quiet though, if there did just so happen to be a bear milling about, it would have no doubt smelt the small sense of fear emitting discreetly from my sphincter.

Anyhow, the tourist breakaway was well worth the risk of getting gang-banged by a pack of grizzlies; as from a small rocky shelf, one was able to observe uninterrupted views of the waterfalls. They seemed to burst out of a rock pinnacle some 100 metres high, a gushing stream of frothy white water crashing down into the Ishikari below. Another moment was in order.

After a few minutes, my moment collapsed in on itself as a small mob of chatty tourists descended, with about as much stealth as a pony on heat. Any grizzlies that may have been stalking me were now keeping a low profile, more than likely through fear of being chatted to death by a gossipy tourist. As the stampede of sightseers got closer, I took my queue to retreat for the day – back to 1986.

Sounkyo - Higashimokoto
88 miles

At 3,388 metres, the Ginga tunnel leading out of Sounkyo was a beast. A safe tunnel one might add though, one which allowed a plentiful amount of sidewalk space for the casual tour cyclist, always a bonus. This did however mean cutting out a small portion of Daisetsuzan's scenic beauty. But I was able to save up valuable energy for the long day ahead. On the other side of the tunnel, the road steadily began to ascend. It was my first mountain climb in some time and nowhere near as straining as I had expected it to be, and upon reaching an altitude of 1,050 metres a leisurely descent would ensue back down into the lowlands.

I was to journey along a laboriously straight road towards Kitami amongst a vast, flat arable landscape. An encompassing smell of shit hung in the air, gently reminding me of home. Having worked with cattle for a number of years, the smell of their sloppy loose stools was something that I was all too familiar with. Hokkaidō was famed for its dairy industry and produces nearly half of Japan's milk. Yet I can't say I care too much for the standard of care given to a large portion of these animals. I consider myself to be a bit of a conservationist and an animal lover, but now unfortunately a bulk of the dairy cattle in Japan seem to spend their lives in battery farmed feedlots, crammed together inside minuscule, badly ventilated shacks with little room to roam.

A herd is generally at their most content when they are allowed to graze for themselves upon open pastures under the grace of the sky. In the harsh Hokkaidō winters, being kept inside was perhaps more applicable, but not in the summer months. Yet, thankfully, these morbid feedlots weren't the entire picture, as I progressed further around the prefecture a small amount of faith would be restored as I took joy in witnessing free-roaming cattle. Some farmers showed that they do have compassion for their stock, caring for their animals' general well-being and not just how well lined their pockets were. It would be encouraging to see more Japanese farmers take up this stance.

Ok, semi-rant over. Next time I'll get into whale farming!

Farther east, I passed through the nefarious streets of Kitami and came to the conclusion that the city's traffic lights, all potentially 4.5 million of them, just didn't like me very much. Their distribution was hideously frequent and they were alarmingly skilled at turning red whenever in my presence, to the point that I had a sinking suspicion that someone somewhere was having a good old laugh at my expense. But there was no time to investigate such tomfoolery as I had some Couchsurfers to meet.

Nearly 30 miles east of Kitami sits Higashimokoto, a sleepy town with no agenda, en route to the Shiretoko Peninsula. There I would find my bed for the night. But getting to my night's locale was particularly draining. Leaving Kitami saw the terrain bulk up with a series of rolling hills that would really test my endurance. Just before reaching the summit of every hill, I would convince myself that it would be my last climb of the day. Knowing that one was so close to the day's final destination a sort of unhealthy eagerness began to inevitably build with each and every passing mile; that all-important end of day beer and fried chicken just wasn't going to consume itself!

Eventually, just before my second wind was about to kick in, I made it to Higashimokoto. Seeking out a Seicomart, I rewarded myself with a can of beer and some fried chicken, naturally. Afterwards, in a demure and cutesy sized Japanese bungalow, I met English teachers Lili from Canada and Miles, from New Zealand. Both of them were completely full of beans and a pleasure to be around. Lili was enthusiastic and chatty and Miles was head smart and slightly eccentric. They made for interesting hosts and an intriguing comedy duo; and for the sake of normality I was more than happy to join in.

And so after breaking the ice and discussing the compulsory cycling venture and our lives in Japan, we lowered the tone somewhat and diverged ourselves into an evening of predominantly cock and fart gags. Doubtlessly, we wouldn't have had it any other way.

114

Higashimokoto - Abashiri
71 miles

The road out of Highashimokoto continued in the same hilly prevalence from where it had left off yesterday. Yet the rise and fall of the landscape would today be the least of my concerns, as a far more brutally sinister enemy raged from the east; an enemy cruel and merciless, one that would take no prisoners. It was the wind, the unrelenting, soul destroying wind that over the coming hours would completely dismantle any progress in the direction of Shiretoko National Park. In some 4 hours, I managed a pathetically meagre 20 miles, I was very much getting my arse kicked. I needed to conjure up a new strategy. Finding a desolate and sheltered wooden shack of a bus stop to the side of the road, I pitched a seat, pulled out my map book and my accompanying thinking cap. With still some 50 miles to cover, the chances of reaching my destination by sundown were looking pretty desperate. Whilst in the process of planning my next move, the wind would pick up further and a hurl a contingent of abuse in the bus stop's general direction; a lose piece of plywood began to flap about wildly as a patch of dust kicked up into my face, blinding me temporarily.

'Fuck this!' I scorned. My mind was made up. I was defeated, which I hated, but I didn't have to be here. Just being in Hokkaidō was enough. Reaching Shiretoko would have made the journey through this exciting prefecture a nice touch, but in the current conditions it just wasn't viable. With my willpower completely diminished, I opted to change direction, heading directly north instead, my tail between my legs.

After a couple hours of cycling, I found Hokkaidō's northern coast, before veering west toward the city of Abashiri and its scenic lakeside camping ground.

There is no ignoring the fact that the wind has the oppressive ability to grind a man down, well this man anyway. But just being able to break free of the wind's binding shackles was a massive relief to me. I was no longer its prisoner. And, in Abashiri, 'prisoner' is not a word that one should take lightly.

Abashiri - Monbetsu
77 miles

At the base of Mt. Tento, just a short distance from my camping ground next to Lake Abashiri, is the repositioned Abashiri Prison. When I heard the story of Abashiri Prison, and the abstract and harsh misery endured by its prisoners, I felt compelled to pay a visit. The curiosity derived from the suffering of others is a strange one, but if anything it would yield a valuable history lesson.

In the late 19th Century, fear of the Russian Empire's expansion further east, led the Meiji government to stake a claim upon the wilds of Hokkaidō. Prior to the intervention of the ruling party, the north of Hokkaidō was just as wild as Siberia; a small conclave of fishing villages cut off from the world by an ocean of forest. However, Abashiri's northerly locale was deemed ideal to open up Hokkaidō, but to truly constitute this, a road would need to be established into central Hokkaidō. But how would this be achieved on an extremely limited budget? *Hmm…how about some free and expendable labour in the form of one thousand prisoners? Yeah, that'll do the trick!* And so from all the far reaching corners of Japan, a bunch of bad-arses were summoned to Abashiri. Firstly, they would build themselves some accommodation, i.e. a prison, and then after that the real backbreaker - a really big fuck-off road into the heart of Hokkaidō. Land had to be cleared and bridges built, come rain or snow it was here that the iron ball clad prisoners were really put to the test. Exploited to the point of exhaustion and starvation, many died to aid the government's advance upon Hokkaidō, in order to claim the nation's right to the land.

Overnight, the wind had become limp; it was now a warm and overcast Sunday morning as I entered the grounds of the prison museum. All was quiet, the weekend day trippers obviously having better places to be. Many materials from the old prison, which had once been located on the northern shore, were used in the replication of the museum, everything exacted as it once was: the main gate to the prisoner's mess hall, bathhouse, prayer room and solitude huts.

A guard tower sat adjacent to the wooden radial five-wing prison chamber, the prison's showpiece. Here one can walk down each aisle and look into the lives of each cell. Many cells contained a puppet depicting a typical day of an Abashiri prisoner. To be holed up here through the winter months would've been a freezing cold hell. The prison was also a working farm, so when the prisoners weren't building a better future for Hokkaidō's infrastructure, they were self-sufficient in growing their own produce. In the mess hall, one could purchase a somewhat typical prison dinner.

Some say that the prisoners were mere petty thieves, others political prisoners sent to the wilds of Hokkaidō to be silenced by the all-powerful Meiji government, whilst others stipulate that the prisoners were just bad, really, really bad. But whatever their sins: theft, murder, poetry or activism, one can't help but marvel at what these prisoners actually achieved during their miserable time at the prison. A prison that quietly came to a close in 1984, yet will forever be rooted deep in the history of Abashiri - thanks to this very informative museum.

In central Abashiri, I made a quick pit stop at Mister Donut for a compulsory gluten treat before continuing in a north-westerly fashion for some 20 miles along a designated cycle path to Tokoro.

Just beyond Tokoro, I passed alongside the coastal Saroma Lake; with a surface area of 58mi² it sits as Hokkaidō's largest and Japan's third largest lake. It was a dull coloured and brackish lake, its appearance clearly echoed by the dreary gloom that had begun to reach over the bright morning skies.

As I traipsed further along, minding my own business, I was again halted by one of the few things that really annoy me about Japan, traffic lights. In Kitami they had ridiculed me, but out in the sticks they were just plain taking the piss. They're bloody everywhere, and with Japan being the 10th most populous nation on Earth, they are of course a sensible solution to an obvious abundance of heavily trafficked roads. But, in the countryside, they are just nonsensical eyesores; completely irrelevant to their locale. So you could be the first vehicle going down a certain country road for the first time since 1963 and... you'll run head-on into a red light.

In Japan, this mental test of patience was surely considered a great incentive to self-discipline. And if you can't wait a couple of minutes at a completely irrelevant to humanity traffic light then you're more than likely to fail the Japanese code of etiquette. Taking a quick look around, I observed nothing but a couple of ominous looking bushes. So, I shrugged my shoulders and broke the code. *A code I would come to break on countless further occasions.* 'What's the fecking point in these fecking traffic lights?' I gestured, in order to buy my law-breaking self some form of credibility. But I was alone and thus no one really cared for my pet hate. Which is a shame, because I really hate them and I just wanted everyone to know that. But now as my Reader, I guess you do.

My evening saw me arrive in the port town shithole of Monbetsu. Along the docks, cardboard and plastic wrapping blew about like tumbleweed as noisy forklift trucks darted about with pallets of scrap metal. If this was Skeggy, then one would expect to see a few burnt out Ford Escorts down by the shore front for nostalgic effect. Yet, in far-flung Monbetsu,

Ford's were scarce. The town though, like many a towns dotted along the shores of Hokkaidō, is a trading post with Russia. In just a short time of being there, I'd already witnessed a few conspicuously tall Caucasian chaps mooching about with plastic bags full of rattling Vodka bottles. The town even had a number of signs in Cyrillic. I'd have to be on my guard tonight, for I hadn't made it this far north to get bummed in my tent by a bunch of rowdy Russian's.

I found an Aeon Mall, which usually has a roof-top car park, from there one can gain a good vantage point of the land and even potentially figure out a suburban green space, i.e. a park for a night's stealth camp. My immediate surrounds were particularly built up, yet casting an eye away from the mall, I saw a procession of grubby and lost looking apartment blocks fizzling out a third of the way up a distant hill; from there vegetation was allowed to reign supreme. It was there that I found my pitch.

I took a glance downwards toward the mall's ground floor car park. A couple of bulky white men were looking up at me with a curious eye, my butthole clenched a little as I took a step back out of their line of sight. Waiting a few seconds, I again approached to have another look and they were still looking at me. I quickly jumped back again. I appeared to be playing subconscious mind games with Russians.

Should I take another peek to see if they are still looking up at me? I thought.

What again? Why?
I don't know.
Just leave it, you fucking idiot.
Yeah okay, good call.
Who are you talking to?
You!
Me?
Yes, you!
But I am you.
No you're not.

Yes I am.

Oh yeah, you are actually, well... good luck not getting bummed tonight!

Thanks, I appreciate it.

Sensibly, I talked myself out of a third glance and hastily retreated from the mall and cycled up into the hills.

It was dark by the time I'd made it through the suburbs and on to the hill's sweaty ascent. Just beyond the last batch of architectural atrocities, I found a park. Loose gravel presented me with a constricted and steep slope as I clumsily scaled further up the hill to its summit. The surrounding park, unlike the rest of Monbetsu, was meticulously well maintained; to camp here now felt a trifle insulting. But thinking of the Vodka swilling Russians in the town centre below and how at some point during the night they would probably end up pissing through some poor old Japanese gran's letterbox, made me feel like the idea of camping on an immaculate Wimbledon-esque Tennis Club lawn was probably the least of Monbetsu's concerns.

Monbetsu - Hamatonbetsu
87 miles

I slept uneasy though; the noise from the docks was prominent throughout the night. A seemingly 24-hour operation; ships being loaded and released of their cargo as an arrangement of sirens and horns sounded out continuously. As dawn began to slowly creep in, the low light projected an army of ants trailing up and down the outside of my tent. I watched them monotonously and just when I felt as if I was about to nod off, I suddenly bolted upright, shaking off my trance. 04:30am, I'd lounged around for long enough. My journey north was to continue.

Heading out of Monbetsu, I was again subjected to another one of Hokkaidō's consistently straight roads, one that seemed to melt into the horizon and offer very little hope of curvature.

My surrounds though were far from pedestrian; to my right lay the sea of Okhotsk, its salted breeze gentle and fresh. And to my left, a landscape very reminiscent of the Scottish Highlands: green wavy hills, boggy marshes, craggy rocks and a pint's worth of midges heading directly for my eyeballs.

The road was to eventually spoil me rotten by offering up a bend and before long, as a set of heavy dark clouds began to loom, I would make it to Hamatonbestu, the last frontier before Wakkanai, Hokkaidō's northern most city.

Over a can of coffee outside a Seicomart, I started talking to a Japanese tour cyclist who that day had set out from Wakkanai. He confirmed that the weather there was very wet, windy and cold. And upon that confirmation I didn't think that I'd be able to make the final 50 or so miles before sundown.

However, on the outskirts of town lay a spot of luck - Kutcharo Lake. It offered convenient and free camping. Upon arrival an eerie mist clung to the lake as close by, a group of gulls gathered around a broken jetty, preparing to roost, they too had given up for the day. And as the drizzle turned to rain, I'd just about finished preparing camp before huddling into my sleeping bag - with a packet of crab flavoured crisps and some fine 20th Century literature. For tonight, the rain wasn't going anywhere, and neither was I.

Hamatonbetsu - Rebun
73 miles

I awoke cold and damp, I hadn't jizzed myself, unfortunately things never got that far. But my tent was to prove that it wasn't the watertight vessel that I'd hoped it would be. In fact, it was shit, just plain shit; a little like Chinese water torture. Yet, for now, the rain had lapsed and the skies sat wearily overcast. I wiped down the inside of my tent with a cloth, in an attempt to absorb a bulk of the moisture, ringing the cloth out frequently. My schoolboy error lay in the fact that my far

121

from suave pop-up tent was only a one season tent, summer minus the rain. I'd need to invest in a waterproof flysheet as soon as possible or face a prominently wet future.

Cycling north along the lake, I came across an old railway line that had been converted into a cycle path. Through a melee of woodland and arable settings, I passed the remnants of long defunct station platforms; the road elevating slightly to offer a panoramic view across the lake. The lake's boundaries though were still undefined by a low-lying band of mist. The further away from the lake I got the more dense and decrepit the forest path would become. Vegetation splayed itself out errantly before me; my legs getting slapped by huge wet dock leaves and my face whipped by a foray of spindly outreaching tree branches. The path came to an abrupt end at an impenetrable wall of flora; with no road signs in view, I was left to navigate via compass.

Being positioned someway inland, I knew that heading directly north would bring me to the coast. Unfortunately, the inland roads were being perversely cruel, a bulk of them giving me a glimmer of hope before suddenly turning 90°on me and leading me astray. My saviour was to come in the shape of young Japanese farm labourer who jumped out of his truck and bundled a couple of hot cans of coffee into my hands. I took this golden opportunity to ask where I might be able to find the road to Wakkanai. He looked impressed with my Japanese and then began to speak at about 400 million miles per hour, assuming that I was a native speaker. I was thankfully able to pick out a few key words though, 'next left,' '5km' and 'ocean'; all I really needed to know. I thanked him for the coffee and directions, before shaking hands and departing. *How did he know that I needed coffee?* 'I love this country,' I said to myself before nearly turning right at a crossroads - instead of left.

A short while later, I found myself back on the coast; a brilliant sea mist enveloping me as I found the road toward Wakkanai - it was all so beautifully creepy. Inside this big, thick, white blanket of obscurity, I could hear the ocean waves crashing against the shore, the occasional hum of an approaching vehicle, accompanied by a blurry frenzy of oncoming lights. Within a few moments, I was in a bright, clear and spellbindingly beautiful summer's day. It was an extremely odd transition as I stopped to look back over my shoulder at this intriguing natural illusion. The abstract wave of mist continued its purge inland, devouring the foothills of the nearby mountains and creating a floating world effect, that was like something out of a Final Fantasy video game. I was impressed.

Ahead of me now the skies were clear as I continued to straddle the coast toward Wakkanai, stopping for a compulsory break at Cape Sōya. It is here that many a mad person - when cycling across Japan - both starts and finishes their journey. I was to meet and congratulate several other cyclists during my short spell there, customarily taking photographs of one another posing alongside a big pointed monument that declared Cape Sōya to be Japan's 'Northern Most Point'. This is a bit of fib, and I do hate to come across as meticulous - but about half a mile north-westerly from Cape Sōya sits the uninhabited island of Benten-jima, this is actually Japan's northern most limit... just saying.

Rounding the Cape and heading along the Soya Bay, one sees a colossally prominent structure some 30 miles away, towering up out of the ocean. Mt. Rishiri is a dormant volcano which rises to 1,721 metres and looks a lot like Mt. Fuji. In fact, its nickname is Mt. Rishiri-Fuji.

Rishiri, and its smaller, low-lying neighbour, Rebun are two islands that make up the Rishiri-Rebun-Sarobetsu National Park, (try saying that with a gob full of Monster Munch!) both of which I intended to conquer visit. Whether or not I was up for trekking to Mt. Rishiri's apparently awkward summit was still up for debate, but whatever my decision, I knew it would be spontaneous.

Making it to Wakkanai, I made a mad dash for the ferry terminal. Upon arriving there at 15:19, I discovered that the last ferry to Rebun for the day would be departing at 15:30. It was at this point that I began to panic, losing every thread of my Japanese language in the process, whilst trying to explain to the buxom young lady at the ticket counter that I wanted to go to Rebun. Fortunately, she had an excellent grasp of caveman speech and, before I knew it, I was being whisked away onto the ferry with my two wheeled companion, happy at how well my pure blind luck had just played out.

Passing the mighty Mt. Rishiri en route to Rebun, I became instinctively put off by the idea of scaling it. A blackness descended over the island at the volcano's peak, yet over on neighbouring Rebun, the skies were still clear and welcoming; just like the Seicomart was upon my arrival at the small island's port.

Grabbing that vital beer and that equally vital box of fried chicken, I sat down upon a sea wall and watched a storm gather speed over Rishiri. With any luck, the storm would get all its atrocities out of its system before I took the ferry over tomorrow. I took a few more sips of my brew as the gloomy clouds began to progress steadily towards Rebun. The sips turned into big messy gulps as I decided that shelter was a definite must. In Japan without a reservation one is often pushed to find accommodation, such was the case with titchy Rebun and thus I would be forced to camp. My decision to jump on the ferry to Rebun was somewhat of a rushed one and now my undoing seemed imminent.

Seeking out the Midorigoaka camp site, a short ride north from Rebun Town, I threw up my sack-of-shit tent. My only modification for tonight was in the form of covering for one side of the tent: my waterproof poncho. On this side I would lay my head, the rest of my body would just have to get wet.

Then… it began to rain.

Rebun - Rishiri
41 miles

The rain wasn't heavy, but it was constant, and within a few hours my tent was drenched. By torchlight, I was able to find a vast bulk of the water's entry points and under each drip I placed a plastic bag to collect the water. Every hour or so I emptied the bags outside of the tent, before allowing them to slowly refill again. Ridiculously, I kept up these shenanigans until dawn, by which point I had 9 bags of water positioned around myself.

I waited for the rain to lapse into drizzle before packing up camp. By the time I'd paid my camping fees to the site manager - who had no idea I had even camped upon his turf - it had started to rain again. Donning my wet weather gear and heading north, I realised the only thing missing from my pack was a pair of inflatable armbands.

Rebun is a narrow, elongated island, stretching 18 miles from north to south and just 5 miles east to west, so despite the on/off rain it shouldn't take one too long to quite literally soak up the sights. I cycled a very touristy route to Cape Sukotan, Rebun's northern most point. A number of tourist buses thrashed past me in the rain; excited and surprised faces pressed up against the windows, eager hands reaching for cameras. I wondered if perhaps the bus passengers thought that I was either one of two things:

1: A hard-arse, or
2: A dumb-arse.

As I spat out an ominously sour tasting piece of muck that had flicked up from the road's surface, directly into my mouth, I knew it was more than likely the latter.

Making it to Cape Sukotan, I was congratulated by a small number of tourists from the bus. As they clapped their hands, my ego took a rare opportunity to bathe in the glory and I cordially accepted a handful of *mochi* cakes from my adoring fans. Fans that like me would no doubt be disappointed with Cape Sukotan itself. Through the marring drizzle one could just about make out a few craggy islets and a couple of fed up seagulls. I shrugged my shoulders and turned south.

I took an alternate route on the way back, hugging the island's eastern coast. A number of battered old fishing houses were dotted along the coast, some were merely corrugated shacks that looked as if they would be lucky enough to stand firm for just one more day. Elderly fishermen and women, were out maintaining their boats or prepping their catch for market. The hard working life of a Rebunite seemed far from a prosperous one, but it was the only kind of life most here would ever know - and that's testament to the courage and the adaptability of mankind.

To the far south of the island lay Rebun's money shot. A steep climb out of Rebun Town saw me picking up a walking trail to Motochi Lighthouse. From a small car park, where I left my bike, I was to be treated to an orgy of delights: absorbingly lush green hills that stemmed from a series of high rising cliffs, carved by either Nature's expertise – or by the wand of a local wizard.

A certain enchantment now encapsulated Rebun, as the occasional front of sea mist passed through, obscuring my surrounds for moments at a time, before again clearing and blowing me away with its scenic beauty. However, south-westerly, an effigy of Mt. Doom from Lord Of The Rings lay prominent, a monstrously sullen looking Mt. Rishiri awaited. And with nothing but misery certain, I caught the next ferry over.

It was a short 40 minute ferry trip to Oshidomari in the island's north; Rebun and Rishiri being separated by just 6 miles. From the blackened summit of Mt. Rishiri, vast dark swathes of cloud were being cast out across the island, forcing me hastily south of town for a couple of miles to one of Rishiri's designated camp sites. A small clearing amongst a patch of woodland saw me set up camp next to a couple of young Japanese campers; they too were bracing themselves for a rough night's sleep.

I had prepared my tent as I had done on my previous night in Rebun, poncho covering one side and an armoury of plastic bags littered across the floor inside. And, as the heaven's burst with all their might, I was ready for Round 2.

Round 2 came and 23 minutes after the first drops of rain began to fall, I found myself abandoning ship; my tent utterly compromised. Torrents of water came flooding into my tent from every angle, no amount of plastic bags being able to bail me out as a thuggish wind swept across the camp.

It was dark outside, as I stuck my drenched head out of my water filled vessel. One of my neighbours was scampering about desperately with a flashlight, trying to find his tent pegs as the wind had just effortlessly whipped his flysheet away. He gave up and by dawn would be found sharing his neighbour's far superior North Face tent.

I though wasn't about to knock on a stranger's tent door to ask if there was any room for one more dumb-arse. But I couldn't stay put; and braving it out was far from an option. About 30 yards from my tent - which I had now dubiously named 'Sir Leaksalot' - was a barbecue gazebo. I ran over to it barefooted with my flashlight. The ground of the gazebo was solid stone with a roof made from wood which was leaking, but the barbecue itself wasn't secured to anything. I pushed it to one side and made adequate space for one terribly shit tent. I then ran back and forth importing all of my worldly goods to their new less than ideal, but perfectly survivable camp site.

Crawling into my moist tent, I waited it out as the rain continued to pour ceaselessly throughout the night.

Rishiri - Wakkanai
7 miles

I'd heard through the grapevine that Hokkaidō doesn't have a rainy season. Bollocks! It was late morning before the rain finally decided to peter out somewhat, offering up a glimmer of optimism.

During the process of packing up my tent, my neighbours found themselves getting harassed by a mob of crows. Whilst one camper was away from his tent brushing his teeth, one opportunist would fly directly into his tent and come away with a packet of cigarettes. As the fellow from the other tent ran to try and discourage the big bird away, another crow would simultaneously swoop down and enter the other unhappy camper's tent, coming away this time with a roll of cling film. It was a pre-planned and well articulated attack upon humanity. And whilst the camper brushing his teeth came running back to his tent waving his hands in the air with a toothbrush hanging out of his mouth, another crow would drop down to the wash basin and take off with his momentarily deserted tube of toothpaste. What these flying heathens needed with such accessories I couldn't quite fathom, but I had no doubt in my mind that something rather malefic was going down in these parts - and I didn't like it one bit. A short moment later, a crow then paid me a visit, perching itself on a rail next to my tent. It looked at me, tilting its head to one side suggestively, trying to be cute.

'Fuck off,' I ushered. 'I'm not in the mood.'

The bird took the hint and swiftly fucked right off.

I really wasn't in the mood.

As soon as I was packed, I said farewell to my disorientated camping neighbours and headed back north toward the coast, in the direction of Oshidomari. With the weather appearing to be on the mend, I had ambitions of circumnavigating the roughly 37 mile island. Yet, just 2 short miles into my little venture, I became saturated; the skies absolutely pummelling me with the wet stuff... again. Rather quickly I decided that Rishiri was no longer the place for me. With luck, I wasn't far from the ferry terminal where I was able to empty about a pint of water from each of my trainers and change into the last of my dry clothes; then I would catch the afternoon ferry back to an equally soggy Wakkanai.

Wakkanai

For three days I found myself holed up in another one of Hokkaidō's classic 1980's themed youth hostels. It was a desolate sort of building that gave off a haunted house vibe; located atop an isolated hill.

Wakkanai was still being deluged by buckets of rain and after a while I began to feel somewhat trapped; the early stages of cabin fever were imminent. I walked around the empty hostel in an attempt to keep myself busy, but there was no one else around. Reception was only open for a couple of hours each day and the elderly gentleman receptionist mostly appeared to be interested in staring at the wall. Each morning I would awake and pull back the curtains to expose the watery world of Wakkanai. Then I'd let out a heavy sigh before trudging downstairs to reception to book yet another night in the house that time forgot. The receptionist would also sigh in disgust at my request and thus the cycle continued. One would have thought that my saving grace would have been the television in my room, yet unfortunately this was only to add to my misery as it allowed me to bear witness to the tragedy of England's offensively disgraceful World Cup campaign, and the less said about that sham, the better.

Wakkanai - Shosanbetsu
74 miles

On my fourth day at the hostel, a heavier than normal sigh ensued as I skulked downstairs to reception.

'*Ohayo gozaimasu,*' good morning, I said to the receptionist who seemed a little disgruntled by the fact that I'd just disturbed his reverie of boredom.

'*Oh... Ohayo gozaimasu,*' he begrudgingly, replied.

'*Mou hitoban onegai shimasu,*' one more night, please.

'*Ano... chotto...*' hmm... erm...well. He was being hesitant about something.

'*Oh, mondai desu ka?*' Oh, is there a problem?

The receptionist then went on to tell me that the hostel was full.

'What??' I said in English, the word echoing down the baron hallway (and probably still is). I then took a good look around me, making a point to observe one of the building's main proficiencies... its sheer emptiness.

'*Honto ni?*' Seriously? I said, marginally miffed.

'*Hai, sou desu, gomen ne,*' Yes, that's right, sorry about that. Before going on to confirm that check out was at 10am.

I looked at my watch; it was 9:50am. I sighed so hard I almost destroyed myself.

11 minutes later and I was reacquainted with a classic drenching as I began to work my way south on the long road towards Okinawa. Although, despite the damp conditions, there was a certain jubilance about being back on the road again. The act of being just ever so slightly more productive than being sat on one's arse in a crummy hostel room, was one of pure invigoration. I was reaping the positives from the negatives. Yes, it was pissing it down, but, I was back in the saddle, and, more importantly, I was happy to be there!

After a couple of hours, I came across an unmanned road side rest area. It was a small wooden structure, immaculately clean, offering toilets, cooking facilities, a dining area and an enticingly huge gas heater. It was open to the weary traveller in a gesture of goodwill and trust; a true pyromaniac's paradise. Feeling the increasing need to take all my clothes off, I stripped away my seemingly non-waterproof waterproofs. Firing up the gas heater, I began to dry my belongings. The rain continued to hammer it down outside, like it had nothing else better to do. Inside, under shelter, and around the now raging warmth of the gas heater, I took it upon myself to learn the Japanese words for human body parts, laughing childishly to myself upon learning the words for both male and female genitalia.

With my clothes subsequently dried, and the onset of boredom beginning to deliver itself once more, I decided to saddle up and head back out into the rain.

I hugged the coast for several more hours, the weather eventually clearing shortly before my arrival in the village of Shosanbetsu. I lucked out here by finding the Misakidai camping ground, perched upon a scenic cliff edge, overlooking the ocean's calm and gentle waters. The sun clung to the horizon, its bright fiery reflection trailblazing across the Sea of Japan. The camp site also had the added bonus of being free. Well, when I say free, nobody asked me for any money. And... the extra prize of an onsite *onsen* was also added to the playlist. This I should note however was not free, but for a meagre £1.80 the price of cleanliness was wholesomely affordable.

I found it hard initially to conquer the idea of having a big bath with other completely butt naked strangers. Was I a prude? Well, yes, but growing up in conservative England where having a bath was a private, behind closed doors affair, would somehow dictate my abstract gingerness.

In Japan, the baths are segregated by sex, as to presumably discourage a modest amount of jizzing. After removing one's clothes and placing them in a small basket, one can collect a modesty towel to cover one's sausage. But a Japanese bathhouse is a place of etiquette, you can't just simply go waltzing in after a long, hard sweaty days work and belly flop straight into the shared bathing facilities... that would be the most heinous of bath crimes. One must shower first, and properly too. A row of stalls bordering on toddler's potties are generally provided, along with a selection of soaps, shampoos and a big mirror, so you can presumably check out your junk in its reflection - or not. Here one must take the time to liberate one's self of a day of grime, scrubbing hard and furiously, so that one is presentable for public bathing.

When one enters the bath, one should essentially be a shiny, clean entity, so, if your elbows aren't sparkling - you're not coming in! When my elbows were eventually gleaming, I'd find that there were a number of baths available for me to explore, all of different shapes and sizes and seemingly varying temperatures - inclusive of an outside bath which would turn out to be my favourite. Again, as I appeared to be the only tourist travelling through Hokkaidō at this moment, the bathhouse was far from crowded. It was an appeasing relaxant after a long day's arduous journeying in the rain. And now that I was familiar with this luxury, it was to become one that I would take advantage of more in the months to come.

Shosanbetsu - Mashike
66 miles

The night saw yet more heavy rainfall, but camping under a picnic shelter I'd find myself smug and unfazed by what would have otherwise been another soggy dilemma. I'd soon be seeing the bright lights of Sapporo again, where I'd be able to rectify my current tent situation.

As I continued south along the west coast, I found very little gradient to contend with; allowing for a productive day's progress. Passing through the charmless industrial city of Rumoi, the grisly Mt. Shokanbestu didn't altogether seem too pleased to see me. For the best part of the day, the weather had been composed, but from the mountain range a dark foray of clouds had assembled. Vast hazy drifts of precipitation were coaxing the far reaching forests that clustered the periphery of Mashike; Rumoi District's last stronghold of civilisation, before entering the gauntlet of the mountains.

As the wind gathered and the rain forced itself in my direction, I was lucky enough to find sudden refuge in a very homely bus stop; a wooden and spacious structure with sliding doors so that one could keep the elements at bay. Inside was spotless, clean and perfectly habitable. And not only was there a nice long bench for me to sprawl myself out upon, but there was also room for my belongings and my trusty steed. I parked my derrière on the bench and uttered a small sigh of relief as the rain began to pummel the world around me. With the drone of the rain loudly rebounding off the shelter's roof, I closed my eyes for the briefest of moments.

Some 12 seconds later, I found myself impulsively waking up, my head spasmodically clanging against the wall of the shelter. I was epically tired, and any ambitions of passing the mountain range this day were truly dashed. I lay back upon the bench, placing my head upon my makeshift pillow of a rolled up fleece. Again, closing my eyes, I slept instantly.

Mashike - Sapporo
74 miles

When I awoke, I was able to add a new tick to the list of places slept upon on my journey thus far:

Hostel - √

Baseball Pitch - ✓
Park Bench - ✓
The House of Pubes - ✓
Hotel - ✓
Tsunami Evacuation Point - ✓
Refugee Shelter - ✓
Wilderness - ✓
Train Station- ✓
Traditional Japanese Home - ✓
Bus Stop - ✓

Congratulating myself, I shoved a banana into my gob before making haste into the overcast mountains of Shokanbetsudake. Before I left though, I swept and tidied up the premises. The Japanese etiquette was almost flowing naturally through me now, apart from the fact that I'd just roughed it for the night in a bus stop... like a quintessential hobo.

The road to Sapporo took me on some of the most testing terrain I'd encountered in all of Hokkaidō, as a continuous flow of mountains lined the coastal route south. And for those with a fetish for tunnels (you sick bastards) you'd be in for a treat. Any semblance of fear that I once had for these man-made shortcuts / cyclist death traps I'd long since lost. After 20 tunnels in the space of just a couple of hours, one soon becomes immune to their treacherous ways. Yet to lose that fear entirely would be unwise; and, as the day wore on, I found myself nearly getting completely erased by a passing truck. To take for granted the gravity of danger on offer in these tunnels, could have cost me dearly.

By early afternoon, I had the big smoke of Sapporo back in my sights. Here for a couple of days I would meet up with some familiar faces, drink some beer, do some karaoke, iron out any bicycle imperfections and, at last, remedy my camping predicament with the addition of a new flysheet for Sir Leaksalot. For, if there was one thing that was certain, Japan's rainy season hadn't finished with me yet, in fact it had barely even begun.

Sapporo – Lake Shikotsu
53 miles

Between an 8-hour karaoke binge and England's next World Cup match, I'd had very little time to rest. Normally, a 4am kick off would have been deemed an unheard of feat, yet I was still running on an excess of alcohol fumes and raring for England's next humiliation to the Uruguayan's. The match inevitably resulted in England being dumped out of the World Cup; the impossible dream living up to its predictable reputation. And with Japan shortly following England out of the back door, football fever soon dampened down across the board. England's loss however would have a sobering effect upon me. I'd been in Hokkaidō for close to 2 months now, and as much as it was an awe-inspiring and grandiose prefecture, I was eager to experience the other prefectures.

At the base of Hokkaidō lay the city of Hakodate, from there I would be able to grab a ferry back to Honshū where 37 other prefectures would await me. But at some 200 miles from Sapporo, Hakodate was still a few days cycling away. So, I began to peddle.

From Sapporo, I picked up the well-forested Shiroishi cycle path that meandered some 12 miles to the town of Kitahiroshima. From there a rather gross and monotonous main road took me to Chitose, where I picked up another cycle path that gradually ascended up into the mountains toward Lake Shikotsu.

The weather was overcast with unclear intentions, but all the same allowed for comfortable cycling. The lake itself remained hidden by the guise of a dense and impenetrable looking forest, before gradually thinning out to reveal a camp site upon its eastern shore. Being a Thursday, the site wasn't exactly a hive of activity, with just a small number of other campers, so finding a suitable spot wasn't going to be an issue.

Whilst I was setting up camp, one of my neighbours came over with a beer to say 'Hello.' Being no stranger to drinking the beer of a stranger, I readily took his kind offering. The stranger introduced himself as Johan, a musician from Switzerland. We chatted a while under the sky's grey lull; an image exacted across the breadth of the big lakes surface. Situated amongst three volcanoes the lake rested in a caldera, said to have been formed some 40-50,000 years ago. It is the second largest caldera lake in Japan with a surface area of 48.72mi^2, and also the country's second deepest at 363 metres. Yet, for now, a vast portion of the lake and its mountainous surrounds lay mostly obscured from low-lying cloud cover and a rapidly fading light. The encroaching evening would consequently lead the surrounding temperature to swiftly plummet, forcing Johan and I to retreat to the lacklustre warmth of our respective tents. Nestling into my sleeping bag, I listened to the discreet lapping of water against the shore's edge. It was dreamy and relaxing, the perfect drug for some hasty shut-eye.

Lake Shikotsu

For breakfast I had a can of eels, a breakfast that I shall never have again... ever, for they left a monstrously dirty aftertaste in my mouth; like an old boot that was left to fester in a pile of dog muck... and then got canned for consumption. One crummy breakfast aside though, I had little complaints about my surrounds. Sitting at the edge of Lake Shitkotsu the sun was beginning to break through the cloud cover as streams of light seeped through - giving the water a turquoise glow. A procession of trees of various shades of green merged up into the mountains, lining the bulk of the lake's perimeter. All three of the lake's surrounding volcanoes were in clear view this morning: the not so actively-active Mt. Eniwa to the north, the dormantly-dormant Mt. Fuppushi to the south, and adjacent, its hyperactive-active partner in crime, Mt. Tarumae. Although having not blown its load since 1982, Tarumae is considered to be one of the most active volcanoes in Japan… and I decided to scale it!

The volcano at 1,041m is a relatively straightforward climb on a designated pathway. I hiked with Swiss Johan, so had somebody to natter with about canned dog muck on the ascent. In about an hour we would make it to the summit; vegetation becoming sparse as a lunar landscape of volcanic ash and debris unravelled before us. Some 100 metres away lay the volcano's steaming crater; an area strictly off limits as white poisonous gases emitted precariously from various cracks in the rocks. I advised Johan that the bad boy could blow at any given moment, before consequently asking him to 'imagine that.' He told me not to say such things.

We stood for a while and ate some snacks. Looking north from the mountain's summit, I saw that the impression of Lake Shikotsu being a crater lake was all the more obvious. I asked Johan how long he thought it would take him to drink all of the lake's 5.0 cubic miles of water, it was then that he looked at me as if I was a little bit special; he was probably right though… probably.

We continued to chat and joke about nothing in particular before suddenly finding ourselves enveloped in a big blanket of thick mist, barely being able to see even a few short metres ahead. It came from nowhere, like a Russian spy sub. The party was thus over and we descended back to Shikotsu.

Back at the lake, the Sapporo weekend getaway crew had arrived, I could barely find my own tent amongst the masses. The barbecues were out in force, the music was blaring, dogs were fighting and the kids were screaming their heads off; it was the perfect weekend getaway.

It was my round, so I bought Johan a beer as we had a little chat with our Japanese neighbours who were quick to cook us up a mean feast. After a couple of beers and some *yakitori*, I was now beginning to feel a holiday vibe; something that I hadn't exactly felt over the previous months. Today was my day off, but taking that rare chance to relax, I still felt some form of guilt at the lack of progress that I'd made. My project was no race, I had time, but it was hard to get that premise through to my brain - especially one as special as mine.

Lake Shikotsu - Oshamanbe
82 miles

A multitude of mountains paved the way for the 60-mile stretch between Lake Shikotsu and Lake Toya. With the comfort of clear skies, I made exceptional progress, my only concerns being the weekend drivers who drove by as if they had just been given a day pass to behave like absolute mentalists. Any regard for the Highway Code was completely shelved at the weekend, it seemed.

Arriving at Lake Toya, in just about one piece, I stopped for some late-afternoon fried chicken treats from Seicomart.

Lake Toya, like Shikotsu is a caldera lake, but its shape is more circular; with a circumference of just over 26 miles. In the middle lies four small forested islands, observantly called Nakajima, Middle Islands. As I perused the lake's perimeter, it appeared that I had arrived during a mass cosplay pilgrimage.

For those not in know, cosplay is an abbreviation of 'costume play'. Fans or nerds - as they are often known - dress up in the clothes of their favourite fictionalised characters: from cartoon shows, comic books or video games. The concept has been doing the rounds now in Japan since the early 90's, but in recent years it has begun to surface overseas as a popular, if not slightly gimmicky attraction, to other like-minded nerds.

The costumes are dramatic, the hairstyles funky, the flesh revealing, and if one had no concept of the idea and happened across such an event completely at random, one would no doubt have to question one's sanity.

The shores of the lake were completely awash with cosplayers as I weaved in and out of the excitable hoards, alongside the most serene of natural wonders. However, when Jigglypuff came over and asked if he/she could take a photograph with me... I knew it was time to bail.

With gusto I would traverse the treacherous Route 37 south to the quiet town of Oshamanbe. On the outskirts lay a desolate country park, perfectly ripe for a quiet night's camping... tomorrow I would arrive in Hakodate, my last port of call in Hokkaidō.

Oshamanbe - Hakodate
87 miles

When I slept, I dreamed of *Pokémon,* most notably an unofficial *Pokémon* that goes by the name of *'Anusmouthmon,'* and the less said about his party trick the better! His ethereal-realm antics however wouldn't put me off my breakfast of chocolate croissants from the ever trusting Seicomart; a supermarket that once away from Hokkaidō I would come to miss dearly. Of the roughly 6.7 billion different convenience stores spanning across the Japanese archipelago, Seicomart will always be held in high regard, its prices inviting and its food delectable. *Now if that free plug doesn't get me free croissants I don't know what will!*

Being a Monday, the sloppy Sunday drivers were now back in the office dreaming up a world of clerical miseries. My weekday competition was again the omnipresent trucker, who would offer up a fine catalogue of near death experiences as I journeyed along a decisively slapdash and wanky Route 5 to Hakodate. To grin and bear it was my only viable option.

To the east of me sat Uchiura Bay, which I would cycle alongside, until the western foothills of Mt. Komagatake; a fine figure of a volcano that towers up into the clouds upon the fringes of the bay. Cutting inland on a more direct and southerly trajectory toward Hakodate, I escaped the torment of Route 5 for the briefest of moments as I passed through Ōnuma National Park. The 35-square mile National Park being a by-product of an ancient eruption of Mt. Komagatake; essentially forming the two picturesque lakes of Ōnuma and Konuma. Both lakes are dotted with a series of minuscule birch and maple covered islands and the promiscuously dormant Komagatake sits leering on the horizon. It was a tranquil and more than welcome interval before falling back onto the dastardly Route 5 for the remainder of the journey to Hakodate.

For many, the prefecture's third largest city, Hakodate, is seen as the gateway to Hokkaidō. It is also one of the main hubs for entry to the Seikan Railway Tunnel, a 33.46 mile stretch of tunnel that runs under the sea bed, essentially connecting Hokkaidō with neighbouring island Honshū. I, however, considering Hakodate's place in history, opted for the more conventional method. Since the opening of its borders to foreign trade back in 1854 - after years of isolation from the rest of the world - the Tsugaru Strait has seen a wealth of ships from across the globe ply its waters. So, for this reason, and the other reason of really wanting to visit the remote Shimokita Peninsula in Aomori's rugged north, I felt it only apt to follow suit and take the ferry.

As it is a port town, I feared the worst for Hakodate, feeling the necessity to stereotype the place before barely arriving. My first impression as I cycled through the city's outlying suburbs, witnessing a contingent of rundown buildings, battered sidewalks, abandoned bicycles and, most of all, weeds, was that I'd had the place sussed. Yet in this instance I was wrong, sincerely wrong. In reality, my only certainty for being able to confidently judge a city by its cover lay a lifetime away in Hokkaidō's far north, for the city of Monbetsu truly was a horrible shithole. Sure, the suburbs of Hakodate had a hard edge to them with an element of rot, but it lacked any sinister undertones. There was no denying however that the city didn't quite share the wealth of Hokkaidō's number one city, Sapporo.

Cycling further into the core of the city, I witnessed a mishmash of architecture; offering up a mixture of days gone by with a dousing of the modern age. The city provoked an element of mystery, but it wasn't until I made it to the harbour at the base of Mt. Hakodate that I was able to begin to appreciate its draw as a tourist focal point; its rich history becoming absorbingly evident.

From 'The Bay' area, with its cobbled streets and dockside restaurants, an assembly of red brick trading warehouses still stand. The rogue cosmopolitan traders of the past long since gone, they have been replaced with an array of souvenir shops, local delicacies, a beer hall and an all grimacing Starbucks.

For the most part, the charm saunters on towards Motomachi and into the foothills of Mt. Hakodate; a former settlement for the city's foreign residents. Today a number of well-preserved buildings still stand such as the British Consulate, a Russian Orthodox church and a Chinese memorial hall. Hakodate was once one of the most important trading posts in Northern Japan; making the city more than just a harbour.

As Motomachi began to peter out, I found the ropeway lift that would take me up 334 metre's to the summit of Mt. Hakodate. I leisurely tied up my steed and joined the brigade of tourists flooding into the ticket office. It is here at this small mountain's summit that the city's artillery of attractions comes to its ultimate climax. The viewing platforms at the summit were packed tight; the city's main earner immediately obvious. Some say that the view from the mountain's peak is one of the three best night views of Japan. A statement which I agree with – and if you wanted to take a picture of the back of a Chinese tourist's head, it was absolutely perfect!

As the sun gradually tucked itself beyond the horizon, allowing day to graciously fall into night, a euphoria of 'ooooo's' and 'ahhhh's' rang out. The lights of the city below twinkled radiantly, showing the scale of the city all the way up towards the darkness of the distant mountain ranges, that I had journeyed earlier.

For the past two months I'd been tackling the bulk of what now lay to the north of me; it had been a fair test, an engaging test, but the real tests were still to come.

STATS

Dates: 24/04/2014 – 24/06/2014
Total miles traversed: 2,405 miles
Total time in the saddle: 242 hours and 48 minutes

9.2 AOMORI
青森県

Hakodate – Mt. Osore
38 miles

It was a short 90-minute ferry ride from Hakodate to Ōma, a small town upon the tip of the axe-shaped peninsula of Shimokita. Ōma is famed for having some of the most delectable and pricey tuna in Japan, an abundance which can commonly be found in Tokyo's rampant Tsukiji Market. A stone's throw to the north was Cape Ōma, the northern most point of Honshū. A black and white lighthouse sits just off shore on a tiny low-lying island, the last rock to stand between Honshū and Hokkaidō; the big island now a mere shadow grafted onto the horizon. The skies were free of cloud cover as the sun shimmered brightly off of the calm waters of the Tsugaru Strait. At a Cornetto incinerating 24°C, I quite rightly slapped on some sun screen before turning my back on Hokkaidō for the very last time.

Cycling south-easterly, I'd see the rise and fall of Shimokita's rugged coastline to Ōhata. There, curious eyes and light-hearted giggles would greet me as I wandered the supermarket in search of snacks and supplies for my forthcoming ascent into the region's remote and mountainous interior.

Outside the supermarket I sat on a bench and noshed on some sushi. An elderly gent approached me, hands in his pockets and a cigarette dangling from his lips. As he sat down next to me, he began to speak; his accent a thick and incomprehensible drawl. I struggled with his line of questioning but told him roughly what I thought he wanted to hear. Acknowledging me with neither surprise nor disgust, he nodded his head humbly, before pulling a packet of cigarettes out of his shirt pocket and offering me a smoke. I declined his offer politely, which led him to ramble on for a while before working out that I didn't have the foggiest. And so we sat in silence for some moments, as I slurped on a carton of spicy tomato juice. Finally, he stood before taking a long hard look at my cycling rig; then he wished me a safe journey. I thanked him as he shuffled away slowly to sit on another bench, less than two metres away from me.

Leaving Ōhata and heading inland to the mountains, my rig felt uncomfortably weighty, yet reading beforehand about the remoteness of the area I had no intentions of running out of fuel, and thus had stocked heavily on supplies. My main concern however was that I'd bought a bunch of bananas back at the supermarket, forgetting that I was now heading into prime macaque territory. Now, I'd heard no rumours of macaque-attacks in Japan, but Google Images clearly details the devastation our distant relatives can cause if they happen to be having a seriously bad day at the monkey office. And anybody that's anybody knows, that a banana is a monkey's best friend, so the last thing I wanted was a bloody fight to the death in the remotes of Shimokita - over the faintest hit of potassium. So... I cycled the steep mountainside in a stealthy silence, observing my surrounds meticulously in mild fear of any sudden macaque-attacks.

I ascended for some 9 miles, up into the crater within the dormant volcano of the 879 metre Mt. Osore. The roads were devoid of traffic and the surrounding forests stood eerily vacant of wildlife.

Descending from the rim of the crater down to the shores of Lake Usori, the first thing that overwhelms one is the potency of sulphur lingering in the air. A number of scalding hot shallow waterways raced around the borders of the volcanic lake, as cracked fissures vented steam amongst the fluorescent yellow puddles of sulphur. The shadows of the surrounding forested hills cast a dismal reflection across Usori's almost lifeless waters. Lifeless for a reason perhaps, considering the area is renowned locally as being a gateway to Hell! The whole area is steeped in mysticism stretching as far back as 1,200 years ago when a Buddhist monk stumbled across the sacred mountain, whilst looking for a land that would resonate the world of Buddha. In fact, Mt. Osore, or Osorezan as it is also known, is considered to be one of Japan's three most sacred mountains. The others are Wakayama Prefecture's Mt. Koya, and Kyoto and Shiga Prefectures adjoining Mt. Hiei.

Osorezan's translation is also slightly undefined; straddling names such as Mt. Death, Mt. Fear, The Daunting Mountain, the Mountain of Horror or just good old-fashioned Mt. Doom, yet whatever the translation, joy and happiness is evidently out the window, that much is clear.

Flanking around the lake's edge is a red bridge which crosses a small waterway, this is known as the Sanzu-no-Kawa, a.k.a. the Sanzu River. It is a Buddhist belief that to reach the afterlife, the souls of the dead must cross this river; yet this can only happen if your karma is sufficient enough. If one has lived an innocent life, then one can just waltz quite gaily across the cutesy red bridge without qualm. If one has been mildly frivolous, but from time to time has helped someone's gran across the road, then one can traverse a shallow water crossing and ideally make it to the other side with a relatively unscathed soul. However, if one has dabbled nefariously in life (*and voted Conservative*) then don't expect a free ride to the Underworld, please ready yourself for some turbulent and demonically hell-bent waters that will ultimately devour your very soul. Gaining a shot at reincarnation was certainly no easy feat.

Through the gates of the lakeside's humbling ancient Bodaiji Temple, a baron, craggy and sulphurous world awaits, a world that looks as though it was once turned inside out. The heavy surrounding silence is dented only by the random flickering sound of spinning pinwheels jutting out of piles of stacked rocks. Close by Jizo stone guardians like those I witnessed back in Nikko's Kanmangafuchi Abyss can be found, caring for the souls of the unborn as they make the tricky transition into the next world.

I explored all of this alone, this in itself gifted the sensation of being in a truly sacred place. Its silent tranquillity was absorbing and beautiful; an artisan's dream. A number of wooden outbuildings lay scattered around the main hub of the Bodaiji Temple complex. I peered inside one and saw a tub of steaming water; it was a hot spring. I smelt my pits, they reeked of the living dead. If I'd have had a God at that precise moment, then I would have looked to the skies and thanked him/her/it. But alas I didn't, so I quickly peeled off my clothing and cast myself into the spring's mineral rich waters. My skin felt instantly invigorated, if not a little scorched as the water was outrageously hot. I relaxed for a good 3 minutes and 24 seconds... until I felt like my head was going to explode. Then I shakily clambered out like a used up junkie. The water's unclear turquoise glow disguised any evidence of my greasy day in the saddle. I sat on a bench and dried off, peering out of the same window that led to me to discover the hot spring in the first place. A monk appeared to be walking from building to building and was seemingly locking up for the evening. I hurriedly finished towelling off and gathered my belongings, exiting the building with haste.

The air outside was now noticeably colder as the sun began to bury itself beyond the crest of the encircling crater. I said my farewells to the monk as we passed one another, before finding myself in a desolate and roomy car park, next to Lake Usori. Content with the stillness of the life here, I set up camp in this perfect nirvana. And as night fell it began to rain... or so I thought.

I lay motionless in the dark, listening to the all-familiar pitter patter of droplets upon my tent; a somewhat soothing noise but one that unfortunately also encourages the bladder. I held on for as long as I could in the hope that the rain would cease; it was by no means heavy but enough to cause a mild dousing. Yet, it didn't let up. Begrudgingly, I unzipped my tent, before unexpectedly becoming engulfed by a small swarm of flying insects. *There was no rain.* I quickly zipped the tent back up and rummaged around for my torch. With the aid of light I was able to work up a sweat and splatter a bulk of the invaders. The light from my torch illuminating the tent would give me some perspective as to what was going on outside. Cast upon the thin nylon walls of my tent the shadows of hundreds upon thousands of bugs were projected, all seemingly piling across one another in some sort of bug orgy. The only thing I can confirm about the strange phenomena was that they were not mosquitoes; their bodies lightly coloured, and their flight and movement more rapid and direct. They lacked the lazy, meandrous floating of the pitiful mosquito, yet I feared that it was the warmth of my blood they too craved. If they were to eat through the very fabric of my tent then, by dawn, I would surely be nothing more than a husk. And then, suddenly, I didn't really need that piss after all.

Mt. Osore - Aomori
78 miles

I awoke early as usual, in sync with daybreak, slightly surprised to have fallen asleep to the sound of desperately hungry bugs. Yet, as I emerged from my tent, all was still; the heathen swarms having dissipated back into the depths from whence they had came. A thick band of mist clung to Lake Usori, partially obscuring its luminous glow, as the pinnacle of Mt. Ozore floated mysteriously above, coaxed in a clear blue summer sky.

My day started with a series of steep climbs up and out of the caldera; I scaled a number of energy zapping gradients ranging from 9% - 12%. This is never a good way to start the day; always more appealing to be able to gradually ease one's stiff muscles into a climb - as opposed to an immediate gung-ho assault. Yet having devoured my banana stash at breakfast I would soon find my rhythm.

After about 3 miles, I'd find myself looking down upon Lake Usori; its dawn mist already spent, revealing the water's intrinsically vibrant colouring. On the opposite side, to the south beyond a wave of pines, lay the city of Mutsu and the Ominato Bay - from there I could straddle close to the coast all the way to Aomori.

Descending from the mountains, the steep gradients allowed me to pick up some serious speed, which saw me smash my previous high speed record of 32.6 mph with a breakneck 40 mph. The adrenaline was pumping and my brain power was truly limited as I maniacally overtook a couple of cars.

Down in the uninspiring Mutsu, I rewarded myself with an ice cream from Family Mart before making tracks along the uninspiring and much more plaintively dicey Route 279 south; along the western axe handle of the Shimokita Peninsula towards Noheji Bay. It was whilst traversing this section that a bulk of my possessions decided to deteriorate in a tightly contested and well synchronised fashion. Wear and tear was always an inevitability, but it's stressful when everything decides to pretty much shit itself in such a collective manner.

Firstly, my front pannier was beginning to dip further and further south, to the point where it was almost touching the front tyre; on close inspection the screw and nut fixture had bored straight through the thread. Using some bigger washers I could remedy this but it would mean having to lighten the load. I then I had a phantom noise coming from within my seat post, a clicking noise from my right pedal and my odometer was running out of battery juice too; which annoyingly meant wiping all the data when replacing the battery. Sadly, my new DWR (Doughty World Record) of 40 mph would henceforth become nothing more than mere word of mouth.

My final cause of concern came from my camera. Whilst taking a picture of a tiny dollop of an island situated just off the coast, I noticed some big black smears on the lens. I sighed heavily in disgust, somehow alienating the temptation to launch the device into the bay. Memories are priceless, but pictures of memories are beyond priceless. Heading to the prefectural capital however would ideally see the problem remedied. Yet, upon my arrival in Aomori, my optimism was soon dashed as I encountered only one camera shop; the owner of which dismissed my custom and, in my stubbornness, I refused to seek out another.

I hung about sulkily for a couple of hours in an otherwise pleasing enough coastal city, visiting the Nabuta Warasse Museum; a bizarre looking building veiled with a collection of blood red slats that within detailed the story of Aomori's big summer Nebuta Festival. If one happened to be in Aomori in early August they would no doubt witness a vibrant party atmosphere of cheering masses; the streets filled with a contingent of huge, immaculately detailed floats made from paper and bamboo, depicting various Japanese mythological characters. *Taiko* drum beats would thrum around every corner and *haneto* dancers and audience members alike would be shaking their booties deep into the technicoloured night. But, like I said, this all takes place in August, and it was currently the back-end of June which put me shit out of luck.

Out of Festival season, the city centre of Aomori had very little else to offer the passing nomad; I wound down the evening in a local curry house before heading out upon an extensive search for a ditch in which to lay my increasingly itchy head.

Aomori - Hirosaki
30 miles

I'd riled up a nest of ants during the darkness of night, whilst slyly parking my tent in the grounds of the Aomori Prefecture

Sports Park. Passing unnoticed through the compound's gates, I'd found solace behind a small congregation of bushes in a blind spot from passing vehicles. Here I would play the part of trespasser, albeit an out of sight and out of mind trespasser - one of the best in the trade. And by dawn, even the ants had settled down and forgiven me, as before the sun had barely even considered flexing its semi-cancerous rays, I was on the road to Hirosaki. *My only evidence to ever having spent the night coming from this very confession, for I am the ever guilty trespasser.*

In a few short and stress-free hours I found myself to the south of the Tsugaru Plain in the castle town of Hirosaki. The town's emblem is the swastika, but it doesn't take long to realise that Nazi Germany had played no part in the formation of this appealing city. The city has oodles of charm with a series of compact and tranquil alleyways lined with a montage of traditional Japanese homes and immaculately maintained gardens.

Sitting amongst the spacious Hirosaki Castle Park, lies the city's showpiece: the 17th Century Hirosaki Castle. Yes, it's been nobbled once or twice, but today it stands very prominent atop a fortress of boulders, some 3-storeys high; its fair white walls and dark green bamboo roof tiles arching out above the lily-covered waters of the moat, 20 feet below. In its presence one can't help but cast one's imagination back to feudal Japan with its spurting blood and roly-poly heads, as seen in the likes of classics such as Shogun Assassin, and the Lone Wolf and Cub series. And without any evidence to back up my claim I convinced myself that I would have been an excellent samurai… most probably.

I cycled further into the Park, stumbling oddly across a very un-Edo running track, the re-imaginings of violent samurai movies suddenly ceasing. It was then that a shirtless white-man foreigner came running towards me.

'Hey!' he called out.

I looked over my shoulder to see if he wasn't perhaps waving at a better person than myself, I saw no one. I looked back at the semi-nude foreigner who was now pointing at me directly. I raised my hand coyly to reciprocate some form of response, my stranger-danger perceptiveness kicking in slightly.

'Hey man, what's the deal?' said the stranger in an American accent, his nipples in turn also pointing at me.

'Oh, I'm just cycling around Japan,' I replied rather modestly, trying my best to look around the nipples but not directly at the nipples.

'Cool, cool, you fixed for a place to stay here in Hirosaki?'

'Err... no, but this town seems nice enough though. I'm pretty sure I'll find a decent gutter or park bench to nuzzle up to.'

'Nah man, won't allow it. Me and the wife have gotta little place just east of here, we'd love to have you over to tell us some stories.'

And like the drop of a hat, his American man-nipples no longer offended me. I wondered about taking off my shirt also, to reveal my English man-nipples, but quickly came to my senses realising that the algorithms wouldn't have quite computed and would've customarily have been deemed as just plain weird. So... I kept my nipples under wraps.

The American's name was Ken, and he and his wife, Eliza, were from Nashville, Tennessee. Ken informed me that they were both English teachers and that he still had a class to teach before winding down for the day, but could meet up with me after work at the train station, after which he would show me the east side.

I had again fluked myself into the home of fellow humans, the kind charity of strangers again gifting me a roof over my head for the night; an overwhelming treat every time.

Not being due to meet up with Ken for another couple of hours, I decided to seek out a camera shop. My saviour would come in the form of BIC camera, where I explained, in

Japanese, to the sales assistant that I had a mucky lens –
suffice it to say this was a trifle tricky. But, when he began to
quickly dismantle my camera in front of me, it appeared that
I'd somehow managed to get the message across. He polished
and blew with the tentative care one would show a prized
possession, meticulously piecing it back together, testing it,
pulling it apart again, before repeating the process of cleaning
the camera's interior until duly content. All the time I worried
about how much it was going to set me back financially, but
being a needs-must scenario, I had little choice in the matter.

'*Hai, dozo,*' said the satisfied sales assistant handing me back
my camera, a slight glimmer of sweat bullying his brow.

Testing the camera, revealed that the lens was now spotless;
like new. I was jubilant with the service offered and began to
rummage through my wallet in order to pay. At which point
the sales assistant began to blush and look deeply
embarrassed, his eyes darting from side to side in the hope
that his colleagues weren't watching.

'*Ikura desu ka?*' How much? I asked.

'*Nai, nai, nai, daijoubu desu, daijoubu,*' No, no, no, it's ok, it's
ok, shaking his hands disinterestedly at my wallet.

'*Hontou ni?*' Really?

'*Hai, daijoubu desu, arigatou gozaimasu,*' Yes, its fine, thank
you very much.

I was a little taken aback, he'd spent a good deal of time
pissing about with my camera and had saved me a great deal
of grief, all for the remarkable price of absolutely nothing. I
feel that I'd struggle to find this sort of bargain anywhere else
in the world. I thanked him and put my wallet away, the tears
in his eyes beginning to retreat as he gave another quick
glance around to make sure none of his colleagues were
watching his shame. He bowed with honour, I bowed back
with sincere gratitude, he bowed even lower, I dared not bow
again.

152

Outside Hirosaki train station I met up with my new Tennessean friends. Ken as good looking as he was, was no match for his amazingly beautiful wife, Eliza, I didn't tell them that though because I didn't want a punch in the head. After being whisked back to their apartment on the east side of town, I enjoyed a relaxed evening amongst new friends. Realising that I hadn't really conversed with anyone for the best part of a week, it was nice to just have a general chinwag and talk of common interests in life: TV shows, music, sports etc. We also did all the things good friends would do like going out for burgers and heading to the cinema to watch a mediocre X-Men flick. It was a warm and homely environment to be a part of and I felt more than welcomed into the happy couple's Hirosaki lives. It was abundantly clear that Ken and Eliza loved life and they loved each other equally as much, and that in itself was a wonderful aura to be around. It was a peaceful interval, before I clashed head on with the full brunt of 'tsuyu,' a.k.a. rainy season.

STATS

Dates: 25/06/2014 – 27/06/2014
Total miles traversed: 2,551 miles
Total time in the saddle: 259 hours and 59 minutes

11. AKITA
秋田県

Hirosaki - Futatsui
63 miles

Along with boasting about having the most beautiful women in Japan, Akita also brags about consuming the highest quantity of sake in the country; I wondered if the two stats correlated? Unfortunately, as much as the sake fan that I am, I just didn't quite have the time to carry out the research myself; for I had my first puncture to attend to. No sooner had I crossed the border into Akita Prefecture, along the mangy Route 7 – complete with its contingent of nails, scrap metal and jagged rubble - had I heard a sudden 'pop'. Descending a hill, I looked down at my rear tyre as panicked air gushed forth. I stopped to inspect the situation. The tyre's tread by this stage had become somewhat mortified and would need replacing soon, yet the main harbinger of doom was a big fat rusty nail embedded deep into the rubber. I plucked it out and the tyre let out an exhaustive hiss before becoming completely flat. Surprisingly however I wasn't angry, I had just traversed some 2,559 miles and had only just received my first puncture, I couldn't argue with those stats. After patching up the inner tube, I raised a greasy hand of fizzy carrot juice to 2,559 more uninterrupted miles.

I continued along the depressing Route 7, through a daunting section of tunnels and steadfast hills, over which the Akitan drivers seemed to pride themselves on getting as close to me as physically possible. An elderly gentleman at one point pulled straight out on me at an intersection, missing me by the narrowest of margins. I gave him a mouthful of my finest English, which no doubt fell upon deaf ears; yet my hand gestures I'm certain were more than efficient in conveying my emotions. It was only when I saw where the gentlemen had just come from that I realised why the dirty old bastard was in such an eager hurry to get away. Settled amongst the rolling hills, the vivid waterways and alpine forests, was an ominous corrugated shack, a half-draped curtain for a doorway and a small sign advertising DVD's.

'Oh, the perfect spot to pick up a copy of Miyazaki's Spirited Away,' I thought to myself.

Actually no… I didn't think that at all. I knew damn well what to expect as I parked up my bike, becoming suddenly overwhelmed by a kind of sleazy curiosity. Like the rest of the perverts I would look over my shoulder for prying eyes before entering the shack. Inside it was dark and musky, the only seedy light available coming from the four caged vending machines that all sat adjacent one another. The machines were plied with more sexual content than you could shake your Aunties big black dildo at. There were an array of DVD's with various depictions of young girls losing their clothing, along with blow-up dolls, lubricant, portable vaginas and other miscellaneous sex toys. Littering the floor afoot the vending machines were a number discarded boxes and ominous plastic bags, I decided not to pry any further. The vicinity stunk of sexual deprivation and I was suddenly quite eager to return to the far less promiscuous Route 7 to catch up with some more classic near death experiences.

At around 6 in the evening I'd made it to Futatsui, a quiet little town perched alongside the gentle flowing waters of the Yoneshiro River. I knew that I'd be spending the night here, so I found a spot just off a walking path which ran parallel to the river. There I pitched my tent, before feasting on some lukewarm soba noodles and battered octopus tentacles. I fell asleep a short while later to a strangely soothing orgy of frog song.

Futatsui – Oga Peninsula
74 miles

I awoke to heavy rain. Not having the patience to linger in my tent I packed up camp and headed to a nearby 7-Eleven for breakfast. With coffee and *gyōza* in hand I took a seat under the eaves of a nearby school gymnasium and waited for the rain to die down somewhat. Being a Sunday, the grounds were empty, so I entertained myself with a game of keepy-uppy with an abandoned basketball.

The on/off rain would be a constant now for some time as I got to grips with the Japanese rainy season, essentially the equivalent of the UK's April showers... but on crack. Getting wet at numerous intervals was, more or less integral to my journey south. If I was lucky enough, I found a hasty retreat out of the random showers, if not I just got a soaking and learned to live with it.

My goal this day would be to traverse the Oga Peninsula, home of the demonic Namahage. Breaching south-westerly through the storm of relentless rain and customary atrocious drivers, I was greeted by two huge, surly looking statues. Each was dressed in a straw garb and displayed distinctly threatening mannerisms; one red-faced martinet wielded a *deba* knife, and the other blue-faced interloper suggestively brandished a mop! Over two millennia ago it was said that a Chinese emperor bought with him five ogres to Oga; a curiously situated peninsula branching out of western Akita into the Sea of Japan. The ogres, or Namahage - as they became known - used to pillage the local villages for their crops and women. This naturally left the local inhabitants somewhat disgruntled; complaints piling into the village elders as the peninsula rapidly turned into the sausage party capital of Japan. Yet one elder had a cunning plan, a challenge if you may, to the thieving Namahage. If the ogres could build 1000 steps up a mountain to a local temple in one night then the villagers would give the demons all of the crops and women that they desired, but if they failed… they would have to fuck right off and know their place in society.

The Namahage, fuelled by greed and lust, set to the challenge in no time, powering through to some 999 steps. It was directly after which however that a wise-arse villager took it upon himself to trick the Namahage. He feigned the sound of the cockerel, leading the Namahage to believe it was the dawn of a new day and that they had failed in their challenge, and thus shamefully they retreated back into the isolated mountains from whence they came.

What the morale is to this story I'm not quite sure; the Namahage's reputation becoming somewhat distorted over time. Their image is now more commonly used in New Year's celebrations whereby men dressed as Namahage will enter the homes of local villagers and scare the shit out of children by chasing them around with sharp blades, incessantly screaming whilst reciting an array of deranged quotations such as 'Any lazy cry babies?' or 'Show me the naughty children' … before threatening to take any idle layabouts back to the mountains with them. Harsh, to say the least.

To begin with the southern fringes of the peninsula made for some easy cycling, as I headed in a clockwise fashion around the coast. The terrain however did soon elevate as some challenging climbs looped around the lush green peninsula, like a complicated knot. A provoking enough task, but when your clothing and the bulk of the possessions that you are carrying contain the extra weight of a hundred or so downpours – it's a merciless task. However, quaint little fishing villages dotted amongst craggy coves allowed for some short breaks from the rain before the exertion continued. Occasionally, I'd stumble across a statue of a Namahage, seemingly goading me on whilst I sweated it out upon another steep climb.

With the sun sitting dimly on the horizon through a thick smudge of gloomy clouds, I passed a row of deserted restaurants and souvenir shacks to make it to Cape Nyudozaki. A lonesome lighthouse sat upon a crest looking out across the Sea of Japan.

I sat for a while, ransacking my emergency rations of food: fish sausage, pea crisps, canned mystery fish and *karintō* - a sickly deep fried snack caked in brown sugar. I'd not eaten since early morning and with the absorption of Oga Peninsula's copious amount of hills, I'd managed to burn up a heap of calories that I wouldn't efficiently be able to replace before day's end. Shops on the peninsula were thin on the ground, and any that did exist were now either closed or abandoned.

From a signboard I saw an Auto Campground advertised just off of a road named the 'Namahage Line.' The road cut into Oga's ropey interior with the same integral rising and falling as the tricky peninsula's coast.

Finding my way to the campground I discovered that it was in fact closed. Which made me wonder - being at the back-end of June and on a weekend - when exactly did they plan on opening for the season? If at all. A signboard indicated the layout of the campground with various plots mapped out. The skies then began to rumble as a mass of black cloud lurched towards me, and at that moment - to my mind - the campground was suddenly open for business.

I cautiously entered the grounds on high alert for humans. The grass had been recently cut and the outbuildings invariably were still being maintained... but, as night shimmied closer and the weather gradually worsened, the only signs of life came from the surrounding forest. Frogs, crickets, bush warblers and the lowly grunting of a wild boar, or was it...no...surely not. I picked an outbuilding with toilets and wash basins at the furthest reaches of the campground, setting up my tent under shelter upon a hard concrete floor. It was to be an uncomfortable night's sleep, but I would be dry at least. And as I lay down upon my concrete bed, the thunderstorm passing raucously above me, I wondered overall if I'd been a good boy, for my fate was clearly now in the hands of the Namahage.

Oga Peninsula - Yurihonjō
66 miles

As expected, it wasn't a tremendous night's sleep, but not being violently stabbed to death in my tent by the *deba* blade of a Namahage was something to be grateful for, at least. The eaves of the outbuilding - still dripping from the night's incessant downpour - made me glad for the umpteenth time that I'd found shelter. At a little after 4:30am, the rain ceased, and the Japanese bush warbler began his sweet dawn chorus. And after a breakfast... of no breakfast, I resumed my assault on the peninsula's turbulent interior. The peaks of Mt. Honzan and Mt. Kenashi were coated in a sombre mist as a small collection of farm houses peered out of an excess of delicate and prominent greens, which coaxed the valley below.

My right knee began to give me some hassle as I started my first ascent of the morning - perhaps a combination of yesterday's tireless graft and the past month of non-stop cycling was beginning to take its toll. Or... perhaps I wasn't as durable as my ego was allowing me to believe.

Breakfast however was key, and finding a trusty 7-Eleven on the fringes of Oga City allowed me to bountifully stuff my face and catch up on any carb and protein intake that my body had duly missed. It rained as I ate and I got wet, but the joy that came with a full stomach was more empowering than the damp. The two cups of coffee probably also aided my overall satisfaction.

Positively charged, I returned to the hideously un-sexy Route 7, a complete fart of a section of road that would only worsen the closer I got to Akita; to the north of which sits the city's

159

industrial zone. Oil refineries, metalwork's, docklands and recycling plants pave the way, and the road was strewn with foreign objects, pot holes, and battered beyond recognition sidewalks. An endless conglomeration of Arctic lorries hurtled past me at panty-shitting speeds; the route was bloody treacherous and the rain only added to the awfulness of the situation. I could breathe a little more timidly though upon reaching the Port Tower Seline. Climbing up some 143 metres into the pallid, overcast skies, the tower near enough marks the border between the industrial renegade quarter and the city's outer suburbs. Here I found a bicycle shop where I'd be able to grab a new rear tyre. My 'Continental Marathon' had served me well - I tossed it onto a hopeless pile of other rubbery memories, in exchange for a brand spanking new 'Schwalbe Marathon.' I would not be able to argue with the quality of either tyre.

With my new tyre, I cycled into the city centre and found Senshu Park, a well preserved site atop a hill, offering up a handful of shrines, temples and castle ruins. Yet unless one is a food connoisseur and primarily here for the *nabemono* hotpot, *gakko* pickles, *junsai* seaweed or *morokoshi* sweets - then very much like Aomori City, Akita would also hold that similar under reaching draw for the casual passer-by. I grabbed some *azuki* bean filled *morokoshi* cakes and hit the road, passing through the city's quaint southern suburbs, before piling onto my old nemesis, Route 7.

I'd wind down the evening some 25 miles later in the pleasant Yurihonjō, my right knee now throbbing. My initial plan had been to set up camp atop the freshly mown banks of the Koyoshi River, but this was dashed as I came across an *onsen* next to a picturesque lake with accompanying woodland. Through the grime of my mud-caked face, a wry smile appeared... I would sleep well tonight.

STATS

Dates: 28/06/2014 – 30/06/2014
Total miles traversed: 2,754 miles
Total time in the saddle: 279 hours and 17 minutes

12. YAMAGATA
山形県

Yurihonjo - Sakata
57 miles

The hot spring waters had helped numb my aching limb, and the good night's sleep aided my mind in preparation for another battle with Route 7. Today, as I progressed into Yamagata Prefecture, I would only have to join the Bastard Route in fits and spurts. For the most part, I'd be hugging the coast as I weaved my way through a number of tightly packed seashell-clustered roads. Boats were docking and unloading their cargo into a ramshackle collection of processing plants alongside the water's edge. The omnipresent stench of fish lingered in the air as the restless, prying eyes of a flock of seagulls watched curiously from the mast of a half-sunken fishing vessel. Out to sea the skies were clear and promising, yet inland, to the east, the horizon hogging Mt. Chokai towered up into a heavyset blanket of gloom.

I braced myself.

The weather however somehow managed to hold out for me, the only main tragedy was not breaking my 40mph DWR. Hurtling downhill at 39.4mph it felt like it would come with ease, until a bumblebee decided to fly directly into my wide open eyeball. I swerved upon the impact of what felt like a punch from a welterweight but somehow managed to recapture control of my rig before bringing it to a halt. I looked around for the culprit with my one good eye. He/she was long gone, laughing his/her arse off in a hedgerow with a free-loading aphid no doubt. My watery eye would go on to wince for the remainder of the day. I'd learned my lesson: don't fuck with Nature.

Drawing into Sakata, the ominous layers of cloud surrounding Mt. Chokai seemed to peel away as a dazzling blue sky conquered. It was here in Sakata – the conservative agricultural and commercial fishing city - where I would undergo a small sub-quest within my journey. Through the sordid underbelly of the Internet, I'd unravelled something wholesomely curious about Yamagata Prefecture. It was here that the Buddhist sect of Shingon once practiced one of the most extreme forms of enlightenment known to man. Very few Japanese I spoke to about the subject seemed to be aware of the local Yamagatan tradition of self-mummification, i.e. *Sokushinbutsu.*

This practice took place between the 11th and 19th Centuries, and is currently outlawed in Japan and in the Buddhist community, as a whole. During its time, it only wielded some 24 sketchily known examples, but was believed that to achieve full enlightenment and to become a Living Buddha, one must punish the body to replenish the soul of its sins. The process however was no easy feat and it was said to take some 10 years to fully achieve.

The first stages were spent eating an extreme diet of nuts, seeds, roots, tree bark and arsenic laced water! You'd also need to live inside a small box with a solitary air tube. The monk's body would be hunched into the lotus position; the small doses of poison being taken daily… slowly killing the monk. His body was stripped of its fat, muscles and brain matter which inevitably aided the preservation of the material body. However, the body was riddled with so much poison that it failed to decompose properly and would in turn keep the maggots at bay.

Each day, the malnourished monk would ring a bell to let his fellow monks know that he was still alive; when the bell stopped ringing, he would then be cast into the final stages of his road to enlightenment. Sealed in his tomb, the monk would be left for a thousand days. After which the tomb would be opened, if he was a pile of bone and slop, the monk had failed in his quest for enlightenment. Yet, if the body remained preserved, he was regarded as a Living Buddha.

Today these monks are still classified as living citizens of Yamagata Prefecture. Making them some of the oldest dudes on Earth… and I needed to to see them.

I pulled up alongside Kaiko-ji Temple, one of three possible places in Yamagata Prefecture that I'd found on the Internet that might be able to help me in my little quest. The temple was small and unassuming; condensed into the grounds of eastern Sakata's Hiyoriyama Park. The inside of the temple is believed to house two Living Buddha's. Yet, judging by the lack of life around the complex, my efforts seemed far from promising. I walked up a set of stairs to the temple doors; a small tug on them revealing that the place was locked up tight. The small temple's exterior was well preserved and sat amongst an equally well-groomed Japanese garden. This told me that the place was still cared for, but just wasn't open for business. Not today, anyway. I sat in the shade of the steps, out of the sun, for some 15 minutes, in the hope I might spot a monk. After which I was bored. *Heaven knows what it must have been like to sit in a box for 10 years, wasting away.* I spent a little time walking around the park, along the tranquil forested byways dotted further with an assortment of shrines and temples. Yet, still, I could find no evidence of the living dead. I was a shit Mulder, and I desperately needed my Scully. Returning to Kaiko-ji Temple, I decided to give it one last go. Again, it was as empty and as void of life as it was previously, yet I couldn't help but feel that I was somehow being watched from afar.

Daunted in my quest, I cycled east through Sakata; the aged port city formidably quiet. On the edge of town, adjacent to an ocean of rice paddies, I found my Couchsurfing host, Akira. He was a softly spoken I.T. Technician in his early sixties with a degree in Japanese Literature. I asked him about this and he said that he gained more satisfaction from computers than he did from books! He was shy in nature and at times it was difficult to prise a conversation out of him. I wondered if it was because I started banging on about the monks of the living dead... I might have scared him into thinking that I was some sort of necrophiliac. He claimed never to have heard of such a thing and changed the subject quite quickly. The potent smell of a conspiracy began to linger in the air.

However, a mutual bond was formed when he told me that he too was once a tour cyclist. Pulling out a rugged scrapbook, Akira showed me some black and white photographs of when he was a young man of 20 and had cycled across Hokkaidō with some school friends.

He had managed to achieve two things that I never quite managed, one was making it to the vastly remote Shiretoko Peninsula in the island's far north-east and the other was seeing a wild grizzly bear. I wasn't so concerned about the latter - as I liked my limbs - but was envious of him for reaching the wilds of Shiretoko. Informing me of the area's grand and timeless beauty, merely dug the heel in a little deeper. Akira was a kindly and generous man; his mannerisms gracious and uniquely Japanese in every respect. He cooked me up a mean burger with green beans, carrots and miso soup. I washed it down with a can of Sapporo beer, before being shown to my soft, gentle and abundantly sleepable futon. Indeed, on this night, I slept like a Living Buddha.

Sakata / Mt. Haguro

The next morning, after marmalade on toast, Akira said that he would like to take me to Dewa Sanzen, The Three Mountains of Dewa. Dewa was the traditional name for Yamagata Prefecture and its three sacred mountains are said to be the oldest worshipped mountains in all of Japan. I thought of my right knee which was still mildly iffy and how resting it for the day would have been the perfect cure, yet of course I was a guest and couldn't afford to be rude. I did also really want to see the sacred mountains.

'*Hai, ii puran desu,*' yes good plan. I confirmed.

'Good, only 2,446 steps,' he said quite proudly, in English.

'Sweet,' I replied, rather meekly.

I was going to need more marmalade.

Pushing the pedal to the metal, we tore out of Sakata in Akira's Nissan Sunny across the prefecture's agricultural hub and up into the slopes of the Dewa Sanzen. Here we would trail-blaze one third of the popular pilgrimage to the 414 metre summit of Mt. Haguro, thankfully for me the smallest of the three mountains and officially the first any pilgrim should climb - as the mountain itself symbolizes 'Birth'. Consecutive mountains being Mt. Gassan, the largest of the three, which symbolizes 'Death,' and then, lastly, the extremely sacred Mt. Yudono, the mountain of 'Re-birth.' Yudono is said to be so sacred that photography is completely off limits. In fact, you can't even talk about it; whatever happens on the mountain stays on the mountain. Each mountain also plays host to its own shrine, but Mt. Haguro's shrine hosts the primary shrine that venerates all three sacred mountains. The Dewa Sanzen is important not only to Shintō and Buddhism but to the more ascetic Shugendō religion; the founders of the art of the *Sokushinbutsu* as discussed earlier. This religion finds itself heavily focused upon spiritual power whereby its delegates known as 'Yamabushi' put themselves through various acts of harsh discipline in order to attain a oneness with God, i.e. epic pilgrimages, exposure to imperfect elements for long periods of time, never masturbating... ever - and of course my favourite, self-mummification.

I again found myself questioning Akira about the mummies as we sweated our way up the steep steps to the summit, but as he began to make grunting noises, I decided to cut back on the small talk and allow him to focus on the job in hand. I stayed at his pace, so as not to rush him, and we stopped for occasional breathers. We passed one of Japan's National Treasures the Gojū-tō, a magnificent Hitachi sponsored five-storey Pagoda made entirely of wood that rose up high into the canopy of surrounding cedar trees. A number of other little shrines, bridges and waterfalls also dotted the ball-saturating climb to the summit.

The summit itself was consistent of several larger shrines and temples, including the principle Sanzan Gosai-den Temple; its thick thatched roofing offering a cool retreat from the rampant heat outside. Akira and I sat and chilled for a while, listening to a monk perform his mantras before a small audience of pilgrims. When Akira was ready, he removed his red tie and unbuttoned the top button of his shirt. He then went as far as to tie his red tie around his forehead in a Rambo-esque fashion before looking at me sternly, '*ikimashou,*' let's go!

'*Hai,*' I concurred, nodding in agreement.

Upon our return to the foot of the mountain, we celebrated by feasting savagely upon cold soba noodles and green tea, before returning to Akira's house in Sakata. I relaxed for the remainder of the afternoon, the living dead playing heavily on my mind. I had to find them, and tomorrow would be my last chance.

Sakata – Yunohama
70 miles

'I saw the mummy when I was a boy,' declared Akira.

'What???' I said, nearly spitting my marmalade toast into his face. '*Doko?*' where?

'It was a long time ago,' he said standing up and collecting our plates. And that was it, I swear he could tell that I was obviously in the midst of 'Mummy Fever' and he was clearly just toying with my emotions, using his inch perfect Japanese etiquette, as some form of torment. And with him clearing the

167

plates it was obviously conversation over; to ask again would have been considered a heathen act and massively uncouth. I'd blown it. Why he had chosen now over breakfast to confess I shall never know. Well, nevertheless, I hadn't totally failed yet, I still had a couple of cards to play.

Saying farewell to Akira, I headed south through the Shōnai plain to Tsuruoka; a similar city to Sakata, specialising in agriculture, fishing and light manufacturing. As the prefecture's second largest city, it was only just a little bit more active than Sakata, yet would it wield me a member of the living dead? I pulled out a shabby piece of paper with the 3 sights in Yamagata where I might find the much fabled Living Buddhas.

<u>Living Dead Dudes of Yamagata</u>
1. ~~Kaiko-ji Temple, Sakata~~
2. Nangaku-ji Temple, Tsuruoka
3. Dainichi-bo Temple, Dewa Sanzen

Abusing free Wi-Fi from 7-Eleven, I tracked down the Nangaku-ji Temple. Despite being 30-metres from a main road, it was though solemnly quiet. A fusion of shiny black and grey obelisk shaped pillars filled a small cemetery plot just before a confined red and white temple. I parked my bike against the wall of the compound and gingerly walked through the gates of the cemetery, again having that feeling that I was being watched by someone... or something. I climbed a short flight of steps to get to the temple's entrance, before peering through a transparent screen at an empty altar. Maybe the mummy was out back somewhere, undergoing maintenance such as the likes of Lenin, Chairman Mao and Ho Chi Minh? To the right of the staircase, I noticed a door, and to the right of that a doorbell. *Hmm...Do I? Don't I?* I thought fleetingly before pressing the button, a little alarmed by my own spontaneous eagerness. Yet no answer came. I then looked at the door, it was a sliding door. *Hmm…Do I? Don't I?* 'NO!' I soliloquized, I don't, that's just plain rude. Agent Fox Mulder most definitely would've snuck in and started skulking around like a lout, but then Fox Mulder had gunny; I only had a puncture repair kit.

The odds were stacked against me. Yet my gut told that in the confines of this unsuspecting temple, a mummy sat timelessly waiting.

Giving up, I returned to my bike, noticing from a small window of an apartment building - adjacent the temple complex - an elderly lady staring at me. I felt somehow that she'd always been watching. I smiled at her and nodded a greeting, but she just continued to stare. A little freaked out, I pulled out and updated my mummy list.

<u>Living Dead Dudes of Yamagata</u>
1. ~~Kaiko-ji Temple, Sakata~~
2. ~~Nangaku-ji Temple, Tsuruoka~~
3. Dainichi-bo Temple, Dewa Sanzen

I was now going to have to do this the hard way. Folding the list and returning it to my front pannier, I looked back at the elderly lady, but she was gone. I pressed on east and back into the sacred mountains, feeling like a failure.

The ascent into the mountains of the Dewa Sanzen was a steady one; the Akagawa River crafting its way through the rugged terrain would never stray far from my line of sight. When a sign for the Dainichi-bo Temple surfaced I left the main road to Yamagata City and was thrown into a steep and narrow road that wound its way up onto the north-western flanks of Mt. Yudono. A small hamlet unveiled itself to me, amongst a cluster of surrounding rice paddies. Signs for the temple were a little thin on the ground, but following the course of the ever steep and climbing road, I eventually stumbled across a very auspicious looking torii gate. It was bland in comparison to many of the touristic torii gates one might find around Japan; yet its natural elegance was suggestive of promise.

Leaving my bike outside the holy compound, I ventured through the torii gateway and along a compact path, which was lined with a selection of rich smelling flora. At the end of the path, a small flight of steps led me to a tranquil looking temple. Silence greeted me, as expected, but then so did the gentle face of a monk. I enquired as to whether this was the Dainichi-bo Temple and he confirmed that it was and that the cost of entry was 500 Yen. I coughed up some Yen as another more elderly monk appeared and ushered me into the temple. I took off my shoes and entered a dimly lit prayer hall, was given a small stool to sit upon and then I was asked if I spoke any Japanese. I stated, 'a little'. He thanked me and then shuffled out of the room. The initial monk who had claimed my 500 Yen, then appeared behind a transparent *shoji* screen and sat before a shrine of gold, money, fruits and ancient artefacts. I scanned the room profusely for mummies. No such luck. The 500 Yen monk then hit a small brass gong, before beginning to recite a mantra. This continued for some time, before he suddenly leapt up and slung the *shoji* doors wide open. Grabbing a pole with what looked like the head of a massive Chrysanthemum on the end of it, he began to flail it around excitedly in a slightly tantric manner. I noticed that his eyes were closed, so I decided to do the same. Upon doing so, I then heard his feet stomping across the *tatami* floor towards me. Quickly opening one eye, I saw that the Chrysanthemum head was being whisked directly into my face, its petals whipping my jowls. I was being blessed. This was unexpected and different, and most certainly a very bizarre feeling. Alone and some 5,715 miles away from home - in the remote mountains of Yamagata Prefecture - I was receiving the blessing of a Shugendō monk, an experience that I found extreme comfort in. Stopping suddenly, the monk shimmied back to the shrine. Clapping twice and then taking a deep bow to the Gods, he ended the service. I was confused, but was swiftly shoved to one side as the elderly monk reappeared to my left. He began to speak very fast, losing me from the outset. I nodded my head in false understanding and looked sincerely impressed by what he was saying. It was only when I caught wind of the words *'Sokushinbutsu'* and *'Mitai'* that I found myself suddenly lighting up.

'Hai, hai, mitai!' Yes, yes, I want to see!

I tried my best not to sound too desperate, but failed miserably. A smile then spread across the monk's face; he knew my game. It was time for the headliner.

I was led into a side-room, away from the central shrine, and my eyes became immediately fixated upon Daijuku Bosatsu Shinnyokai Shonin - a monk who in his 96th year on Earth, left his mortal body behind after a lifetime of extreme penance.

The elderly monk accompanying me spoke about the life of his fellow monk; his voice soon petering off into a white noise as I observed the dead guy in the glass box. Sat in the lotus position, he was fitted in orange garbs and a glossy pointed hat. His skeletal features had a darkened and waxy glow, his skull sunk heavily upon his chest with eyes fixed upon a set of prayer beads that were draped around his shrivelled hands. He'd been sitting here like this since 1784 as an act of compassion towards a famine that was at the time ravaging central Honshū, ultimately leading to the deaths of over a million people.

I began to feel a little sad, *is this what he really wanted?* Eternity in a box and to be ogled by sweaty cyclists from the other side of the planet? Or was I missing the spiritual point? Having made the ultimate sacrifice in his mortal life, was he now living the perfect nirvana as a so called 'Living Buddha'? I truly hoped so.

Leaving the temple, I felt slightly entranced by my experience. Sitting on a bench in the temple's grounds with a can of Coca-Cola from a very un-Buddhist like vending machine, I contemplated my day's finds. Shinnyokai Shonin had made me sweat to find him, but in doing so he had given me a very surreal moment in my life. Maybe that was what he wanted.

Returning to my bike, I continued east to Yamagata City; all visions of reaching the city swiftly dashed after being informed by a maintenance crew that the road ahead was closed. Funnily enough, I wasn't too phased by the fact that I wasn't able to venture any further up into the mountains, I'd achieved everything I'd set out to do in the prefecture and was ready to take on the next challenge of Niigata. I freewheeled most of the way back down the slopes of Mt. Yudono and returned to Tsuruoka.

On the coast I found Yunohama, a tranquil hot spring retreat just west of the city. I made camp under a picnic shelter, just a few yards from the beach. Walking close to the water's edge, I took a seat on the sand, before pulling out my scraggily list of the dead.

> Living Dead Dudes of Yamagata
> 1. ~~Kaiko-ji Temple, Sakata~~
> 2. ~~Nangaku-ji Temple, Tsuruoka~~
> 3. Dainichi-bo Temple, Dewa Sanzen ✓

I felt a cheeky smile begin to wash over my features. It was then that a seagull passed over and decided to casually defecate upon my head.

I was truly blessed.

STATS

Dates: 1/07/2014 – 3/07/2014
Total miles traversed: 2,881 miles
Total time in the saddle: 292 hours and 34 minutes

13. NIIGATA
新潟県

Yunohama - Agano
85 miles

Entering Niigata Prefecture meant that I was officially leaving Tōhoku, the north of Honshū behind, and saying a hearty 'Hello' to the Chūbu Region, Central Honshū.

Niigata is a prefecture that prides itself on producing some of the best grades of rice in all of Japan, its output of rice is second only to the much more sizable Hokkaidō. This much was evident as I cycled through the prefecture's coastal plains, surrounded by a limitless splendour of photogenic rice paddies. As a steady westerly breeze shimmied across the low-lying landscape, the rice plants' vibrant green shoots rustled together like the sound of a scrunched up plastic bag slowly unravelling itself. I trailed inland as far as the foothills of the Echigo Mountain Range, where the rice paddies, known as *'Tambo'* in Japanese, would abruptly come to a halt. The mountains were not requiring my exclusive company today, so I skimped alongside them, before arching back towards the coast - in the direction of Niigata.

The weather gradually worsened, forcing me to stop in the shrink-wrapped city of Agano, some 14 miles short of my goal. The centre of Agano was home to the lily pad encrusted Hyoko Lake. There I found a small cluster of trees out of the plain sight of suburbia. Not that anybody would want to look out of their window, as no sooner had I erected my tent, did the heavens vivaciously open, spelling an immediate end to the day. Yet, I lay snugly in my tent, as a burly thunderstorm gradually billowed around me. The surrounding trees jostled wildly as the insides of my portable bedroom were occasionally lit up via sudden bursts of lightning.

The rain would continue to hammer down throughout the night upon my stoically impenetrable tent. I was proud of Sir Leaksalot now; almost as if I'd won a bout against Mother Nature herself. A guileless instinct to have nonetheless; one that sooner or later would undoubtedly see me come undone.

Agano – Sado Island
41 miles

The skies were clear first thing and the day was already well on its way to becoming hot. Instead of heading directly to Niigata, I took a bit of a detour further into the depths of the prefecture's lush agricultural heartland. For a prefecture that prides itself on having the best rice in the country, it might as well brag about producing the best sake in the country... or even the world - this is Japan, after all!

During the winter months, the mountains on average will produce some 30ft of snow, earning Niigata the nickname of 'Snow Country.' And as the prefecture borders the Japanese Alps, it plays host to vast swathes of snow boarders and skiers alike, as they all commit themselves to the powdery white slopes. The snow however is not for the abuse of adrenaline junkies alone, for it is also cherished by the piss-heads of the nation. Considered somewhat of an air purifier, the snow contains very little pollutants or nasty microbes and this fact allows for some pretty pure water for the process of sake brewing. The snow-melt from the mountains flows through the endless contingent of pristine paddies, allowing one to soak up just how much of an important part rice plays for the Niigatans. Surrounded by the preliminary makings of the perfect piss-up, I was beginning to feel a little thirsty. Casting an eye to the west would reveal the big smoke, Niigata City. I pedalled on over.

With a population of some 810,000, Niigata City is the biggest Japanese city facing the Sea of Japan. A city with strong

174

trading links with Russia, China and the Koreas, yes, even the dodgy Northern one. During World War II it was on the shortlist to become the second Japanese city to be nuked, and through fear of an imminent bombing, the governor of Niigata had the whole city evacuated. Yet, in the city's favour lay its relatively inconvenient distance to any nearby US airbases; eventually seeing it dropped from 'The List.'

The city today is thriving with commerce; saturated with an ocean of apartment stores, designer shops and glitzy restaurants. Being a Saturday, the happy shoppers were out in force; girls dressed lackingly as they pranced along the high street in sparkly high heels and skirts disguised as belts whilst the boys followed behind carrying bags full of sparkly high heels and skirts that would soon been disguised as belts. The midday sun beat down upon the lightly coloured sidewalks; its rays bouncing off the bitumen with a heated intensity. A number of shoppers defused the extremes by donning umbrellas. The beastly rays saw me take to the city's coast, which was also being taken full advantage of by the weekend crowd; the beach dwellers were out in their droves. I grabbed a beer, got my tits out and decided to give my bike the once over.

My bike had been performing well of late and naturally I encouraged it to stay that way. Scrubbing it down and oiling my chain a lingering thought surfaced; I imagined myself being up in the remote mountains amongst the wind, the rain and the grizzly bears and then... my chain snapping. For if that fear was to become a reality, then I would be truly fucked. I risked not carrying a spare chain for two main reasons though, one was weight, there are only so many spares and tools one can carry before becoming hampered down with possessions and feeling like an immovable object. The other, was largely because I just plain didn't have the knowhow. I'd always meant to teach myself before I left England, but it was just one of those things that I kept putting off until it was too late, like an STI test. I comforted the presumably inevitable by

175

taking a big sip of beer and cast my eyes out into the Earth's great abyss. Somewhere out there was a place of exile, a place called Sado Island, an apt name perhaps. *I should go there*, I thought. *Right Now*!

Sado Island
77 miles

An evening boat would take me to Sado, some 30 miles west off the coast of Niigata. I'd arrived in darkness and quickly found myself an unkempt stretch of coastal parkland to set up camp. Sado is a place with a morose history, and that's even before you consider the slave labour and North Korean kidnappings. For centuries, shamed emperors, political dissidents, outspoken poets, controversial monks and all-round rebels were sent to this remote island - as a form of punishment. To be banished here was a life sentence; very few saw the mainland ever again.

Cycling south-westerly through the Kuninaka Plains I cut right through the centre of the island between two rugged mountain chains that stacked-up either side of me. The stunning vistas made me wonder if being a shamed emperor would have been such a bad thing after all.

The Kimpoku and Kunimi mountain ranges respectively offered up a selection of abrasive looking peaks, caked in thick layers of vegetation. A harsh and unforgiving terrain no doubt and perhaps little explored, but a marvel to the eye all the same. Its highest peaks were mollycoddled in a white cotton-candy blanket of cloud cover, giving the mountains an added touch of mystique.

The road cutting through the rich and fertile centre of the island however was an equally inhospitable place, and far from mysterious. In little over 5 miles I'd nearly been maimed by passing traffic some 7 times. That's 1.4 near death experiences per mile, an alarming statistic. The drivers of the island's 63,000 inhabitants were presumably acting out an apparent real life rendition of the 1997 crash 'em up video game 'Carmageddon,' whereby the more brains that get splattered across the road, the more points you gain. Alas, this was the same year that saw Final Fantasy VII entering the video games market, so I guess I should be at least a little bit thankful that I wasn't getting pecked to death by a Golden Chocobo. Apologies for the blatant sidetracking here, but I couldn't very well go and write a book about Japan without referencing the game of all games a few times, for that would be just plain sacrilege.

Upon hitting the coast and heading north, I would soon clash with the rugged terrain. Each steep and sweaty climb awarded with another equally steep and sweaty climb; it was going to be one of those days. I imagined that amongst all of this constant exercise, I would probably be able to get a job in a freak show when I got back home to England - my body having evolved into just a pair of quads with a face. Now who wouldn't pay to see that?

Sado's northwest would bring me to Aikawa, the home of Sado Kinzan, the island's infamous gold mine. The first ore was extracted in 1601, which brought great prosperity to the Shogunate, and during its peak produced some 400kg of gold a year. But this came at a great expense to human life. During the 1800's, many of Japan's big and overcrowded cities were inundated with homeless people. To help out these stricken beings, the Shogunate gave a number of them a one-way ticket to sunny Sado Island, where the hours were long and the pay... well, non-existent. It was backbreaking work in hellish conditions and failure to comply rewarded the insubordinate with the loss of their head. Life expectancy was short and escape futile. The government however were laughing their cocks off; in just 388 years they'd managed to stack up some 78 tonnes of gold.

The mine today allows visitors to walk two sections: a modern mine that was used up until 1989 and an older mine that allows one to soak up a small slice of the hell that for so many years deprived mostly innocent Japanese citizens of a life. A number of robots are used to animate the harsh daily lives of the miners, from the removal of large rocks to the siphoning off of water to the earth's surface. Conditions were most certainly always cramped and no place for a claustrophobe. A sign read 'Please don't touch the Roberts.' I pondered upon whether or not if it might be okay to just touch one Robert, but to conceivably go on from there and touch up too many Roberts would perhaps be deemed somewhat taboo; socially unacceptable behaviour. And thus through a fear of being swiftly escorted to a secret third mine, I decided to keep my non-Robert touching hands to myself.

From Aikawa I continued in a clockwise motion around the coast; the traffic thinning out tenfold, allowing me to concentrate on the perpetually steep inclines. The turquoise waters of Senkaku Bay seemed alluring in the afternoon heat, yet deceptive as the ocean was still as cold as stone. Old, crooked-backed ladies tended to their coastal rice paddies as their husbands' worked alongside them, strimming the banks.

Another rapid descent would take me down to sea level to Oonogame Rock, in the island's far north-east. Here, at the end of an elongated spit branching out into the Sea of Japan, sits a bulbous, fist-shaped rock that rises some 167 metres. It looks awkward and misshapen; its steep cliff edges hanging out on a limb, magnificently battered by a millennia of hard hitting waves. From here yet another gruff and gradual ascent unfolded up into the mountains, before finally bringing me back down close to the water's edge. I steadily found my way back and at dusk I sought out my previous night's dwellings; an over grown park that seemed to me abandoned, wild and free.

Sado Island – Joetsu
39 miles

The rain would return as I cycled the southern half of Sado. Yet perhaps on this day it was a good thing as I'd long since forgotten the last time I'd actually taken a shower - or a bath. I'm not normally a stinky person, but when you can smell yourself you've got a problem - and I smelt like a wide selection of vomits.

The southern coast of Sado was less challenging than its north; its rollercoaster-esque terrain being less formidable. The dreary inland mountains were obscured by heavy lashings of rain and thus the view out to sea was equally impregnable. My sole focus for the day was to get to the town of Ogi, in order to take a ferry back to the mainland.

And upon my arrival there late afternoon I'd find that the ferry wouldn't set sail for a few more hours. The spare time enabled me to catch up on some reading and get some much needed wall-staring time in, before journeying over to the city of Joetsu.

At nightfall, just before disembarkation the rain came to cease, as a steady flow of beating drums carried across the night; the city being in the midst of a summer festival. The beating drums drew me in, taking me to a park alongside the Seki River, where I found a group of youths - all dressed in white garb - donning navy blue head banners. They were taking it in turn to beat the booming *taiko* drums to a chorus of excitable chanting. The British youth culture I encountered growing up, could have learned a lesson or nine here from its Japanese counterparts, replacing a 3-litre bottle of Strongbow with drums would've no doubt remedied a whole number of hangovers, blackened eyes and disastrous teen pregnancies!

Towards the coast, I found a thick hedgerow running along a large section of beach which would act as a windbreak. There I

179

settled down for the night, the distant drums suddenly dying at midnight, leaving me to the sound of the ocean's lapping and swilling. It was then that the Japanese Alps began to play prominently upon my mind. *Was I ready for some of the highest roads in Japan? Were the highest roads in Japan ready for me*? I farted a little, and slept nervously.

STATS

Dates: 4/07/2014 – 7/07/2014
Total miles traversed: 3,123 miles
Total time in the saddle: 316 hours and 10 minutes

14.1 NAGANO
長野県

Joetsu - Yudanaka
50 miles

Nine of the twelve highest mountains in Japan can be found in Nagano; a fact alone that was enough to make me break out in a cold sweat, and this was before a hearty old man with the essence of doom paid me a visit whilst I was packing up camp. He informed me that a typhoon was on the way and that I should be wary. The typhoon he was referring to was Typhoon Neoguri, and having just recently devastated parts of Okinawa it had now made landfall in the south and was bang on track for Nagano. I sighed and thanked him for the news, as he rewarded me with a can of coffee and a goodwill gesture of *'Ganbatte,'* Good luck.

Many of the mountains across the Japanese Alps are well over 3,000 metres in height, so it was no place to be cycling if a typhoon should hit. Landslides, flooding, falling trees and slippery terrain could all quite easily get a cyclist mullered. Yet I'd been in touch with a bagel shop owner in the mountain town of Kusatsu - just over the border into Gunma Prefecture – who confirmed that her and her family would be delighted to offer me refuge for a couple of nights. By my calculations it would take me two days to reach them, bang in sync with the typhoon hitting central Japan. So now I had to make an executive decision, do I wait it out on the coastal flats of Niigata or try and make it to my saviours, embedded deep within the mountains of Gunma. I downed my can of coffee and looked toward the crystal clear skies, they were sexy, enticing and appeared to yield little danger. To the east a set of beautiful forested vistas trailed off into a hazy infinity. And, like a reckless fool, I began to chase them.

Nagano – host of the 1998 Winter Olympics, was a prefecture of scenic splendour. Yet, with its formidable array of mountains, it is an absolute gauntlet for a cyclist; it was going to be a long, hard week. Rivers cut through the vast network of alpine clustered mountains as the rich volcanic soils of the foothills offered up an agricultural haven to the local farmers. At just above sea level - the inland prefecture with towering peaks - gives one a slightly caged in feeling, it was only as I climbed higher and out of the plains that the true contrast of my challenge became clear.

As I reached the city of Liyama, it was swelteringly hot, so I decided to break for lunch. The city's hidden talent is that it held the World Record for building the most snowmen in an hour... 1,585 to be exact. The current heat though made it difficult for me to imagine that snow was even a possibility in such a blazing inferno.

In the local supermarket, I bought a couple of ice creams before sitting outside on a bench in the shade. Next to me was a fat man, who looked at me with hungry eyes... I felt bad to be honest, but my hunger was raging and I needed all two ice creams for myself. It was selfish of me, but in the long run fatso would surely understand that I was doing him a favour.

Ice cream gormandizing aside, I would soon be slung into a ruthless ascent. The sun consistently remorseless, wearing me out fast. Making it to Nakano, I headed east along Route 292; there I found a brief refuge in an uphill tunnel. The north end of the tunnel allowed a cool vacuum of air to pass through it; soothing me somewhat and distorting a headache that had been gradually building. A little up ahead, I found the *onsen* town of Yudanaka. Stopping there for sushi and yet more headache inducing ice cream, I decided that it was time for a bath.

The area of Yamanouchi where Yudanaka essentially lies, is famed in winter for its Japanese Macaques. Coming in from the surrounding mountains, they bathe and relax in luxury amongst the area's natural hot springs. Their berry-red faces and their icicle infested beards are a famed depiction of Japan in the winter time. However, in the summer months, the mountain forests are flush with fresh running water and an abundance of wild fruits, so the macaques venture out of town. Which is perhaps why - as I pulled up outside the train station and discovered a public foot spa - I felt like the next best tourist attraction. With little thought, I prised my shoes and socks off and doused my cheesy blocks into the mineral rich waters. It felt sublime. An elderly couple watched with some fascination as a teenage girl took a photograph of me on her iPhone, then ran off into the mountains, laughing.

Adjacent the foot spa was a bathhouse. I entered respectfully, placing my shoes in a wicker basket on the wall, before walking through a set of drapes and into a reception area. The lady behind the counter seemed hesitant as I ordered myself one bath. Having had mustered the odour of an evil poo spirit over the past week I guess she had every right to be concerned; for I had no doubt that evil poo spirits hadn't been seen around these parts for a very long time... until now.

The *onsen* was full as I entered; some eight men packed tight into the bath, arse cheek to arse cheek. It was awkward to know where to look as I began to loiter amongst the nude beings. I observed the ceiling for a bit and found a hairline crack in the wall which I followed with my eyes for a bit in order to keep myself busy. By the time the crack had worked its way down the wall towards another, err... crack, the sausage party had mostly sizzled out. And with the space for one more, I dived in. The scorching hot waters opened and purified my clogged pores and massaged my stretched, tired muscles. As was tradition, in exactly 3 minutes and 24 seconds, I was fully baked and ready to flake out.

Well into the groove of keeping up with the act of cleanliness, I did some late evening laundry until the skies became moist. I hoped it wasn't the typhoon finding its way into the mountains a day early.

After washing and drying my fetid clothing, I sought out a public park alongside the Kakuma River. There, I set up my tent on the concrete foundations of a picnic shelter. It would then proceed to hammer it down as a thunderstorm unfolded. A superstitious man might have crossed his fingers. I, however, did no such thing.

Yudanaka – Kusatsu
31 miles

Breakfast started with a brutal 10% incline which set the pace for the bulk of the day's journeying, as I traversed Japan's highest public road - amongst its abandoned summertime ski slopes. I wondered if I was insane to be lugging some 30kg of property up into the skies with me; nobody else seemed to be doing it. But then I thought of my entire plan again and relented that all of this had been my choice, so I just had to get on with it and stop doubting.

Again, it was a roasting hot day, and sweat built heavy upon my brows; long frenetic beads pouring down my face or seeping into my eyes, the stinging sensation unkind. My excretions would wet my drying, cracked lips, as the taste of salt became omnipresent. It was thirsty work, and I was having to rely upon the fresh mountain streams and waterfalls to keep my water supply replenished.

The deeper I ventured, the more I began to feel like the mountains were trying to smother me; they towered up high above me like giant myrtle-coloured fortresses. And with each and every grinding turn, came that all too familiar optimism - I might be close to the top of the mountain chain. As usual though, a long and drawn out tease was in order. It was only when the vegetation began to spread out, and a contingent of craggy, ochre-coloured rocks emerged amongst a jaunted precipice, that progress could be formally acknowledged.

From a high enough vantage point, I could see a road levelling out along the jagged spine of a volcanic peak - Mt. Kusatsu-Shirane: the gateway to Gunma Prefecture.

<u>STATS</u>

Dates: 8/07/2014 – 9/07/2014
Total miles traversed: 3,204 miles
Total time in the saddle: 326 hours and 30 minutes

15. GUNMA
群馬県

I climbed a little higher, until I was above a vast swathe of cloud. At a junction, to the side of the road, a sign stated that I was at the highest point of any public road in Japan. And at a lofty 2,172 metres above sea level, the road ahead of me was completely bound in a thick mist. This would make my descent a little dicey. Yet somewhere down there lay the town of Kusatsu. To my south, a storm beckoned; clouds as black as night beginning to cast shadows across the land.

I began to descend with caution; my view becoming completely obscured the moment I hit the great wall of mist - the smell of sulphur rich in the air. Stopping briefly, I turned on my lights, before continuing into a slow and painful descent with my brakes constantly applied. I was in dangerous territory; seeing the blurry lights of passing and oncoming traffic almost too late on several occasions. Not being able to see a metre in front of me also made cliff edges extremely difficult to gage. It was an eerie sensation; like something out of 'Silent Hill.' Even when I eventually made it down into Kusatsu at 1,200 metres, the whole town was engulfed in the thickest mist I'd ever seen.

There, I sought out 'The Worthy Bagel,' where politeness and extremely hospitable etiquette tore me away from the town's supernatural environment. At the entrance to her café, Mai Nakamura and her large family, greeted me. I felt like a celebrity - without the red carpet - as they led me into my very own welcome party. My bedraggled appearance was not a concern for the Nakamura's, as they went on to treat me like a Rock Star; plying me with enough fine food and beer to sink a pedalo. Mai had owned her bagel shop for a couple of years and business was booming. Her husband Kenji and brother Akihiro also ran another couple of restaurants in town; they saw to it that I wouldn't starve during my time in Kusatsu.

After a couple of hours of socialising with this kind and generous family, it dawned upon me that today was one of the most physical of my campaign and that I barely had another 5 minutes of energy left in me. Thankfully, Mai - a caring mother of two daughters - suggested I take a bath and then hit the hay. I obliged willingly.

Kusatsu

The day started with embarrassment. Passing a bowel movement on somebody else's property is always something that I feel should be done with some form of discretion - especially when it happens to be one of my ungodly bowel movements.

I awoke before any of the Nakamura's were awake, in hope that I might just be able to get away with the most perfect of crimes, and thus I tiptoed across the landing and discreetly into the toilet, like the stealthiest of ninjas. The movement that took place was, as always, spectacular, and - as always - very stinky. It was only when I began to reel off the toilet roll that my master plan became foiled. Would you believe that the toilet roll holder was musical? With the smallest of tugs of the roll, the holder performed a traditional Japanese folk song. I panicked and tried to suffocate the holder with my bare hands, but it was no good; it refused to be muffled. The music blared out loud and proud, and at 6am it was declared to the household (and probably half the 7,000-strong population of Kusatsu) that I, Daniel Doughty, was taking a big fat dump.

The silence over breakfast was admirable, the less said about my morning movement the better. Although, Mai did suggest that I take a walk into town and check out some of the local hot springs. Whether there was a hint in there somewhere, I couldn't be too sure, but I took her advice all the same.

Kusatsu Onsen, 118 miles west of Tokyo, is one of the most famed hot spring towns in Japan. Its steaming hot volcanic waters - served directly from Mt. Kusatsu-Shirane - are said to cure every ailment known to man, bar love sickness. Its waters are some of the most acidic in the land and can dissolve a 6-inch nail in just 10 days. They can also reduce a 1-Yen coin to nothing, within a week. In this acidity, it is virtually impossible for bacteria to thrive, thus allowing only rich minerals to exist.

A little drizzle coaxed the streets as I took the short walk into the town centre. Yet 120 miles to the south of Nagano Prefecture, Typhoon Neoguri was wreaking havoc. It had already caused a fatal landslide that took the life of a 12-year-old boy. The typhoon brought a front of heavy rain that would eventually press out east and dissolve, soon after in the remotes of the North Pacific Ocean. In its wake, it left a trail of destruction and broken hearts.

In town, I stood looking at the marvel of the Yubatake, a huge hot water field of cooling wooden conduits that allows some 5000 litres of luminous-coloured water to flow through every minute. The waters feed the town's guesthouses and public baths, giving them the wherewithal to ply a tourist trade. A sign at one end of the Yubatake reads '1 of 100 scenic spots of peculiar smells in Japan,' referring to the familiar egg-like smell of sulphur that dominates the air. I wondered if my bowel movement this morning would have been Japan's 101st.

The umbrellas were slowly beginning to emerge about town as the rain began to get heavier. I felt the only way to remedy the situation was to fight fire with fire, and, naturally, in the case of Sainokawara Park, water with water. The Park's open air bath has the capacity to house up to 100 customers, though today - with a typhoon in attendance - only a handful of clientele were present. The hot spring situated just outside of town, amongst a forest of pines, was the perfect accompaniment to my nagging muscles. Submerged up to my neck the hot volcanic waters soothed my aches as the rain poured down, cooling my head in the process and thus allowing me to stay submerged longer than the standard 3 minutes and 24 seconds. In fact, I stayed closer to an hour… it was bliss.

Feeling pure and revitalised, I visited Mai's brother Akihiro at his restaurant aside the central Yubatake. His thin-rimmed glasses suited his well-rounded, cheery face as he greeted me with the grace and sincerity of an old friend. He cooked me up some divine soba noodles and we joked and laughed as the rain trashed the town around us. Discussing the Japanese weather, I described it as '*Inu no kuso otenki,*' dog shit weather. This made him and his customers roar with laughter, in fact every time he saw me thereafter he would chuckle with glee and refer to my comment. It appeared that I had tickled his funny bone.

Running back to The Worthy Bagel, Mai was already laughing as I entered her café. '*Inu no kuso otenki ne?*' Dog shit weather isn't it? Word travelled fast around these parts. She offered me a seat in her café and gave me a blueberry bagel and a coffee. I'd never had a bagel before coming to Japan, but I already knew after my first bite that there'd probably never be a better bagel than this. The warm doughy texture with the added assortment of blueberry chunks fulfilled the sensual desires of my substantially sweet tooth. I told Mai how amazing her bagel was and she blushed and retreated behind her counter shyly. She had a delightful family and in just a short time had accommodated me as one of her own; they all had. It was a warming feeling, since I hadn't seen my own family in some 4 months. The Nakamura's treatment of me was priceless.

Kusatsu – Ueda
40 miles

Before leaving the Nakamura's, Mai would again mother me by packing me some *bento,* for the road. An exquisite smell wafted from out of the packaging, making my nostrils twitch

189

excitedly. I then said a fond farewell to my Japanese family, as they waved me off. I cycled to the end of the street and, upon turning out of sight of the family, came to an abrupt stop. I couldn't contain myself, my desire was too strong. As I unwrapped the foil of my *bento* box I found that my hands were shaking as my sticky mitts got to grips with the food of the God's, a.k.a. 'Worthy Bagel' bagels. I unloaded them greedily into my mouth; looking over my shoulder from time to time, as I didn't want any bagel fiends to steel my doughy goodness.

All bageled out, I began to descend.

There was very little effort involved with the day's ride, after my having done most of the hard work muscling my way up to Kusatsu during the previous couple of days. I traversed one of Japan's three Melody Roads, and, as passing cars wound past me, a song called "Memories of Summer" amplified off the bitumen… using a tactile vibration system formed of 2,559 grooves etched into the road. *Only in Japan.*

The road south to Naganohara jarred quickly from left to right, at times becoming extremely steep. Traffic ascending the mountain in the opposite direction squealed past me in high gear; engines sounding reluctant to complete their respective journeys.

Reaching a fiery 35mph, I nearly found myself rocketing into the back of a parked truck. Quick reactions or just plain luck kept me intact.

West from Naganohara saw me pass an ocean of cabbage; one of Gunma's most notable agricultural products. In the background, Mt. Kusatsu-Shirane soared, keeping a watchful eye over her land. This was the last silhouette of Gunma, as I slipped between Mt. Azumaya and Mt. Asama - and back into Nagano Prefecture.

STATS

Dates: 9/07/2014 – 11/07/2014
Total miles traversed: 3,244 miles
Total time in the saddle: 336 hours and 10 minutes

14.2 NAGANO
長野県

Ueda – Norikura Kougen
65 miles

Judgement day pulled closer; apprehension and dread becoming a commonly frequent fixation of my latest dreams. All because of the Norikura Skyline, a road that scaled the roof of the Japanese Alps at some 2,715 metres, officially making it the highest road in Japan. But not the highest public road, for the road to the summit is limited to just taxis, tour buses and cyclists (yay!). I wagered that I wouldn't be beginning the ascent until the following day, thus allowing myself to focus on the job in hand of making it through another cluster of mountains and on towards Matsumoto.

I started the day within the castle grounds of Ueda, next to an aviary full of squawking budgerigars. It was a busy little city with malls, malls and more malls. I'd crept into the grounds close to sundown, knowing that the budgies wouldn't mind because they knew that they'd get the guilty pleasure of acting as my alarm clock... come the ungodly hour of 5am.

Taking in a breakfast of *gyōza* and strawberry cream sandwiches, I directed myself west, out of the city. The alpine flora soon hitting my nostrils; a smell that I'd most certainly miss upon return to the 9 to 5 grind.

The climb up through the mountains was steady and gracious, the cool of the woodland shade welcome. The road narrow saw very little traffic and close by there an alternate toll road that cut directly through the mountains, but this was strictly off limits to cyclist scum such as myself. In the odd car that did pass by, passengers' cast glances. A small red Subaru passed at one stage; a child in the rear seat with his face pressed up against the window smearing the glass with his breath. I imagined the in-car conversation to keep my mind occupied.

'Hey Dad, look at that wanker,' says the child, pointing at me.

'I see him son,' replies the despondent dad.

'Look at all that shit he's lugging up into the Alps with him.'

'Yup, it's all shit son, it's all shit.'

The mother in the passenger seat turns her head to take a fleeting glance at the wanker on the bike.

'There certainly seems to be an increase in wankers these days,' she adds.

'Silence woman,' demands the dad.

The mother hastily returns to her Sunday supplement and reads about space lepers.

'Dad?'

'Yes, son?'

'That man really is a real life wanker isn't he?'

'He sure is kiddo, he sure is!' At this point the father comes to a tricky incline and so he puts his foot down upon the accelerator like a complete prick. 'Buckle up son, it's time for daddy to start driving like a total twat… for no reason.'

'Ok dad,' the child buckles up, taking one last look at me.

'Wanker!'

Simple things for simple minds they say, and to be honest, these are the kind of workings that would constantly spill through my mind as I scaled an endless foray of mountains across the country. Having no music, radio or company one is left with nothing but one's own imagination. For better or for worse it's difficult to say, but for the best part it bought me a little light entertainment along the way, and… it was free!

Cruising back down the mountains and into the plains of Matsumoto, Nagano's second biggest city would offer a temporary release from my imaginarium. The city's central hub thrived with students and their *mamachari* as they clogged the streets, often making it difficult for a wide-boy like myself to pass. My bicycle bell, which I had rarely made use of, would inevitably come in handy here. The locals respected its monosyllabic chiming as I neared them. To ring my bell at a student or an obstructing pedestrian back in the UK would more often than not lead to me getting lambasted with an indignant medley of both verbal and more than likely physical abuse. Something culturally that the British wouldn't have any other way, as opposed to the Japanese, who often give way to a stranger, as if it is ingrained into their cultural makeup.

I came to a halt for lunch, alongside the moat to the rather splendid Matsumoto Castle. Completed in the early 1600's, its 5-storey tower sits prominently upon a motte of boulders as one of Japan's oldest existing structures. The moat contained a burly fleet of koi carp, all contesting for feed that the tourists could buy from an elderly lady by the glistening water's edge. I watched the tourists come and go, whilst sat under the shade of a vine clustered trellis; occasionally peering out to the west and observing the inevitable. Stacked high, climbing up and piercing the clouds, snow still formed upon several peaks. My palms began to get a little clammy. The mountain air was again so close I could almost inhale it. I looked back at the koi carp, they glubbed at some grain on the surface; they were living the high life. Averting my gaze west again, the skies were bright and clear. And there Mt. Norikura loomed, all 3,026 metres of it on full vivacious display, the perfect day perhaps to begin an ascent upon the country's 3rd largest mountain. I gulped, looking back towards the calmness of the moat. The frenzy of carp were beginning to disperse and so I sighed and stood up, returning my glance to the beautifully gruesome chain of mountains to the west - the Japanese Alps.

'Fuck it,' I said, like a gung-ho champ. I then headed west.

I wouldn't be the first Englishman to tackle Mt. Norikura, and certainly wouldn't be the last. In 1878, a: professor, mining engineer, mountaineer, foreign advisor, writer, archaeologist, better man and fellow Englishman, William Gowland, became the first to summit Mt. Norikura. He noted then how the beautiful, multi-pinnacle terrain was reminiscent of the French Alps, and was the first to christen the area, the Japanese Alps. From the basin of Matsumoto, with its panoramic views of the mountains, its title becomes just, it truly was a beauty. But like some beauties I've met in my life, it would perhaps also have the potential to be stubborn and uptight.

It was whilst waiting at one of the many red traffic lights on my way out of the city, that a Japanese gentleman skidded up alongside me on his mountain bike, grinning. His look suggested that he was just on his way to the shops to fetch a pint of milk: faded black t-shirt, joggers and a pair of Nike's - prime convenience store going clobber. The stranger asked me my destination and I confirmed Mt. Norikura. His grin widened as he told me he knew a better route out of the city, and, before I knew, I had myself a guide. Mr Hazuki would lead me along a number of quiet back roads, away from the bustling down town traffic, and out into the eastern foothills of the Alps. He kept a good pace up in front, turning occasionally to make sure that I hadn't perished. His intentions for the day were actually unclear to me, but I hoped that his wife wasn't in a hurry for her pint of milk. Stopping briefly, we had a little chat in broken Japanese and English. He was a semi-retired salaryman with a big passion for cycling and showed me some pictures (on his smart phone) of his racing bike. I saw another photo of him dressed in his skin-tight cycling habiliments, to prove his point. I told him that he looked nice, which instantly felt like a weird thing to say. He then put his phone away and looked at the road ahead.

'*Hai, dozo,*' said Mr Hazuki, ushering me forward into the mountains.

I wasn't too sure if this was goodbye, but as I began to cycle up front, I turned my head around to see that Mr Hazuki was following. *Your wife is going to be so pissed when you get home!* I thought.

195

The terrain got steep fast, and before long we were both sweating and dribbling in the mid-afternoon heat. Mr Hazuki tailed me close, so I felt slightly under pressure to set a certain pace as we ascended. I was cycling a little faster than I normally would; my baggage adding to the strain. Passing a number of dams en route, things suddenly got intense as we entered a cramped and hideously gloomy set of tunnels; reminiscent of a Victorian London sewer system. Dark and wet, I felt pressed to the tunnels' slimy walls by the now heavy flowing traffic. The monotonous drone of engines filled my ears and the smell of fumes was excessive as the rutted asphalt made the road juddery.

Things got even spicier when the tunnel decided to split in two, something I'd never witnessed before. One way would lead directly under the Alps and the other up and over them. I of course needed the up and over option, which meant I'd have to risk life and limb etching myself across the dark and busy tunnel to make sure that I was in the right lane. My adrenaline was pumping savagely, allowing me to focus, my quads clocking up some overtime with the hope that this intoxicating nightmare would soon be over.

As much as I wanted to, I couldn't look around to see if Mr Hazuki was still following on, as one small blip could've cost me my life. Cutting gradually into the correct line, the traffic would ease greatly, allowing me to realise that Mr Hazuki was not far behind. Up ahead I could see daylight. I sighed with relief; as did my colon.

Stopping just outside the tunnel's entrance, I was again glad to be amongst the fresh mountain air. Mr Hazuki emerged soon afterwards, still grinning.

'*Yabai ne?*' dangerous isn't it? I said, starkly.

'*Sou, sou, sou,*' he agreed. '*Chotto...*' he began to point up ahead as if we were now close to something significant.

Again Mr Hazuki would lead the way as I slumped a short way behind upon the gradient's increase. Shunning a few more switchbacks, the terrain eventually levelled out, and at

1,400 metres we had made it to Norikura Kogen, the Norikura Plateau. This roughly marked the halfway point in the mountain's ascent. A small number of houses, hotels and shops clustered the plateau... and a bottle shop. Barely was there time to blink before Mr Hazuki and I were sinking a beer together. Taking a seat curb-side we drank in silence; a well-rewarded silence.

In Matsumoto, I had briefly visited the local tourist office and they confirmed that Norikura Kogen had a camp site. I quizzed Mr Hazuki on the matter and he knew exactly which way to go; in fact he led me there! Awesome was obviously his first name.

Trudging up a stiff ski slope and along a dusty mountain bike path, amongst the shade of evergreens, we would cut through a wild meadow, before emerging out onto a small grassland clearing. The site had an out of season feel to it with a closed reception and shop area, a locked up shower block, a clapped out looking diesel generator and only one other tent set up. There was however a beer vending machine.

I treated Mr Hazuki to another round of Asahi's, which sadly would become a reluctant goodbye drink. Eventually, we shook hands and I thanked him for his legendary deed, then he headed back east to get some milk for Mrs Hazuki. I hoped for Mr Hazuki's sake that his wife was an extremely patient woman.

I set up camp and drank another beer. The peak of Mt. Norikura peered down upon me gloriously as the sky turned the colour of crimson; the sun setting beyond the great mass of rock. The climes today had been ideal and I could only ask for the same again tomorrow on my journey to the summit. It had been a long and difficult trudge, yet thanks to Mr Hazuki, I was unexpectedly half-way there. *I was surely at the point of no return?*

Norikura Kougen – Takayama
37 miles

Up and away by 06:30am the skies were dreary; contrary to the weather forecast.

The climb was slow and steady and a number of race cycling enthusiasts passed me en route to the summit. Each wished me good luck as they went by, some would comment upon my heavy load. I agreed as up in these mountains - at an average speed of about 4 mph - I was like a *mamachari* compared to the speeds that some of these boys could reach.

A gentle drizzle set in as I came to a switchback that revealed the peak of Mt. Norikura was no more. The skies above were now painted in a variety of gloomy shades and, around me, random clumps of snow still sat on the ground. For the better part of the year, the roads up here are impassable, as the surrounds become enveloped in some 7 metres of the white stuff.

Approaching Sanbondaki at 1,800 metres, I reached the point where private cars were no longer allowed to traverse the remaining 915 metres to the summit. My only fight now would be with taxis, tour buses and border control.

As I came to a closed gateway, a stern-faced man in uniform and a black cap appeared from a small roadside shack. He was directing a crossed forearms salute in my general direction, suggesting to me that there would be no entry. It was a sign also given by West Ham fans like myself in proud support of their team. I brandished my irons right back at him, copying his stance.

'Come on West Ham,' I chanted.

The stern-faced man from border control failed to see my humour and looked around at one of his colleagues with a little confusion. His colleague quickly ducked back down behind his counter and out of sight. He wanted nothing to do with my kind.

'*kono michi shimette desu,*' this road is closed, confirmed Stern-face.

This was foul news. '*Hontou ni?*' Really?

'*Hai.*' Yes.

'*Nande?*' Why?

'Racing Carnival,' he said, in English.

'A Racing Carnival?'

'*Hai.*'

'*Demo Gifu ikitai,*' but, I want to go to Gifu, I pleaded.

Gifu Prefecture, has a split border at the summit of Mt. Norikura, with one section of the mountain belonging to Nagano and the other respectively to Gifu. I could only presume that the race was on the Gifu side, as all was relatively quiet in Nagano and far flung from a 'carnival' atmosphere, especially with Stern-face on watch.

He confirmed that I couldn't go to Gifu. I suggested that this would be a bit of a problem for me as I had come all the way from England to cycle the world famous Norikura Skyline. Stern-face would then aggravatingly agree with me, before solemnly pointing back in the direction of Matsumoto and suggesting that I descend back down the mountain. Quite naturally, he just didn't give a fuck for my predicament but… *it's a race, and like all races, it must come to a timely end.*

'What time does the race end?' I blurted out excitedly, making Stern-face shudder slightly.

He looked at his watch, '11:00am,' he confirmed.

I then in turn looked at my watch. It was 09:30am. It would take me a few hours to reach the summit at my pace; the carnival would be long finished by then. In terrible Japanese I tried to explain this to Stern-face by fast-forwarding my watch to 12 o'clock, in order to purvey that I wouldn't reach Norikura's summit until then. He didn't know what an earth I was going on about, he just kept telling me to go back to Matsumoto. My blood by this point was beginning to boil. I'd just have to keep working on him until either he got fed up or

I self-combusted. With the rain intensifying I hoped that either of the two possibilities would conclude with haste.

'*Ja, 11:00am, Gifu no michi, daijoubu desu ka?*' So, at 11:00am, the road to Gifu is ok?

'*Hai.*' Yes.

'*Watashi wa chou osoi ne,*' I'm really slow. Pointing at all my luggage, '*takusan garakuta ga arimasu kara,*' because I'm carrying so much junk.

'*Hai.*' Yes. His stern expression began to lighten a little, as he now merely looked weary.

And after a short and depressing sigh, he turned to face the road to the summit. '*Hai,* ok, ok.' He said, as he reluctantly waved me through the barrier.

There was a small pause of shock on my behalf before the realisation that I'd won kicked in. But rather than linger and relish in the glory, I peddled through the now opened checkpoint barrier as quick as I could - just in case old Wearisome-face changed his mind.

Overwhelmed as I continued with my ascent, the skies would congratulate me by absolutely pissing all over me. And, as I cast a quick look over my shoulder, the checkpoint barrier was down again and the artist formerly known as Stern-face had disappeared back into his glum shack. If I'd have played the wrong card in that little mind game, the moment could well have ended in devastation. Alas, the day was still young and as I breached ever closer to the summit there was still yet plenty of time for a well synchronised dosing of drama.

Heading above the alpines, I came across an empty ski field; the snow still plentiful at this altitude. Torrents of rain fell, crashing down deafeningly upon my safety helmet as a northerly wind occasionally whipped across the exposed dips in the mountain's jagged terrain. Drains to the sides of the road were filling up fast and the road itself was converging into a fast flowing stream; progress becoming formidably slow. I passed a bunch of wet and miserable skiers huddled together under the shelter of a mountain hut; their eyes offering me sympathy. Things were getting unhealthy, *what was I doing up here?* It was possible that I'd bitten off more than I could chew, as suddenly the idea of 'Amsterdam to Amsterdam' began to have a much more nourishing ring to it than 'Tokyo to Tokyo.'

Taking time out, I huddled up against a snow wall, which offered some refuge from the now almost horizontally falling rain. Soaked to the bone, I quickly began to strip out of my drenched waterproof clothing and into another back-up set. Japan's rainy season had made me wise to its elements, or so I had thought. And as I made a lingering ascent to the summit of Japan's highest road, I approached the border into Gifu. I'd made it. A moment of contentedness hit me, as I knew a descent would soon follow. At this point things couldn't possibly get any worse than my ascent – or could they?

STATS

Dates: 12/07/2014 – 13/07/2014
Total miles traversed: 3,346 miles
Total time in the saddle: 348 hours and 22 minutes

16. GIFU
岐阜省

It was whilst atop Mt. Norikura, amongst a dirty grey mist, that I stumbled across a graveyard of abandoned racing bicycles. It appeared that the 'Racing Carnival' was no more as up to 100+ of some of the most expensive bicycles on earth lay strewn across the mountain top, not an owner in sight. Their abandonment made me feel somewhat nervous; no sane cyclist painstakingly trudges some 2,750 metres up a mountain to skip out on its adrenaline infused descent. Something was incredibly wrong. Freewheeling slowly amongst a showcase of shiny carbon frames and their wafer thin tyres, I wondered if it was perhaps time for an upgrade; the pelting rain however discouraged my criminal intent.

I breached what felt like the vertebrae of Norikura with caution, visibility poor. Cornering a huge rising piece of rock, facing north, any visions of the perfect descent were instantly and utterly dashed. A violent wind suddenly ripped into me and jolted me uncontrollably. 'Fuck!' I exclaimed as I battled to regain control of the steering, whilst continuing to pedal pointlessly at the rate of about 0.01mph. This must have really hacked Mother Nature off, as several seconds later she'd throw everything she had at me.

It was a wind that, to this day, I can still feel tearing through me. There wasn't even time to exclaim this time as my helmet flew off my head and its support straps began to throttle me. I piled on the breaks and stomped both feet on the ground, as firmly as possible whilst the wind howled viciously. Absolute control was now in the hands of the mountain goddess; I was a pathetic sack of skin against her fearless wrath. Putting my head down into the wind I tried to remain as static as possible, whilst trying to conjure up a rapid counter-measure. The horizontal rain smashed into me, as I struggled to stand firm; every second felt like a personal vendetta.

The best option was to get off the road, for one side was a sheer drop and the other a rock face. As I threw one leg over the handle bar to get off my bike, the wind took my grip away from me and my bike crashed to the ground. I tried to raise it but under its weight and the pressure of the wind my efforts were futile, so I was forced to drag my steed to the side of the road, like a wounded soldier. There I would crouch and wait it out, my only option. Again I was completely soaked through, how long I could stick it out was unclear. By the side of the road, I was blown around like a ragdoll; the wind so fierce that the front of my bicycle began to levitate up and off of the ground, as if possessed by some demonic force. Thankfully, the heavy load to the rear of the bike prevented it from actually taking off and being cast into oblivion. This was one of the few times that I was thankful for the burden of a heavy rig.

In the face of danger, I was surprised at how calm I was able to remain; in my earlier years I might have gone mad and jumped off the cliff edge, like a half barmy lemming. Yet now, as I crouched marooned on a mountain top, I somehow felt that I was being taught a valuable lesson by Mother Nature; her cruel ways testing my reactions to new challenges. In the flatlands of Cambridgeshire these challenges were just completely unimaginable. She was giving me an adventure. Yet I won't lie when I say that I could have thought of a whole array of better places to be in at the time. Apart from the adrenaline, the only other thing keeping me warm atop the mountain was the thought of being back home; looking after cheery cows and calves upon the calm of the Washes. Just one year previously, life just seemed so very normal. And whilst thinking of home so many, many miles away, an amber glow began to emerge through the thick grey murk.

The hazard lights drew closer, until they stopped in front of me. From my crouched position, I looked up to a small white mini-bus. An aged band of heroes peered back at me; a side door suddenly slid open as an elderly gentleman ushered me in. I didn't have to think twice, I grabbed my front pannier of mostly valuables and my all-important speedometer and dived in, the door swiftly closing behind me. I pitched a seat next to a drenched racing cyclist, amusingly, we just nodded to one another, before both looking directly ahead. Lost in our thoughts, we were the last of the evacuees.

The venomous wind rocked the minivan from side to side as everyone inside groaned with uncertainty and awe. The driver in his late 70's, one of the three elderly stewards who were helping at the day's racing event, escorted us down the mountain slowly as we passed a number of other deserted bicycles. The wind was tossing them about, as if they were mere particles of sand. I feared for my own bike, what may become of it and all of my other possessions, whilst at the same time feeling robbed of one of the grandest descents in all of Japan. Yet if there had been no 'Racing Carnival' on this very day, I dread to think what may have become of me. I was grateful.

We were dropped off a third of the way down the mountain in safer climes, where 100's of other cyclists were waiting anxiously on the return of their bikes. All cast their eyes up into the mountain's fearsome summit, it's surrounding black clouds gruesome. An American from Utah scoped me out and we related our stories to one another like excited school children; both cold as our teeth chattered manically. The Utah chap had just about made it to the summit before the weather took a sudden turn. He told me that he would've still descended - despite the hairy conditions. But then one look at my face and demeanour had him change his mind quite rapidly.

Two hours later, all the cyclist's bikes were returned to them. However, the chills would continue to eat away at me and by then I was shaking uncontrollably. The evacuation buses had been sent back up into the mountains to fetch all the contestants' prized possessions - plus one. It was an uncertain and anxious wait and it was the furthest apart that I'd actually been from my bike since purchasing it. So to see it getting unloaded from the bus was a joyous moment, even more so when all of my bags and panniers were returned unscathed - including my camera and laptop.

Before leaving, I tried to find the elderly band of heroes who had plucked me off the summit, to say thank you. I failed however as they were off someplace fearlessly committing themselves to another good deed. If I should ever make it to my 70's, I could only aspire to be as helpful as the stewards had been at today's event; but sadly I fear a retirement of mostly farting my pants to pieces and shaming my family is a more than likely scenario.

I pressed on some 40 klicks west to Takayama; my head constantly relaying the day's madness over and over. *Luck or destiny?* I couldn't decide, or I just didn't want to. Checking into a hostel in Takayama, I took a long hot shower before throwing on the last of my dry clothes. I then headed out to the nearest convenience store to grab myself some much needed beers.

Whilst in Circle K purchasing my booze, it started to rain heavily, so just outside the convenience store, I waited it out under some dry eaves as I knocked back one of my beers. In the car park, I witnessed a moth flapping about and struggling in a shallow puddle, as the rain crashed down around it. I've never been too certain about karma, but in some small part I felt that I had to offer thanks for my safety. Walking out into the pouring rain, I scooped the little guy up out of his soggy coffin and bought him back under the shelter with me. He gripped tightly to my thumb, shaking frenziedly. I delicately removed a couple of droplets from his wings as I let him continue to sit upon my thumb. Once I'd finished my beer, his shakes had subsided somewhat, so finding a small, dark, sheltered cove to the side of Circle K, I set him down - upon a piece of brickwork and hoped he'd survive the night.

Takayama

'Control Gifu and you control Japan,' was an ancient saying, dating back to the Sengoku period. Its central positioning between Tokyo and Kyoto made it an important crossroads along the Nakasendō route, linking the two major cities. An area no stranger to social upheaval – it saw a number of significant battles stain the prefecture in blood. I was also here to conquer Japan in some small way - but I'm certainly not the controlling type. All I really wanted was to kindly reach every prefecture on my push bike, whilst spilling as little blood as possible in the process.

And after yesterday's full-on assault, I decided that 'conquering' Japan would have to be put on hold for the day; I needed some quiet time. I decided to mill around Takayama's cordial old town and through its narrow alleyways. Around me were old wooden merchant houses that offered up local handicrafts, sake, cakes and the regionally popular Hida beef. Contentedly, I eat and drank myself through a stress-free day… just what the doctor ordered.

STATS

Dates: 13/07/2014 – 14/07/2014
Total miles traversed: 3,346 miles
Total time in the saddle: 348 hours and 22 minutes

17. TOYAMA
富山県

Takayama – Toyama
64 miles

The ride north to Toyama City saw me leave the Japanese Alps behind; it had been an intense week and I had been feeling a longing for the coast again. Toyama means 'many mountains' and it would certainly live up to its name; a riotous cluster of alpine greenery sprawled coarsely across the land, continuing on from where Gifu left off. Yet cutting through a gorge some 20 metres above the placid flowing waters of the Miyagawa River, I was saved a bulk of strenuous climbing, which felt like a pleasing pay-off after the effort it had taken me to get into the Alps.

Toyama City itself had no special draw though. During World War II, 95.6% of its urban area was decimated by American B-29 fire-bombings - bringing its thriving aluminium, steel and ball-bearing industries to an abrupt standstill. However, today, like many a once destroyed Japanese cities, it has been fully resurrected. It is now a regionally important manufacturer of metal, electronic and pharmaceutical products. It is fundamentally clean, accessible and habitually sound with its refurbished and aesthetically pleasing castle, green spaces and attractive waterways that wind through the city and out into the Sea of Japan. Toyama will never be one of the big hitters, but as a passing space it served as an inviting enough city in which to have a gander and set up a stealth camp.

   Cycling north of the city, along a canal that pranced along the hem of a peaceful residential area, I'd find a small wooden gazebo - atop a grassy knoll. Setting up camp there I found limited sleep; the night fast becoming humid and uncomfortable. Unzipping the entrance to my tent offered me a small modicum of relief, but an invading army of ants soon saw to the eventual demise of a once perfectly ideal looking stealth camp. My grassy knoll retreat had essentially become shitty and wank; words that at the time seemed to flow so naturally off my damnable tongue.

The cold now was indefinitely gone, and, to the best of my knowledge, so too was the rainy season - a new challenger had entered the equation.

Over the coming weeks, the south's heat and humidity became one of my greatest new challenges; a burden that I would just have to learn to bear.

Toyama – Mitsukejima
98 miles

The day would start like many a day on the road, by seeking out the nearest 7-Eleven. There, I would have a breakfast of noodles and *gyōza*, accompanied by two coffees whilst abusing the free Wi-Fi on offer and seeing how many Facebook friends had called me a 'cock' in the past 24 hours. After this, I would then hasten to the bathroom, brush my coffee-stained teeth, fill my water bottles up and then drop some mates off at the pool. It got to a point whereby I couldn't imagine starting my day in any other way. Take a 7-Eleven away from me and you're essentially taking away a limb. I'd become religiously dependent upon them, which in itself was quite sad. Yet, their convenience just felt so damn necessary, and if there's one thing that the Japanese do well - it's convenience.

Proceeding north of the city, toward the imaginatively entitled Toyama Bay, the humidity remained rife. The city's manufacturing industry was becoming evident, as lorries chugged past at an alarming rate and smoke poured out of factories; up into the dingy skies above.

Encircling the bay westerly, away from the Toyama industrial zone, soon saw me pass an enclave of quiescent fishing villages. A short climb over a mountain chain brought me down into Nanao, the gateway to the remote, Noto Peninsula.

STATS

Dates: 15/07/2014 – 16/07/2014
Total miles traversed: 3,508 miles
Total time in the saddle: 363 hours and 4 minutes

18. ISHIKAWA
石川県

Nanao would greet me like an old enemy; the skies rumbling with hate as the tension in the atmosphere finally snapped, saturating my surrounds. I found refuge in a local supermarket where I feasted ravenously upon 6 *gyōza*, 2 *onigiri*, 1 banana, 4 chocolate éclairs and an anonymous item of limited palatability.

After brunch, the skies would temporarily clear, allowing me to progress farther north into the Noto Peninsula.

The peninsula branches out some 60 miles into the Sea of Japan; like an accusingly crooked finger. A vastly remote area that the pioneering 8th Century poet Ōtomo no Yakamochi would write about:

> *From the Shiwo Road across*
> *the mountains to the morning*
> *calm of the sea at Hakuhi, I*
> *wish I had a boat!*

The east side of the peninsula, which faces the mainland, is somewhat sheltered, compared to the more rugged and exposed western coast. A sprinkling of farmsteads and fishing villages dot the peninsula's inner coast, before the isolated north becomes apparent.

I rolled up and down the coastline in stereotypical fashion: under grey, dreary clouds. Then, I came across Koiji beach: Koiji meaning love road, a place for lovers apparently. Set on a small islet, just off of the coast, a story goes that in ancient times two young lovers used to meet here every night for a romp. The lady would light a fire on the islet, so that her man could find her amongst the darkness. Yet, unbeknownst to the two lovers, a jealous bastard lurked in the shadows. One night, he tricked the young man by lighting a fire of his own, upon a treacherous part of the islet. Fooled by this devilish plan, the young lover fell into a hole and perished. When his girlfriend found him, she was so distraught by the discovery that she drowned herself in the sea.

The bastard went home, job done.

I scanned the islet to see if anybody required my rubbish love. Alas, as predicted, no fires burned; I'd be spending another night alone.

A few more miles further north would lead me to Mitsukejima, *found rock.* This was said to have been founded by Kōbō-Daishi, the curator of the Shingon sect of Japanese Buddhism.

Climbing up some 30-metres out of the ocean, the odd-shaped rock would also gain the nickname Gunkanjima, *Battleship Island* – as it resembled exactly that of a battleship.

As daylight began to dim, a noisy flock of crows headed to the island to roost. *I should roost too,* I thought. Doing a 180-degree turn, I saw a small copse. After setting up camp amongst the cover of trees, I greeted another tour cyclist who also set up camp, close by. I hoped for my sake that he wasn't a bastard.

Mitsukejima – Kanazawa
111 miles

I'd managed to survive the night without being coerced into any deep crevices; in fact, as I left surrounded by a spooky sea mist, I could hear my camping neighbour snoring contentedly. If I wasn't so eager to push on, then I may well have been jealous of his sleeping abilities.

Pressing on to the nearby town of Suzu, I'd fail to find breakfast; it was the kind of town that looked like it had gone to sleep in the early 1980's and had never quite got around to waking up.

I travelled further around the northern tip of the peninsula, before taking on its wild and rugged Sosogi Coast. Steep cliffs stooped down into the ocean as a steady wind ushered forth, slowing my progress. Running on fumes, I made it to Senmaida, *one thousand rice paddies.* It was here that the tourist scene made a cameo, as a series of miniature rice paddies cascaded down from the mountainside towards the fringes of the coast. Due to their awkward positioning, the paddies have to be maintained by hand; without the aid of modern machinery. White-clad farmers tended their crop delicately; a physical job requiring an abundance of skill and patience - for the lush green rice plants still wouldn't be ready for another couple of months.

Just south of Senmaida was the city of Wajima, one of the peninsula's most populous cities that would finally offer up a convenience store.

I was now 70 miles from Ishikawa's capital city, Kanazawa. At the start of the day, I would have said that I had been a couple of days away from the capital (from my starting point at the tip of Noto's peninsula) but after two cups of iced coffee, I felt inspired to break my personal daily record by traversing a total of 111 miles.

Once away from the peninsula I felt like a man on a mission; the roads levelling out considerably, allowing me to make some excellent progress. The only trouble I had was when I misread a road sign and found myself cruising recklessly onto a boisterous expressway. Bicycles were forbidden there and it wouldn't take me long to work out why, as cars and trucks roared past me at death defying speeds.

One car shot past, a child's snotty face pressed to the window.

'Hey Dad, it's that wanker again!'

'I see him son, I see him.'

The expressway's exit couldn't have come soon enough, and after leaving the horrific road, I came upon a 7-Eleven! Being situated on the outskirts of Kanazawa, my chances of reaching the city's core now sat at 99.3%. I decided to flick a quick e-mail to a Brazilian Couchsurfer called Jimmy. His response to my request was rapid, informing me that he and his boyfriend could host me for the night.

Traversing the suburbs, I arrived in the city centre just as night had set in. A sudden downpour saw me take shelter at a convenience store for a good hour or so - meaning that I wouldn't arrive at my hosts' until quite late. Yet, Jimmy and his Chinese boyfriend, Lei, were not fazed by my lateness. Both were students studying Japanese at the city's University – so they were no strangers to late nights. I however was. We bantered for a while before my eyes started to close.

Kanazawa – Fukui
60 miles

After coffee and a high five, I left Jimmy and Lei to their Japanese studying; something that I was struggling to find the time to do. I had been averaging anywhere between 60-100 miles a day in the saddle, so the very thought of sitting down to study Japanese at the end of the day made me want to commit *seppuku*.

I cycled through the busy streets of Kanazawa, a city once synonymous for being a samurai town. In Nagamachi, one can still witness well-preserved structures from the Edo Period where samurai once resided. To the east of the old samurai district sits the city's castle grounds, where one can find the star attraction, the Kenrokuen Gardens. Bicycle parking here was limited to an area marked out in a small'ish yellow grid. I could only manage to fit my titanic-esque vessel half in and half out of the yellow grid by propping it up at the end of the row of parked bicycles. *That's good enough.* Yet as I began to walk away, it clearly wasn't good enough... as an angry parking warden came running across to me, blowing a whistle

213

and shaking his finger at me. The fact that the bike was overhanging the line by a good 0.42cm was clearly a cause for concern and a major health hazard to the entire nation! The warden's tone was irate and his Japanese beyond me, so I had no choice but to play it dumb as he spoke.

'Err....what?'

The angry warden - in a uniform of navy blue with pearly white buttons - then began to motion for me to move my bike into the yellow grid.

'No space,' I said, whilst trying to gesticulate with my hands.

'Ok, ok,' he said, before turning away from me and yelling for back up.

Oh, I'm fucked now.

His portly colleague waddled over courageously, more jovial than the angry warden who would soon bark an order at him, wiping the happy grin off his face in a heartbeat. *How dare you smile on the job, you knucklehead!* The two men then began to move all the bikes from right to left, until there was enough space for me to squeeze my bike in at the end. The angry warden watched me closely, checking to make sure that I was thoroughly within the parameters of the yellow grid. Content, the angry warden then became the happiest parking warden in Eastern Asia. I thanked him and as he reciprocated, his colleague nodded too. They then bowed to one another and strolled off in opposite directions. *Only in Japan...*

The Kenroku-en Gardens first opened to the public in 1874 and today they're considered one of the three most beautiful gardens in all of Japan, alongside the Kairaku-en of Mito and Kōraku-en of Okayama. But, for many, Kanazawa's Kenroku-en Gardens are the real deal; a designated "Special Place of Scenic Beauty." Spread across some 25 acres, the gardens envelop the six fundamental qualities that - according to an ancient Chinese book of gardens - are required to make a garden sublime: spaciousness, seclusion, artifice, antiquity, water courses and panoramas.

Not being much of a gardener however, I only counted five - seclusion clearly out of the window, as with many tourist attractions within Japan. But the gardens were enchanting enough, with an aged Edo feel to them; a selection of novel tea houses, intricately crafted bridges, koi clustered waterways, moss laden sculptures and ancient trees with roots as solid as steel. An idyllic spot for a feudal lord to show a Geisha girl his willy.

STATS

Dates: 16/07/2014 – 18/07/2014
Total miles traversed: 3,679 miles
Total time in the saddle: 380 hours and 45 minutes

19. FUKUI
福井県

Heading out of Kanazawa, I met up with my old flame, Route 8, as I journeyed into Fukui Prefecture. Route 8 was as feckless as ever, with its limited hard shoulders and hordes of trucks that bounced along the heavily fractured bitumen without a care in the world. The sides of the road were in a process of being invaded by some hefty vegetation which emerged from out of the surrounding alpines in a true 'Day of the Triffids' fashion. The most annoying of these triffids were a number of large and soggy dock leaves that flogged my legs and thighs; a sensation far from sensual.

At the time of writing this, there was much debate surrounding Fukui; a prefecture that hosts some 13 nuclear power reactors - the highest number for any prefecture in Japan. With so many reactors, it was no surprise to learn that the stretch of coastline that the reactors inhabit was referred to as, 'Nuclear Alley.' Talk of putting some of the reactors back online was a popular topic around Fukui, with the government keen to start saving money again, without having to import expensive oil and gas from overseas. This move would cover the lost energy from having all of the country's 48 usable nuclear reactors sitting offline. Yet, in the wake of Fukushima, public opposal was rightfully strong, but the Phoenix had a right to speak. The Phoenix was the city of Fukui's national emblem – and the city's name means 'fortunate'. Fukui was in fact levelled twice, once during 1945 in an American aerial bombardment, and then again by the devastating post war earthquake of 1948. Yet, like the Phoenix, the city would rise from the ashes of destruction and again thrive. The true epitome of the Phoenix are the Fukuian's, and they alone possess the right to have an important say in the future of nuclear energy.

By nightfall I reached the prefecture's capital, a moderate city of some 267,000 people that, like many of Japan's cities, seemed to bear no scars of its gory past. Buildings aimed for the skies, neon lights trailed off into the unknown, and vibrant boulevards got pounded by the footsteps of commerce.

Being hungry, I fancied something dirty like a burger and chips from a certain global conglomerate burger chain, but that would have meant a calamitously long wait. Now, I fully agree with your thinking, "...why would you go all the way to Japan and eat a burger and chips like a yobbo?" And I wholeheartedly agree, especially when I'm sat with cold chips, waiting patiently upon my burger, or an empty burger and cold chips, or green tea - instead of cola - and a portion of cold chips. Or... a burger containing mystery meat and cold chips, or worse still... nothing... with cold chips!

I think growing up in the UK - and becoming somewhat of a connoisseur to eating filth has had a psychological effect upon me. Meaning that I need to eat detritus, every now and again, to prevent myself from going completely cold turkey.

Due to years of this dietary abuse, I appear to have derived a standard in my mind of how my Western fast food should be served up, and in Japan sadly it fails nearly every time. Their Western fast food is served incredibly slowly, but the Japanese version of fast food has been more than mastered, and it's certainly much healthier, too.

So, resisting my cravings for amateur Western fare, I opted for the Japanese quick-fix. Ordering a pork cutlet and rice, saw me feasting within the minute, and then afterwards - with the comfort of a full belly – I found myself disgusted with the fact that I'd ever fancied a dirty burger and chips in the first place. A limited feeling however that of course would soon wear off. For it's what 'they,' 'the corporation', 'the machine', or 'the man' with their additives and bags of grease wanted. Resistance will and always will be futile, for they will always get you in the end.

Under the dim glow of my cheap 100 Yen flashlight, I sought out the Asuwagawa River, which runs directly through the centre of the city, alongside a number of quaint riverside parks.

Finding a dark and unobtrusive spot, I set up my tent and bunkered down for the night. I'd soon be dreaming of burgers being fed into my greedy face by scantily clad Geisha girls.

Fukui – Nagahama
83 miles

I awoke early to a selection of lurching footsteps, creeping around outside my tent. Fearing that I was about to get molested by the walking dead, I grabbed a pile of wits and chanced a sly glance through my tent's involuntary secret peep hole. I was relieved to find that it was just an elderly gentleman walking his dog. The elderly rise early in this part of the world. I rose at about 5am and would often encounter parks full of elderly men and women, performing morning exercises, whilst chewing the cud; an Akita dog often not far away, scoping out some local snatch, whilst urinating up my tent.

On this very morning, whilst exiting my tent, the elderly gent's Akita didn't take too kindly to my presence and began to bark vehemently in my direction. The dog was clearly a racist. The elderly gent apologised before they went on their way.

Heading westerly from Fukui, I sought out the Echizen Coast, a dramatic stretch of coastline bludgeoned timelessly by the ocean's distorting waters. The road packed tightly to the water's edge made for a gracious ride; the clear skies bringing a hive of activity to the coast: windsurferists, snorkellists, barbecueists, sun-absorberists, volleyballists and, of course a mandatory selection of screaming adolescents for good measure.

The coastal road stretched some 60 miles toward the rather uninspiring city of Tsuruga, from where I switched inland in a southerly trajectory towards Japan's largest freshwater lake.

STATS

Dates: 18/07/2014 – 19/07/2014
Total miles traversed: 3,762 miles
Total time in the saddle: 387 hours and 16 minutes

20. SHIGA
滋賀県

Lake Biwa is a grandiose lake, holding approximately 27.5 billion tonnes of water, with a perimeter of about 143 miles. It occupies a 6th of Shiga Prefecture's total land mass. The lives of 15 million people are dependent upon its vast reserves; the lake being the source of the naturally formed Seta River which runs a course of some 47 miles out to Osaka Bay.

Approaching from the north, I traversed the fringes of the lake's swarthy waters, along the more populous eastern plains. To the west, a shadowy outcrop provided a continuous silhouette of the sparsely populated Hira Mountains. It was overcast and muggy; my sweaty skin acting like a piece of flypaper that would sap up all manner of roadside grit and impurities. *I should go for a swim,* I'd think to myself on a number of occasions… but as enticing as the waters may well have been, I was making some personally ground-breaking progress. Not that this was a race, but once I had found a steady rhythm, it was very hard to tone down the daily expected output of mileage. I had a self-imposed daily quota, and with the terrain being as flat as a pancake, it was important to carry on at full speed.

By the time I'd made it to Nagahama, the sun was beginning to slip behind the mountains; a radiant amber glow bouncing off the great lake's surface. The mild stress of finding a place to stealth camp was relieved by a free lakeside camp site, which was opposite none other than an opportunist 7-Eleven. I'd found my heaven. Purchasing a 4-pack, I set up camp next to a fallen tree. There were only a small number of other campers about, as I perched myself upon the tree trunk and sank my beers in silence.

The sun gradually ebbed beyond the horizon and cast me into darkness. For now, I was massively content with life, I'd by no means found the meaning of it yet, but supping on a beer alongside one of Mother Nature's finest, definitely had a certain feel-good factor to it. Wandering over to the shoreline, I wondered if I might finally take that plunge. Dipping my big toe into the lake's ice cold waters, I shuddered violently. *Nah.* Downing the rest of my beer I retreated to my tent to dream about sleep.

My tranquillity was shattered moments after resting my head upon my makeshift pillow (a dry bag of pants and socks). The shrill sound started from a nearby car park; the monotonous drone of a diesel generator powering up, shortly followed by cheers of joy, and then moments later an endless *boom, chicka-boom, chicka-boom…*

Basil Brush on acid? Not quite. Unzipping my tent I discovered that I was in the midst of an all-night lake side rave.

From then on, music of a discriminate nature pounded haphazardly from a stack of amps deep into the night as a collective of lairy youths waved neon sticks about guilelessly as they danced and drank themselves silly. Slightly perturbed, I zipped my tent back up and lay back down.

Boom, chicka-boom, chicka-boom.

And then closed my eyes.

Boom, chicka-boom, chicka-boom…

Nagahama – Kyoto
58 miles

Boom, chicka-boom, chicka-boom…

Come 7am and I was still wide awake. The same song continuously blasted away without remorse. I'd just experienced my first Japanese all-night rave and the Japanese themselves at their most unruly. On a plus note, I did manage to survive the night without getting my head kicked in by a pillhead, so by and large I shouldn't complain. Making my

221

way to the communal toilets, I bore witness to the last of the ravers; one man bounced up and down with sunglasses on, wearing a long white nightshirt... his rhythm was boundless as his fingers gyrated to the skies suggestively. Another man lay passed out on the ground, his friend leaning over him slapping his face. 'Nobu-san, okiro, okiro,' Mr Nobu, wake up, wake up. The friend smiled politely at me, as I entered the toilet block.

Now for a shithouse that had just undergone an all-night rave, I was remarkably surprised at how clean the facilities still were... what was wrong with these people? Cleanliness in the face of anarchy was an incredible feat to achieve, yet these kids seemed to have pulled it off effortlessly. The Japanese are a festival organiser's dream... partygoers across the world take heed.

After a considerably nasty poo I took the walk of shame back to my tent. Mr Nobu still in a heap on the floor was now alone; his friend off dancing with Mr Sunglasses, together they pointed at the skies as they jived.

Mr Nobu had since gained a cigarette, pursed tightly between his lips he puffed away contentedly with his eyes closed. Certain that he had everything under control, I left him to it.

Leaving the campsite, the invasive drivel of *boom, chicka-boom, chicka-boom* would remain etched into my head for the remainder of my journey south around the lake. Even stopping for ice cream, I found myself sub-consciously nodding my head to the non-existent beat. It was a cruel blow, but it felt better knowing that Mr Nobu would be having a worse off day, nursing his hangover.

By lunchtime, the temperature had soared to a sizzling 31°C: windsurferers, snorkelers, barbecuers, sun-absorberers, volleyballers and the essential quota of screaming children plied Biwa's pristine waters.

The southern section of the lake became more populous with camp sites, hotels and tourists as I etched closer to Ōtsu, Shiga's capital city. A city that is largely overshadowed by its big neighbour - one that I also - in an impetuous hunger to further my progression - chose to ignore, as I forced myself up into a sticky ascent of the Higashiyama mountain range and down into the baking hot oven of Kyoto. *Boom, chicka-boom, chicka-boom...*

STATS

Dates: 19/07/2014 – 20/07/2014
Total miles traversed: 3,820 miles
Total time in the saddle: 392 hours and 40 minutes

21.1 KYOTO
京都府

Kyoto

I would awake with a hangover.

Kyoto was only my second prolonged stop since Hokkaidō, some three months previously, and it acted as the perfect excuse for an absolute skinful. Arising out of bed, yawning like a barbarian and then groaning like a zombie, I stumbled from my hotel room and out onto a balcony.

My hotel sat embedded into the slopes of the Higashiyama Mountains and offered a panoramic view across the city. A city that doesn't intimidate with an abundance of skyscrapers, unlike in many Japanese cities; a law having been passed that forbade the building of structures over a certain height. This was in an effort to allow the city to retain its cultural relevance and identity.

Obviously, this doesn't completely overrule modernity and there are still some exceptions to the cause - such as the Kyoto Tower that thrusts itself up into the skyline. Historically, however, Kyoto's roots surge deep, spanning back to 794 when Emperor Kammu first designated the area - then known as Heian-Kyo - as the countries imperial capital... a title it would relish for well over a thousand years. Emperors and Shoguns would come and go and civil war would occasionally decimate the city, but every time it would be rebuilt - restoring the city's historic values. It is also the headquarters for Nintendo.

Venturing down from the mountainside on foot into the Kyoto Basin, I was greeted by some menacingly hot weather. Being surrounded on three sides by mountains, means that Kyoto is seasonably predictable; its summer's really fucking hot and its winters really fucking cold.

Having a grid style layout, Kyoto is easy enough to navigate around. Strolling through the delicately cobbled backstreets of Gion, amongst the old tea houses, a procession of Geisha shuffled past; a silhouette of the past projecting into the present; an endearing sight. The immaculately detailed Geisha in their exquisitely decorated kimonos, holding their red brollies, wearing their clunky *geta* slippers and with beaming white faces are one of Kyoto's oldest and most familiar sights. Contrary to popular belief, they are not actually hookers... but for a generally hefty fee one might acquire the services of the Geisha to enlighten certain social settings. They joke, sing, dance, play musical instruments, serve drink and food, light your cigarettes and entertain with the kind of etiquette you can only really associate with the Japanese.

I hadn't quite budgeted for the services of a Geisha (estimated £500) during this specific trip. But to see them scoot through this ancient district to their next appointment was enough to satisfy my ogling touristic eyes, √.

The old district of Gion soon merged into the new district, with modern shops and arcades offering a world of goods. These range from the latest designer clobber and filthy burger joints, to more traditional retail outlets - offering up a reasonable selection of: handicrafts, textiles, lacquerware, pottery, ceramics, fans and a multitude of other souvenirs and local delicacies.

I discovered the claustrophobic and ramshackle Nishiki Market, or 'Kyoto's Kitchen' as called by many a Kyotoite. The market dates back to the 14th Century and yields some 126 shops - and if beans, rice, pickles, tea, seaweed, fish, crackers and other obscurities are on your agenda then this is the place to be.

I opted for some *tofu* ice cream, not quite hangover fodder - it was bland to say the least – instead, I felt an urge to smear it all over my sweaty face in an attempt to save myself from the city's clamminess. Reluctantly, though, I managed to restrain myself from such clear madness in an effort to keep my sanity on a neutral par with that of my fellow tourists. And speaking of tourists, today would be the first day in a considerably long time when I actually felt like a tourist. With no pressures, time restraints or mountains to scale I was completely free to wander the country's 6th biggest city in an aimless fashion. It felt almost like I was on day release...

The remaining days were spent temple gazing, and with over a thousand Buddhist temples and four-hundred Shintō shrines, one can't help but run into a few of them. The big hitters being spread apart from one another led me to unshackling my bicycle of its panniers to enable me to tour the city with a sweat infused ease.

Highlights included the Arashiyama bamboo grove - as seen in *Crouching Tiger, Hidden Dragon* and Fushimi Inari Taisha, a network of over a thousand closely linked vermillion torii gateways, that run amok over the slopes of Mt. Inari in Kyoto's South East.

The true icing on the cake though would have to be Kinkaku-ju, otherwise known as the Golden Pavilion. *Lonely Planet* will tell you that to avoid the masses you should attend early - upon arrival it would appear that 94.7% of the camera toting tourists in Kyoto had read that exact same passage in their respective guidebooks. The place was absolutely crammed and I'm not so sure if there will ever be a good time to visit, due to the majestic nature of the structure. It will indefinitely always attract the masses.

The 14th Century three-tiered pavilion is dressed in gold leaf to reflect its qualities onto a surrounding pond, amongst a fine *Muromachi* period garden. The structure is integrated with Nature in such a way, that it becomes a work of art. Photo opportunities were scarce, as stewards were keen to move me on, as to allow them to pour in as many *Lonely Planet* guidebook wielding tourists as humanly possible. Yet, the contrasting beauty of the temple alone, was more than enough to burn a generous mental image into my memory for at least half a lifetime.

Before I knew it, my 4-day break in Kyoto was up and it was definitely that time again. I hadn't wholeheartedly relaxed, nonetheless, the cultural heart of Japan had been an embracing pit stop and it was plain to see why the city was on the itinerary for the bulk of travellers to the country.

Having been saved from allied bombings during World War II, the city had retained a sense of historical dignity; something unfortunately that not every Japanese city can boast.

Kyoto – Kobe
47 miles

Plying the concrete jungles of the Keihanshin, the metropolitan region where Kyoto, Osaka and Kobe all meet, saw me exposed to a brutal 37°C heat. The sun beat down fiercely upon the road as its rays refracted upwards, giving a constant mirage effect. I found myself going through some 2 litres of water an hour, whilst the sweat poured out of me, profusely.

Losing enough sodium through a concentrated bout of sweating has the potential to be disastrous, so the replacement of salt in the now hot and humid climes had become essential. Enter the *umeboshi,* an extremely sour plum rammed with an abundance of salt that will leave you scrunching your face for days to come, but they get the job done. Reluctantly tossing a couple of these nasty fruits down my gullet every couple of hours, was certainly more than enough to prevent me from keeling over. Gross plums and flat gradients were to be my saving grace for the day as my body looked to play the acclimatisation game.

When the cloud cover came, which was rare, it was much appreciated. It didn't take much of an edge off the sun's wrath, but it was something, and as an opportunist I had to take it.

Reaching Route 2, I cycled westbound to Kobe. The change of direction was noticeable on the dry, hot wind that blew head-on resembling that of the dirty heated breath of the Devil himself. Perhaps this was an immoral reminder of what he still had in store for me over the coming months.

STATS

Dates: 20/07/2014 – 25/07/2014
Total miles traversed: 3,867 miles
Total time in the saddle: 397 hours and 2 minutes

22.1 HYOGO
兵庫県

Chaotic scenes greeted me, upon my entering the country's 5th largest metropolis of Kobe. At an intersection, the traffic was grid-locked and - cycling on the sidewalks being legal in Japan – I was able to escape the encroaching jam somewhat.

A little farther ahead and a steady crowd had gathered. My curiosity drew me over, but I wished it hadn't. Several elderly women were standing agasp; hands covering their faces in shock. Peering through the cracks of the crowd, I saw a twisted and claret soaked body trapped under the wheels of a bus. The reasoning behind the tailback of traffic was now unpleasantly clear, and I, head hung low, cycled on.

At my hostel, I granted myself a much needed shower and a rare siesta, after which, I awoke with a ravishing hunger. Heeding the call of my stomach, I headed to the city's central hub of Sannomiya, where a ramen shop - resembling a photo booth – set me straight.

Kobe is a vibrant and fast paced city; one of the earliest of Japanese cities to have traded internationally from its much famed port. Venturing there revealed an extremely cosmopolitan vibe. An exotic boulevard lined with light clustered tress paved the way to a selection of upmarket restaurants and shopping malls, that sat pretty alongside the water's edge. A huge Ferris wheel, the city's glitzy red landmark port tower and accompanying maritime museum illuminated the night sky. I took a seat in the wharf as the humid night was kind enough to allow a gentle breeze to pass.

Much of what I was witnessing was relatively new, as during the early hours of 17th January 1995, a devastating 6.7 magnitude earthquake struck, causing widespread damage across the entire Kobe region, claiming 6,434 lives. The Great Hanshin Earthquake, all but decimated the city's infrastructure and port area, setting the government back some £66.3 billion in expenses. At the time it was Japan's most destructive earthquake - since the Great Kantō Earthquake of 1923, which led to over 100,000 deaths.

It's quite hard to remain positive when one thinks of the history of these islands, both Mother Nature and humankind have played some decisively cruel cards to its citizens over the years. But with a bold, determined defiance, as always, the Japanese would again rise from the realms of uncertainty.

Kobe – Himeji
52 miles

By the time I'd readied my bike for the day, I was already a sweaty wreck; the dial again well on its way to another 37°C scorcher. Racing out of central Kobe toward the suburbs, I found the coast of the Seto Inland Sea, a predominately caged in body of water, home to hundreds of islands, islets and a border for the three main islands: Honshū, Shikoku and Kyūshū.

Many of the larger islands of the inland sea are connected by a network of bridges, with a vast swathe of the smaller inhabited islands being served via frequent ferry connections.

Clinging to the coast, I avoided a sizeable portion of heavy traffic that traipsed along Route 718. The fragile coastal breeze allowed for some marginally comfortable cycling, yet my forever perspiring palms began to corrode my handlebar tape, revealing a sticky adhesiveness that plastered my hands in a tar-like residue. A problem I should probably have sorted out at some point, but never did.

Whilst trailing a coast, you can't really go wrong, with or without a map… unless you're me, of course. It was around about the time that I was closing in on the city of Himeji that the midday sun must have sent me a little mental. Missing a vital turn-off, I found myself heading up into a set of mountains, and, as far as I was aware, this wasn't part of the day's agenda. But being a stubborn wretch, I was determined not to go back upon myself, *all roads must lead somewhere*. I slaved skywards for a while; the road seemingly less travelled and slightly worse for wear. Before long, I was out of water and *umeboshi*, the inland sea had now also gone astray, leaving me with an only slightly more than a lacklustre grasp of my geographic locale. Fortunately, the knackered-to-shit roads would soon reveal a lonely traffic controller. You might have thought being stuck up on a mountain all day, in the middle of nowhere under the blazing hot sun, that you'd be pleased to see a stranger. The traffic controller's reactions however would clearly dictate otherwise. As I approached the man, he began to wave his sparkly orange baton about frantically, before brandishing me with the sign of 'The Irons.'

'Come on West Ham!' I said, as per usual.

Unfazed, his face remained expressionless.

'Erm...*Himeji wa doko desu ka?*' Err...where's Himeji? I asked, hesitantly.

He pointed his baton back over my shoulder... an inevitability which I had half expected. I sighed. *'Arigatou gozaimasu.'* There was no reply. His eyes were cold and eerie, so I turned and went back down the mountainside, sulking slightly, but never at any point looking back over my shoulder - as I could feel the traffic controller's eyes burning into the back of my cranium.

When I reached the junction that I'd initially missed, I tutted at myself and shook my head in the utmost of disgust. Rank amateur. The new found road to Himeji would soon bathe me in an abundance of 7-Eleven's, so that I could replenish my thirst and get my ice cream fix in check - before heading into town.

Himeji is home to one of the most famed castles in the country, a castle that since 1333 has undergone various incarnations, but still sits prominently atop a hill bearing down over the city. It was one of Japan's first entries into the

UNESCO World Heritage list and was a survivor of both World War II and the Great Hanshin Earthquake.

The brilliant white building stands proud, earning itself the nickname of 'White Heron Castle,' yet initially not all were happy with this architectural marvel. It is said that one of the castle's early carpenters was most displeased with his own grafting; a sinking cliff close to the keep meant that the castle's tower lent a little too much to the southeast. This fact would inevitably lead the carpenter to his own grave. Scaling the walls of the castle's 150ft tower - with a chisel in his mouth – he cast himself off the top and down into the courtyard below. Today, however, I witnessed nothing but the work of master craftsman, the two huge cranes on one side of the six-storey structure carrying out reconstruction work, slightly marring the castle's majesty to some extent. But all in all, the building still acts as a perfect embodiment to the country's ancient, feudal past.

In the same district, amongst a peaceful neighbourhood, a network of narrow lanes and traditional Japanese homes, I found my guesthouse. It was a harmonious-sized little place that could handle just a small handful of guests at any one time; more than idyllic when compared to some of the gruesome party hostels that habituate the big cities, across the world. The last thing one wants after a battling day on the road is to get vomited upon by a drunk, greasy 18-year-old backpacker on a gap year.

Once in a 24-man rat infested dorm in Perth, Australia I witnessed a fellow Englishman piss himself in his sleep. From his bed, he was somehow able to direct his heavy stream of urine out of the side of his shorts and directly into the mouth of the neighbouring passed out Irishman. True story!! This was a sickening reminder of what some of the world's hostels have to offer.

Yet, here in Himeji, I felt a long way from all that sort of tomfoolery, and I for one was glad. Amen.

STATS

Dates: 25/07/2014 – 26/07/2014
Total miles traversed: 3,919 miles
Total time in the saddle: 401 hours and 38 minutes

23. OKAYAMA
岡山県

Himeji – Okayama
56 miles

The sky today was overcast, blocking out the sun's keen intensity. There was still an element of stickiness to the day but, with the sun in hiding, it made my surge fourth into Okayama Prefecture all the more durable.

Rural life was becoming a common sight again, after days of passing through a vast concrete sprawl that seemed to stretch all the way from downtown Kyoto some 80 miles away. I was now entering Chūgoku, the western most region of Honshū. If I cycled to the south of the current prefecture, I would be able to gain entry via ferry to Japan's third main island, Shikoku.

I spent the day in Okayama city, a more than copacetic and liveable city with its handsome black castle and popular Kōraku-en gardens. The girthy Asahi River splits up into varying courses and these flow elegantly around the city, under a number of causeways.

A man who would call Okayama his home would also claim the right to be my Couchsurfing host for the night. Bryan was an American from America, Kansas to be precise. Now in his early thirties, he had settled here as an English teacher, some eight years previously, with his then wife. They did some sex and made young Eddy, whom Bryan still looked after. However, Bryan didn't want to talk about his former wife – so we didn't. He had just recently mortgaged himself a charming little traditional Japanese home: *tatami* flooring, *shoji* sliding doors and lots of wood, you know the drill. The three of us sat upon the porch in some deckchairs, tucking into some home-made burgers. Bryan and I had beers and young Eddy supped a glass of milk. Bryan seemed content and happy to be in Okayama, as did his son who was full of questions about life.

He still though needed to be reminded a good four times that it was time for his homework; each reminder leading him to eat his burger with increased sluggishness. Eddy is a wise one, he'll go far.

Okayama – Naoshima
47 miles

The morning started slow; my solitary rear mud guard and brakes annoyingly chaffed my rear tyre as I headed west, out of Okayama. Love diminished fast for mud guards on this trip, yes they repelled a certain amount of water and random street guff, but at the same time when it was absolutely pissing it down as tends to be a common trend in Japan then one inescapably ends up getting soaked to the bone and filthy regardless. Finding some shade, I spent an hour or so fine tuning my bike, before it was good to go again. After which, I was eventually able to make some good progress with my day.

Breaching farther into the morn, saw me ride through the Kibi Plains, here I would encounter a serene and traffic free cycle route that threaded through a cluster of rice paddies. The scenery was dotted with shrines, temples and burial mounds – which dated back to somewhere around the 4th Century. The area was known as the Kibi Kingdom, and it spawned the Japanese folklore legend Momotaro, a.k.a. 'Peach Boy.' A name well known across the country as Peach Boy featured in his own comic book and TV show. If you're not an Anime icon in Japan, then you're most certainly not a legend.

The story goes that one day an old woman was milling about down by the river, when a giant peach came floating past. Catching the peach, she rushed home with it to show her lumberjack husband. The childless couple eagerly prised open the giant peach, to discover a little boy hidden inside the core. The boy told them he had been sent from heaven as a gift to them. The elderly couple named the lad, Momotaro (Peach Boy), and raised him as their own.

The middle part of the story is a tad hazy, but one can only assume that he was a law abiding Peach Boy. Although some critics have gone as far as to say that the heavenly gift was a little bit of a work shy freeloader, but I for one don't always believe everything that I read, do you? Well anyway, when trouble did rear its ugly head, Momotaro was more than willing to get his hands dirty, especially when it came to demons – which he hated. The dirty demon scum had overrun an island called... Demon Island, and so hence forth Momotaro would take the law into his own hands and with the aid of a monkey, a dog and a... pheasant, set off to Demon Island. Upon seeing the demons' back to Hell, Momotaro confiscated the entire stash of the demons' treasure from their fort and gave all the loot to his parents. From that day forward, everybody lived happily ever after. So, I'm guessing in a roundabout way the morale of the story is too be good to your parents because of everything they have done for you, essentially this can be achieved by raping and pillaging other people's homes and then giving all of the spoils to them as a gesture of respect and thanks. Well, something like that anyway.

The plains ended at the small city of Sōja, and from there I negotiated some bulky traffic, as I trailed southerly alongside the Takahashi River. At Kurashiki, an old trading quarter once governed by the Shogunate, stands a series of bleached-white, rice storehouses. They now function as museums and touristy boutiques, a reminder of the towns importance of yesteryear.

Just a woodpigeons queef away from the elegant Bikan historical quarter, lies a noisy, dirty and venomous lorry-cluttered road. A road that would eventually quieten down, allowing me to sweat my way south across a cheeky bunch of mountains, towards Uno.

I had to act fast upon my arrival at the port of Uno, as a ferry to Naoshima was close to disembarkation. And so, with haste, I purchased myself a ticket and wheeled myself over to the council-housed sized vessel. In 20 minutes, I found myself on the shores of Naoshima, a land of modern and contemporary art, pristine beaches and more importantly... James Bond!

STATS

Dates: 27/07/2014 – 28/07/2014
Total miles traversed: 4,022 miles
Total time in the saddle: 412 hours and 38 minutes

24. KAGAWA
香川県

At Miyanoura Port I was greeted by a massive artificial red pumpkin. The 12ft-tall larger than life incarnation of the popular cultivar, was modelled by Yayoi Kusama. This was to be the first of a plethora of public art installations that I'd see. Various artists from across the globe found themselves indulging in the Naoshima project; whereby art and Nature are simultaneously fused as one.

In the early 1990's the island of no more than 3 square miles in size (and 3000 inhabitants), underwent an overhaul. This once dwindling island, known for its copper smelters and polluted fishing industry, would be propped up by the introduction of the Mitsubishi eco-friendly metal recycling plant. More interestingly, it established a mass scale art scene, funded by the publishing tycoon and chairman of the Benesse Corporation, Soichiro Fukutake. What started off as a few small scale art projects, would duly grow over the course of two decades into an aspiring art Mecca; attracting the attention of both artisans and art lovers alike.

At the information desk in Miyanoura, I enquired about camping sites. I was politely scoffed at; the receptionist slowly crossing her arms at me to reveal that she too was a budding West Ham supporter. It was too hot and humid for fun, so I decided not to rise to the occasion and thus settled for a guesthouse just a short distance from the port. Dumping my belongings at my digs, I decided to take a leisurely stroll. And it wouldn't take me long to find exactly what I was looking for... Bond, James Bond.

An ominous looking white-walled building with a couple of James Bond posters lured me inside. I'd read about it on the Internet and it had always seemed like a slightly surreal place in which to have a 007 Museum. Inside, it was no bigger than your average village hall, yet instead of a solemn set of faces, sat in a circle of plastic chairs craving the bottle, there was an invariably pro-Connery affair. An array of film posters and glass cabinets full of Bond memorabilia decked the halls: manuscripts, guns, action figures, nude pictures of Bond girls, novels in a multitude of languages and a copy of the January 7th 1966 edition of 'Life' magazine. This featured Sean C. in a ripped gimp suit, chest suggestively exposed. Sean aside however, the main emphasis was on Raymond Benson's 2002 Bond novel 'The Man with the Red Tattoo,' which sees Bond return to the Japanese archipelago for the first time since Ian Fleming's 1964 novel 'You Only Live Twice.'

Storyboarding for the Benson novel surrounds the outer walls of the hall, along with a cheesy low budget film adaptation playing on loop in the corner of the room. In the story, Bond is on the hunt for a ruthless terrorist assassin who is knocking off a number of important diplomats - with a deadly virus. The search takes him to little old Naoshima – hence the reasoning for the museum's general existence as a very promptive sort of petition to get the next fully fledged Bond film officially bought to the island. So James, what are you waiting for? Naoshima's calling… pick up the phone.

Naoshima – Takamatsu
20 miles

Heading east across the island from Miyanoura, I ventured towards a day of contemporary artistic infusion and confusion. Then I became mud guard-less. Ascending a brief and desolate hill, my mud guard would again frustratingly begin to catch upon the rear tyre as the heat was allowed to dictate my impulses as I dismounted from my vessel to manhandle the rear guard beyond recognition. Now though, as an added bonus, my rig was now a fraction lighter, my hot-headedness clearly paying off, well… sort of.

The island's east revealed Honmura; a sleepy fishing hamlet with a big artistic presence. A number of once-abandoned homes are now new-fangled art house projects. A little farther south, lay the grounds of Benesse House and the ChiChu Art Museum. There I found a garden of animal sculptures, piles of obscure metal objects and another one of Kusama's pumpkins, this time yellow. Close by was an idyllic and well maintained beach; the sun glittered fanatically on the inland sea. The area looked like a cross between something out of the 1960's TV show 'The Prisoner' and a wily hideout for a surrealist Bond villain. *Pick up the phone James, pick it up!*

I wouldn't actually be able to cycle up the hill that led to the Benesse Museum, as a security guard turned me away. Nevertheless, I proceeded the rest of the way to the pricey museum on foot. Now I'm a terrible artist, but when I look at works such as a staircase leading to nowhere, an all blue canvas simply entitled 'Blue,' a heap of deteriorating wood and a set of completely bollocksed pots and pans - I often find myself quite confused. Am I actually looking at contemporary, innovative works of art – or pieces of garbage. Was that reaction though the point of contemporary art? If so, then I was missing the point, entirely.

'*Did you like that, Dan*?' I thought to myself.

'It was all right.'

'*Wanna go on a boat, mate*?'

'YEAHH!!!'

'*Come on then…!*'

And off I trundled.

The ferry to Takamatsu, Kagawa's capital city, took about an hour. I spent the duration nervously eyeing a map of the rather mountainous Shikoku and snapping photos… of the rather mountainous Shikoku.

To head directly through the sparsely populated central mountains in the current heat seemed like a suicide mission; the coast would have to be the way to go.

Coming down the gangway off of the ferry and onto dry land, my front brakes decided to fall to pieces; instantly draining any feel good vibes. In the melting sun, with a pounding headache, I stood aside the rather vulgar 151-metre high Symbol Tower, the apparent 'Symbol' of Takamatsu. It was there that I re-re-fixed my brakes and began to head east.

My mood then became really quite terrible and I began to feel extremely negative. Passing a shopping complex, I noted a cinema and saw that Godzilla was showing. To not watch Godzilla in the nation that spawned the great beast seemed to me like a great insult. And considering my rather charmless mood, I wagered that it might also cheer me up, somewhat. So... for some 2 hours, I sat in a cool darkness, mindlessly watching a modern-day telling of the King of Monsters. The carnage was strangely soothing, for a while, anyway.

When the film had finished it was dark outside, yet still as humid as hell. It was time to search for a stealth camp; my first in over a week. I cycled the coast for 5 miles, until I was on the fringes of Takamatsu. There I found a truckers' rest stop; a number of big rigs lined up in a car park, whilst their engines chugged away idly, air cons blazing and cab curtains drawn. *Come morning, the car park would be silent and littered with tissues and pornography.*

Just to the side of the truck stop was a small park; a locked chain across its pathway entrance. Accidentally on purpose, I slipped through unnoticed. An out of service steam engine sat in the park, accompanied by a defunct station platform. Casting my eyes out to sea, a storm was well in the works, if it should head inland I would be sheltered. Satisfied with my find, I set up camp.

Sleep though, rarely came, the humidity too much to bear as I could scarcely breathe inside my tent. Unzipping the tent door, welcomed an army of mosquitoes. Zipping up again, I trapped a handful of the bloodsucking freaks inside with me, as I flapped about in the dark - in order to disperse them one by one. However, this activity was only making me sweat even more freely. When I thought that I'd finished with their extermination, I lay down to stew in my own juices. Breathing heavily, I felt that a meltdown was imminent. I closed my eyes.

Takamatsu – Tokushima
50 miles

'WWWWWEEEEEEEEEEIIIIIIIAAAAAA!!!!' another mosquito whizzed past my ear.

'Right that's it!' I proclaimed. I'd had enough, I looked at my watch, 3:30am. But it didn't matter, I was packing up camp, regardless; exhausted, angry and disgustingly sweaty.

I cycled a short way in the darkness, before deciding that it might be a good idea to do a video blog. Finding a reclining iron bench, I lay back on it, as if I was on some kind of medieval psychiatrist's couch. There I fumed and rather bleakly talked about how the heat was beginning to get to me, wearing me down and demoralising me. I was actually very angry. And that after some four months on the road the notion that I didn't actually have to be here was beginning to take a hold. *What was I doing anyway? What the actual fuck was I doing? Who does this? To what end or cause?*

I just didn't have to be there, robbing myself of the luxuries of home with my great family and friends. Not to mention: a permanent roof over my head, an Xbox and a solid double bed with a mattress, a daily bath/shower, fish and chips, Melton Mowbray pork pies, Ben's Cookies and my beloved West Ham United.

However, the fact of the matter was that I was there, doing what I was doing and I couldn't stop - even if I really wanted too. I just couldn't. The fuming did help though, as un-poetic as it was, it needed to happen. Watching the footage back, I'd somehow fall asleep with the camera on my chest, completely drained.

About an hour later, I awoke, with dawn just about to break I found myself covered in a new set of mosquito bites. Fuming, I packed my camera away, then bumbled bleary eyed and itchy over towards my bike.

Encircling Shido Bay I was rewarded with one of the grandest of sights of being up so early. The sun was beginning to climb from the east, casting a delicate glow across the inland sea and outlining the rugged interior of craggy islands and islets. It was quite simply, beautiful. I tried a smile on for size, but it hurt.

An elderly fisherwoman passed me by with a bucket full of crabs, an even earlier riser than myself, no doubt.

'Kirei ne?' she remarked, beautiful isn't it?

'Sou desu ne!' I replied, it is - isn't it?

The moment calmed me and allowed that much needed smile to coax my face. Feeling more positive, I journeyed away from Kagawa, Japan's smallest prefecture.

STATS

Dates: 28/07/2014 – 30/07/2014
Total miles traversed: 4,092 miles
Total time in the saddle: 419 hours and 40 minutes

25. TOKUSHIMA
徳島県

With the ocean over my left shoulder and the bulk of Tokushima's 80% mountainous land mass to my right, I was all set for some steady progress. Shots of caffeine at regular intervals played a crucial part in allowing me to attain full consciousness at the helms. Without this most perfect drug I would surely be done for.

En route to Naruto, I began to encounter a phenomenon that one can only associate with Shikoku, the *Shikoku Henro* - 'The Shikoku Pilgrimage'. Spend long enough on the island and you can't help but notice pilgrims plying the roads of cities and countryside alike, donning white garbs, wicker hats, with a walking stick and very little else. These pilgrims are retracing the footsteps of Kōbō-Daishi, the founder of Shingon Buddhism, who some 1000 years previously committed to a 750-mile trudge across the island. To mark the way, there are 88 temples spread across the island; the pilgrims will stop at each temple to pray before moving onto the next. The whole ordeal takes roughly 50 to 60 days to walk and is completed by people from all walks of life, who are maybe looking to reflect upon their lives and discover or re-discover what it is that makes them tick.

Naruto brought me to Ryōzen-ji, a temple that due to its close proximity to the sacred mountain of Mt. Koya - lying across the Kii Channel on neighbouring island Honshū - is considered both the starting and finishing point for the island's pilgrimage. In Ryōzen-ji, one can find many a pilgrim bantering about their journey and either preparing or congratulating one another for the road ahead or the road just conquered. The city of Naruto itself though about as exhilarating as nits, its only other draw being the whirlpools across the strait, between the city and the neighbouring Island of Awaji.

From Naruto, the traffic congested all the way into the heart of Tokushima City; a city again that pulls no real punches. It is known for its indigo dye industry and its Awa Odori dance festival, that attracts over a million tourists each August, for a massive dance off. At the back-end of July though, the streets were empty, trailing along endlessly in a copy and paste fashion, numerous 'No Bicycle Parking' signs dotted about to which I had no choice but to be offended by.

I would spend the night with Miguel, a food nutritionist student, self-confessed Lady Gaga fan, and Couchsurfer from sunny Spain. We went to a local izakaya for beers and snacks, the usual crowd habituating the vicinity; the loud unnecessarily raucous laughter of pissed-up salarymen, accompanied by the uncomfortable false laughter of their female counterparts.

Whilst tackling a deep fried chicken cartilage, Miguel informed me that he had hosted another cyclist just the previous night; an American who was planning to do the Shikoku Pilgrimage via pushbike. This not only impressed me but also put a crazy little idea into my head. What if I encapsulate an achievement within an achievement, by not only cycling to every single prefecture across the nation, but also by cycling to all 88 temples of the Shikoku Pilgrimage! I thought about it over a couple more beers, amongst the izakaya's white noise, before finally coming to a conclusion. 'Nah!'

Tokushima – Ikumi
65 miles

I slept well in Miguel's air-conditioned apartment; recuperating handsomely from the previous night's lost sleep. Having a late'ish lie in, I left Tokushima at around 8am.

245

By 8:10am, the furnace of the sun had reduced me to nothing more than a fleshy puddle of sweat. An hour or so later, I'd reach the Tachibana Bay thermal power station of Anan. A huge metal rod towered up, fingering the sky, accompanied by the groan of industry, it was gross yet somehow intriguing.

As I stopped to gawp, a man came over to say hello, before ushering me into the cool of his portacabin office. There he and his colleagues fussed over me by showering me with cold drinks, food and souvenirs for the road – and, most importantly, a paper fan. Another random but welcome act of kindness to add to the ever growing tally of random and welcome acts of kindness. It is said that in Shikoku one can encounter some of the best hospitality in all of Japan, and with some 5000 pilgrims walking across the island every year, the locals will often be seen presenting the pilgrims with home-made rice balls, local fruits and treats, some even offer a roof for the night.

Further south along the coast, in the town of Minami, I met one such pilgrim. Stopping by the town's train station to fill my water bottles, a young Californian approached me and kindly asked where I was headed. I reeled off my tale and he revealed his. He planned to head to all 88 temples of the Shikoku Pilgrimage - via bicycle. It was then that I realised that we both had a mutual Couchsurfing friend! The young Californian's story however did not end well - just two days into his journey, he had decided that he'd had enough and was returning back to the States – via Miguel's pad. He confirmed that he hadn't quite realised just how physically demanding the journey was going to be and just how ridiculously hot it was going to be, either. Admitting his lack of preparation, he vowed to return home, do his homework properly, and the following year return. I hazarded a guess that this little promise would never come to fruition, yet I hoped that I was wrong.

Towards the afternoon the coastal route got a little more ropey, heading into Shikoku's rugged interior for a while - before eventually emerging towards a coastline of numerous switchbacks. A wind was on the rise now, as the once crystal clear skies became blotted with cloud cover - allowing for some cool climes. The waves along the coast also became more intimidating; the beaches enticing droves of surfers who now piled joyously into the blue. I myself would sneak across the border into Kochi, my third of Shikoku's four prefectures.

STATS

Dates: 30/07/2014 – 31/07/2014
Total miles traversed: 4,157 miles
Total time in the saddle: 425 hours and 1 minute

26. KOCHI
高知県

Tucked just over the border is the quaint little coastal hamlet of Ikumi. Here I would meet Satoshi, a tomato farmer from Yokohama. I'd been in contact with him via a website called Warmshowers, the website - although nowhere near as popular as Couchsurfing - offers up a similar policy and is purely dedicated to tour cyclists. Satoshi, an avid tour cyclist himself - having cycled for 6 months across Central and South America - was more than willing to put a roof over my head for the night. He lit up a barbecue upon my arrival and offered me a can of beer, which I snatched away from him like a dehydrated alcoholic.

We both then proceeded to chat enthusiastically about our days in the saddle. Satoshi had decided that the city life was not for him, so took up residence in the thinly populated Kochi Prefecture, opting for the quiet life. Kochi, although the largest of Shikoku's prefectures, is covered in 84% forest and houses just a little over 750,000 inhabitants - making it the 3rd least populous prefecture in Japan. I asked him if he yearned to be back in the saddle?

'No,' his reply was swift and assertive. We both laughed.

Ikumi – Kochi
84 miles

Over breakfast, Satoshi informed me that I should be on my guard as there might be a typhoon making landfall over the next couple of days. Kochi is completely exposed to the Pacific Ocean and is often prone to the full brunt of typhoons. And on this morning - with the skies moodily overcast and the coastal waters dramatically battering the coast - the onset of a forthcoming climatic disturbance became more than obvious.

As I journeyed south toward Cape Muroto, I saw that the prospect of storms was not deterring the surfers who were either ridiculously brave or extremely stupid. But then, what did I know? For I was about to cycle directly into the path of a typhoon.

The gradient south, being mostly flat, allowed for an encouraging ride. I even saw wild monkeys for the first time in Japan. Oh sorry, Japanese Macaques. A bulk of them milled about on the sides of the road as I slowly passed them by. They seemed non-fazed by my presence at first, a couple giving me a curious eye, but nonetheless continued on with the business of de-fleaing one another, and hurling their babies about. It was only when I stopped to get out my camera, that I was suddenly alone again, the entire fleet scurrying up into the mountains. Shrugging my shoulders, I wheeled on.

Edging around Cape Muruto, with the wind by my side, I surged toward Kochi City. A city about as appealing as Tokushima and Takamatsu by being about as equally unappealing as Tokushima and Takamatsu! The looming grey skies did not aid the city's stance in the slightest. Although I did read that the women of Kochi are a force to be reckoned with. Locally referred to as *Hachiki* - meaning eight testicles - they are said to possess the ability to be able to drink booze to the humble equivalent of four men. Something I would have liked to have witnessed, but then the thought of an approaching typhoon suddenly shook me out of my new quest. I would need shelter tonight, camping out would be too distressing.

Asking around, I found that there were two guesthouses in town. Scoping both out, I was doubly disappointed to find that they were both fully booked. And, as light began to fade, it began to rain terribly. I sought a temporary refuge under a railway flyover and began to sulk.

I would have been in trouble if the typhoon had hit whilst I mooched around trying to make a stealth camp; I'd need some Internet to find out its exact course, as winging it along the coast could well see me towards a complete smattering. Unfortunately, Shikoku boasts absolutely zero 7-Eleven's, which effectively limited my connection to the World Wide Web, I would have to find an Internet cafe.

After an hour or so, the rain relented somewhat, allowing me to head out in search for the Internet superhighway.

Internet cafes in Japan are often referred to as 'Manga Cafés.' Here one can purchase their own private booth with a computer workstation, widescreen monitor, futon with accompanying blankets and pillows, wanking tissues, slippers, unlimited tea, coffee, soft drinks, ice cream and more comic books and porn than the most depraved of sex zealots could possibly dream of spaffing too.

Generally, I'd been a little bit standoffish in my approach to them, having never ventured inside one, I guess the unknown had seen me garner a certain sense of intimidation towards them. Yet, despite the journey that I was undertaking, I did still sometimes find myself struggling to engage with certain elements of Japanese society. This was a massive mistake as the whole process of checking into a said Manga Café couldn't have been any easier. Finding one such café in the city's suburbs, I parked my bike up outside, wrapping it up with my tent's fly cover sheet. 'Goodnight my friend,' I whispered, before venturing into the café.

Inside, I was greeted kindly by a bewildered looking receptionist; readjusting her glasses, she offered me a laminated list of options. It felt sordid, but right. The writing was in an incomprehensible jumbo of Japanese, yet with the lucrative aid of photographs, I was able to make my selection with ease. For 8 hours I could get a booth for a tenner. Bargain. Being shown to my booth, I quickly made myself at home and checked the Japanese Meteorological Agency's website for any information I could find on the upcoming typhoon. On a map of Japan, the whole of Shikoku was lit up red, this indicated a regional warning.

'Oh dear, oh very dear!'

Kochi – Matsuyama
89 miles

No longer considered a typhoon, but still an unprecedented threat, 'Severe Tropical Storm Nakri' - as it would become known - was bang on course for Shikoku. According to the Japanese Meteorological Agency, it could well be with me by lunchtime. This would lead to a change of plan, as traversing the coast would now be deemed suicide, yet so could my other option - the mountains. The Shikoku range to my north had long been something that I would have rather avoided, but with limited opportunities for a roof over my head, Matsuyama would be my only chance of refuge during the onslaught of a severe storm. Reserving a room online at a guesthouse, would however officially condemn me to the mountainous task ahead.

I slept for a few hours in the Manga Café, getting up shortly before dawn to prepare myself. It was humid outside and still dry. Heading out early enough would ideally see me halfway through my journey before the storm caught up with me. I crossed my fingers.

One mile later, it was pissing it down. I sought shelter under the eaves of a Lawson's convenience store in the town of Ino, where I took it upon myself to get some breakfast. After a short wait and with two coffees drained, the rain suddenly ceased. Quickly I hopped back in the saddle with a bag of donuts and progressed a little further. Just five minutes on, and it was pissing it down again. This time I found refuge at Ino's train station. The rain was so heavy that I literally had to ditch my bicycle to the ground in the station's car park, whilst

251

I ran inside the station and under cover – myself clearly taking precedence. I also had to keep my donuts dry.

Thunder cracked above as the mountain tops to the north became shrouded in a grimy, dark mist. I watched for about 10 minutes; the rain relentless. I took a seat in the waiting room, trying to read my book. It was going to be a long day, this much I already knew.

As the heavy rain persisted, my reading suddenly became disrupted by the sound of an air-raid siren blaring out from somewhere in town. This was alarming to say the least and at first I had no idea what it meant; there was no one in the train station to ask. I went and looked outside, the rain was absolutely hammering the town. *A town doesn't just simply issue a warning siren for no good reason.* Logic told me that 'Severe Tropical Storm Nakri' had already landed.

I cursed my luck and went back to my book, reading the same words over and over again. My brain refused to process anything, so I gave up. After an hour, the rain would reluctantly clear up, and with it the warning sirens faded. I made a break for it.

I played hide and seek with the rain for the next 4 hours, as I coerced myself further north through a valley, alongside the Niyodo River. Its banks swelled up fast; huge tree branches, plastic materials, car tyres and other random items all floating rapidly down the river. Farming plots by the banks of the river were beginning to flood, as water levels crept up to the doors of a row of parked farming vehicles. Things were getting pretty wild.

Approaching the town of Ochi, the randomly dispersed lashings of rain were now beginning to catch me out. A tunnel though saw me catch a break momentarily, before earmarking my next disaster for the day.

Route 33, which should have guided me all the way to my destination of Matsuyama, was cordoned off. This wasn't good, not good at all. A series of luminous yellow and orange road blocks stood in my way, along with a traffic controller in a big white anorak who was waving his baton at me as I closed in on him. He was already shaking his head; I knew my chances of getting past him were going to be nigh on impossible.

'*Matsuyama ni ikitai,*' I said hopelessly. I want to go to Matsuyama.

'*Kono michi shimete desu,*' he replied, lifting up his arms and showing me his irons; rain dribbling furiously from the hood of his mac. This road is closed.

'*Hmph…demo, ima nani wo shimasu ka?*' I asked. Hmph…so what do I do now?

'*Err…chotto matte kudasai,*' he turned and went to find a colleague.

Being some 20 miles north of Kochi City now, I was adamant that I would not return, I'd rather shit myself at my own wedding, than cycle back upon myself now. I'd already come too far.

I watched two men in their huge white anoraks have a debate in the pouring rain. There were lots of words and head shaking and when the traffic controller returned, I already knew the answer. Up came his arms again to form a big 'X,' thou shall not pass.

'*Gomen nasai,*' said the traffic controller, sympathetically.

I huffed a little but it wasn't his fault, he was just the middle man and there was a damn good reason why the road was closed. In the mountains of Japan, landslides, flooding and death are frequently rife during periods of heavy rainfall. Yet here I was, the stupid idiot, trying to get in, knowing the risks that I could face.

I retreated back to the nearby tunnel where, under shelter, I pulled out my map book. Running my finger down the index page, I found Kochi Prefecture, page 26. Quickly darting to the supposed location of page 26, I could find only pages 24 and 29, everything in between bailing on me. 'Oh for fucks sake,' I bellowed out, my cursing echoing all along the tunnel, in sync to the rumbling of thunder. I threw the map book across the road and then quickly went and picked it up again. Maybe one day it might actually come in handy. Pissed off, I cycled a little further along into Ochi and found a convenience store and again some shelter from the endless lashings of rain.

Inside the *conbini*, I grabbed a map book from the magazine rack and stood in a row of variously aged gentlemen who were all reading comic books. The map book of course was all in Japanese, but with a little initiative I was able to find my current locale and, more importantly, a way out of my current predicament. As expected, it wouldn't come easy. A turning off just out of town would take me up onto a mountain road that seemed to zigzag across the Shikoku range for an eternity, before dropping back down onto Route 439. In theory this should guide me back onto the very much currently closed Route 33. It would come at huge peril of course, and before I set out I knew that it was going to be one hell of a gruelling task, many a mountain pass being in ill condition and rarely maintained. Signs would also be thin on the ground, often gifting an element of uncertainty to the actual road's destination. Also, these roads could be closed. *Why wouldn't they be*? Yet at 10am, having managed just 20 miles in some 5 hours, I still had some 70 more miles to achieve. I had to get moving. And thus my own stupidity would urge me forth. *Fuck it*, I thought. *I'm going to Matsuyama even if it gets me killed.* It being the biggest city in Shikoku, I'd still have to go there anyway - even in a body bag.

Finding the start of the Route 18 mountain pass would of course lead me to another road blockade. This was unmanned so I'd sneak past without issue.

It was a gentle ascent at first, the road narrow and well maintained, yet soon to be challenged by the return of some cumbersome rainfall. Torrents of water flushed out of the surrounding forests, forming rivulets on the road's surface, which I had to forcefully cycle against. Water now crashed down upon me from above and below; I wished I'd had some mud guards!

Thunder growled fearlessly from the rafters as the mountain road began to shrivel in size to something more consistent to a mountain path; becoming ever narrower, steeper, trickier and all the less inviting. I was beginning to wonder if paying heed to those initial warning sirens back in Ino might have now been a good idea. *A bit too late for that now.* No longer finding myself playing a game of cat and mouse with the elements - Mother Nature was now firmly in control, as she pissed all over me. Soaked to the bone, I couldn't possibly get any wetter, the only way now being forward, regardless.

My bike wasn't enjoying the occasion much either: a horrible creaking noise began to resonate from the front axle, my brakes absolutely drenched began to fail and the electronic display screen of my odometer was filling up with water fast - its numerical digits slowly fading to a nothingness. A certain stench of doom lingered upon the horizon, I certainly didn't want another Norikura Skyline incident.

The more I climbed, the more the road twisted and turned. Then, I came across a small settlement tucked away precariously amongst the mountains, that reeked of self-sufficiency. Rickety little houses bundled together tightly, alongside a cliff face - amongst tea plantations, rice paddies and varying other crops that ascended up high into the dreary mists above. An insanely attractive sight to behold in such extremes. I passed an old lady bent double to the side of the road, tending her crop; she was weeding with one hand and an umbrella in the other.

'*Konnichiwa,*' I offered upon passing.

She nodded back in kind, smiling sweetly with a toothless grin. She was as hard as nails.

Away from the settlement, I hit a fork in the road, each path no doubt leading to someplace mythical; unknown to mankind. Both paths were decrepit, extremely steep and completely void of signage, yet both tore off on a tangent, further into the remotes of the mountains. *Left, right, left, right...err...left! Probably!* My decision was made on gut instinct.

The old path was steep and covered in wet moss; my tyres began to lose traction, slipping often. It was now that I began to worry slightly, finding myself paying attention to every little noise that pitched out of the surrounding forests. The water oozed passively out of the sides of the mountain, bringing with it traces of earth and debris; if a landslide was going to happen, then this was the place, and if it did... I wouldn't be found for weeks.

The path wound on and on for what felt like hours and I was certain now that I'd completely lost Route 18 altogether. My imagination began to wander. Perhaps I'd stumbled into a time vortex along an old and mysterious samurai trading route of the Edo Period. *Would I lose my head to the blade of a rogue rōnin?* I sincerely hoped not. Eventually, when the path did finally begin to descend, my imagination gave way to great relief. I still didn't know exactly where it would lead me, and I had to get off my bike and walk down; as my brakes were now completely defunct.

Through a gap in the tree canopy, I just about made out some sort of village settlement in the valley below. And with that I upped the ante slightly. Sitting back on the saddle, I used the soles of my trainers to brake when necessary, more than once nearly flying off a cliff edge in the process. I could see civilisation though, and that psychologically bought with it an easing of mind; just like a McDonalds in a war zone. For now I was invincible.

As I ventured closer to the mountain village, I could hear a calamitous crashing of water. The river ran savagely through the village and from my vantage point, I could make out two bridges crossing the wild, wild river: one solid and stern, the other minuscule and feeble. I knew which one I would be crossing. The village itself was lifeless, its inhabitants either hiding in their homes or already evacuated to someplace safe; a common procedure come typhoon season in Japan.

The road wound down to the daunting riverside where there were some public toilets and a small shelter. Lunchtime. Despite being drenched through; my hands shrivelled like walnuts - I wasn't actually feeling that cold, the exorbitant humidity levels seeing to that, or perhaps it was just the adrenaline. Nonetheless, I still changed into some dry clothes and feasted on rice balls that I'd bought at the *conbini* back in Ochi. It was quite unsettling to be standing so close to the river's unabashed ferocity, but all the same it was an absolute spectacle and the noise it produced was completely deafening. On the opposite side of the bank was a house; the rapids just feet from its front door. The owner must have been shitting himself. If the whole valley was to be suddenly swept away it would've come as no surprise. And upon picturing the news headlines, I made haste.

The large bridge across the river was part of Route 439 and it just so turned out that I wouldn't even need to cross the bridge, but I would have to straddle through the valley, alongside the fearsome rapids. I knew at least though that I was headed in the right direction; that was some comfort.

Further ahead, I'd encounter another road closure sign with a picture of a uniformed man bowing in apology, and this was no comfort whatsoever. The road that was part of a descent towards the river, was more than likely flooded - yet to the side of the road was a notice board with a shoddy map indicating a diversion. Having no choice, I tried my best to follow it, as it led me down a narrow track way. Here I found myself steering around huge boulders and rubble that must have just recently tumbled down from the mountainside.

At the end of the track I came to the foot of a huge dam, and... a complete dead end. Shaking my head in disgust, I tracked back on myself. On my return, there was a man in a bright blue anorak taking photographs of the lairy rapids and we greeted each other. For a fleeting second I took my eye off the track; which cost me dearly. Running over a pile of landslide rubble, I heard a sudden pop and then a whoosh as all of the air from my front tyre was immediately expelled. This devastating blow was so very cruel. I looked back at the man in the bright blue anorak who had since returned to his water photography. In my devastation, I partially blamed him; my mood soured. Buckets of water now beat down upon me, as I began to feel a dull ache form at the base of my very soul.

Remembering a saw mill I'd passed along the track way, I wheeled my casualty there to carry out an operation under its limited shelter. The front tyre being buggered though was at least a marginal bonus, as opposed to the heavily laden rear. That would have just increased my time in the mountains, time I just didn't have. Studying my tyre, I came to the conclusion that I must have either ran over a shard of obsidian rock or a sea of knives, as my tyre revealed a great gaping tear whilst my inner tube had a laceration utterly beyond redemption. I quickly chucked in a new inner tube and made a mental note to get a new tyre ASAP.

I was feeling quite low by this point, but considering my predicament it was for the best that I didn't let any emotions get the better of me; they would have only worsened the situation and clouded my thoughts.

Heading back to the beginning of the track way, I assessed the discreditable Route 439 diversion map once again. Upon doing so some white smoke began to waft over my right shoulder towards the sign board; I was on fire! Oh no wait, no I wasn't, it was just the condensation from a creepy old man's warm breath – of whom stood directly over my shoulder.

'Ahh!! Where did you come from??!?' I blurted out in startled English.

He laughed, his accompanying umbrella also appearing to bob up and down in delight.

'*Daijoubu?*' He asked. Are you ok?

I confirmed that I was all right but just needed to find Route 33. He then pointed me in the direction of a bridge that crossed the river, telling me to go up a steep hill before turning left directly onto Route 33. I thanked the old man for his wisdom, before acting out his instructions. All of which went to plan as I branched left at an intersection and onto Route 33. There I'd find a signboard indicating 69 km to Matsuyama.

A sigh of relief was then duly in order as I trailed the Niyodo River toward the border of Ehime Prefecture. I still had a long way to go, but I'd been mucking around in the mountains for some 10 hours and sorely needed to find Matsuyama. Things were looking up. The rain even momentarily petered out, and then decided against that idea and started back up again.

A blast of thunder decisively put me in my place, or was that a mass landslide? *Shut up Daniel, just keep peddling!*

STATS

Dates: 31/07/2014 – 2/08/2014
Total miles traversed: 4,330 miles
Total time in the saddle: 441 hours and 27 minutes

27. EHIME
愛媛県

A feeling of déjà vu came over me as I approached another manned road block. I was now so deep in the mountains that I wouldn't have anywhere to turn, should they not let me pass. Through the heavy streams of rain I could barely see the traffic controller, but the orange baton he was waving around was depressingly obvious. Upon stopping in front of him, he showed me his dreaded forearms and a formidable shaking of the head. I decided that I couldn't speak basic Japanese anymore; it was just easier to appear as a tourist. So I started to chunter away in English, telling him how I needed to get to Matsuyama as I had nowhere else to stay and it would be unhealthy for me to have to go back. The traffic controller soon took a step back, he didn't have the foggiest as to what I was banging on about. Turning, he called over to a superior and explained that I was obviously a moron. The superior looked me up and down, his eyes a little wild. He wasn't happy. He asked me in Japanese if I spoke Japanese, I stupidly said no… in Japanese, quickly diverting away from this minute faux pas by pointing to the road ahead… and much like a cave man blurting out 'Me, go Matsuyama!' Before quickly pulling my best puppy dog face expression. The temptation to also throw in a quivering lip also present, but feared that that might well have been regarded as slightly over doing it somewhat.

The superior rubbed some water off of his forehead. '*Chotto matte*,' and returned to the hut by the side of the road to pick up a phone. His colleague then smiled at me enthusiastically. I repaid him with the exact same gesture before looking away awkwardly.

The sound of rain thrumming upon a close by building's corrugated roof top, intensified, as a sinisterly cold droplet of water ran the course of my spine, causing me to shudder, I would soon be completely soaked through again.

I looked back at the superior of whom was yapping away on the blower before turning a look back towards his colleague again. He was still smiling directly at me, looking like he could quite possibly explode at any second, it was odd. Again, I quickly diverted my eyes away.

Hurry the fuck up, I thought as I closed my eyes and began to shiver some more.

The next time I looked up, the superior was stood gravely before me.

'Ok,' he said as he moved a barrier to one side ushering me forward. *'Abunai yo!'* It's dangerous!

I nodded in agreement, it was.

As I proceeded further along Route 33, I encountered various farmsteads and settlements. The potential for a life changing natural disaster was merely a heartbeat away, yet for the inhabitants it was a way of life - they were truly living on the edge. Yet, despite the dangers on offer, having the road to myself would also gift a certain mystical charm to my surrounds - the area being a constant marvel to the eye, even more so in these Biblical conditions.

By the time I'd reached the town of Kumakogen - some 20 miles from Matsumoto - it was early evening and the rain was beginning to finally ease. Finding a *conbini,* I feasted like a gannet, safe in the knowledge that I should now make it to Matsuyama without the assistance of a body bag.

Whilst feasting, a mother and child combo walked past holding hands, the child looking at me in some sort of awe... or shock.

'Don't look at it!' Said the child's mother, probably.

I checked myself over, I looked like a drowned bear. The shivers were also now becoming quite unsettling. Jumping back on my bike I would participate in one last moderate ascent for the day and be rewarded with some captivating views across the city of Matsuyama.

Lights began to twinkle, like the turning on of some far distant galaxy. And with no vehicles to share the road with, the descent could be described as nothing more than sweet!

Just shortly before 10pm I found my guesthouse. I'd spent roughly 17 hours muddling through the rugged mountains of Shikoku - from one prefectural capital to another - and it would prove to be one of the most physically and mentally draining days of my journey thus far. I felt truly obliterated, but thankful all the same as things could well have been a lot worse... a lot worse.

I would later go on to learn that 'Severe Tropical Storm Nakri' bought with it record amounts of rainfall to Shikoku - 1,000 millimetres of the wet stuff being measured in Kochi Prefecture alone. That in one day equated to three times as much rainfall on average to what the prefecture would normally see in an entire month. Other news I would also learn - before going to bed – was that a Category 5 Super Typhoon was now in the process of barrelling its way towards the south-west of Japan with winds of up to 150mph. *Yay!!*

Matsuyama

Matsuyama was a breath of fresh air, when compared to the other three capital cities of Shikoku. The largest of the island's cities with over 500,000 inhabitants, it's a city beautified with an abundance of green space, pilgrimage temples, a steep hilltop castle and the rather special Dōgo Onsen. The mineral rich waters of the area have been known to the Japanese for well over a thousand years, and were said to have cured the ailments of a deity.

The Dōgo Onsen Honkan, the oldest bathhouse in the country - dating back to 1894 - is a three-story wooden building inclusive of a watchtower. This building became the inspiration behind the bathhouse of the spirit world in Miyazaki's timeless classic 'Spirited Away.'

A bulk of the sights, bar that of the castle were fairly close to my guesthouse, this allowed for some limited walking. For today, as a result of yesterday's trauma, was consequently a rest day and all forms of physical exertion were strictly off the menu. Beer however, wasn't.

Matsuyama – Onomichi
72 miles

Morning saw me around Ehime's coast, the climes lacking any hint of a typhoon with clear skies and a skin-blisteringly hot sun that would see me burnt red raw – when I had forgotten to apply sunscreen.

Trailing the coast eventually led me to Imabari, the last mainland city of Shikoku. From there - and across the Seto Inland Sea spanning some six islands - runs the Shimanami Kaido. This is a 40-mile long toll road for both cars and cyclists, connecting Shikoku with Western Honshū. It's a popular route once plundered by buccaneers and pirates between the 14th and 16th Centuries. Today, however, there is safe passage for cyclists from all walks of life.

The cycling route is some 6 miles longer than the actual toll road for motor vehicles; allowing one to concentrate on nothing more than one's fellow cyclists and the contrasting views across the inland sea from the island's interconnecting bridges.

Local fishermen cart their catch to neighbouring islands, as holidaying family's island hop - on rented bicycles. The weekend cycling enthusiast is also amongst them with his latest multi-Yen vessel - the type that love to stop and take pictures of their steeds in idyllic settings, which in turn seems to cause a strange set of stirrings within the never regions of their tight spandex shorts. Not that I was looking of course, I'd already had my lunch.

STATS

Dates: 2/08/2014 – 4/08/2014
Total miles traversed: 4,402 miles
Total time in the saddle: 448 hours and 22 minutes

28. HIROSHIMA
広島県

Ikuchi Island marks the beginning of Hiroshima Prefecture. Crossing the bridge from Omishima, I waved goodbye to Shikoku, as I cycled forth across the open expanse of the inland sea - in harmony with a gentle ocean breeze and a plenitude of spectacular island gazing opportunities.

Reaching Mukaishima, the 6th and final island of the Shimanami Kaido crossing, saw me fumble about amongst the island's interior until close to sundown. This island once saw 100 RAF Prisoners of War stationed here, after their dreaded journey from Indonesia on one of the Japanese's fearsome Hell Ships - the *Dainichi Maru.* These men would soon be joined by 116 American's, shipped in from The Philippines. Those that managed to survive the perilous journey were soon put to work and used as slave labour on the island's shipyards; many being worked to death or dying of malnutrition. Just a small chapter from the history of a prefecture that would eventually become synonymous with the build up to the end of World War II.

The final bridge connecting Mukaishima to Onomichi on the mainland was not suitable for cyclists, so I took a short ferry ride across a narrow stretch of ocean.

In Onomichi, I tracked down one of the most impressive guesthouses in Japan. A guesthouse seemingly poised in the past, sitting inside an aged shopping arcade that seemed as if it might slowly be gearing itself up for a long nap. From the outside, the guesthouse could quite easily be mistaken for a place of limited appeal, for in fact the fascia of the building is one of deception, a trend unique to the old townhouses of Onomichi. In an attempt to reinvigorate this part of town, this old townhouse - known as *'Anago no Nedoko'* (bed of an eel) stems back some 100 metres or so and has been renovated to a

265

traditional yet quirky standard. It contained a chic coffee house, kitchen, lounge area, garden and a number of comfortable dormitories.

It was a warm and welcoming place, in a town that is unrushed and more accepting to the slowness of time. I settled in for a couple of days as some heavy rain poured down around me - Typhoon Halong looming ever closer, its exact path still uncertain.

Onomichi – Hiroshima
65 miles

The day was uncomfortably muggy as I took the coastal road west to Hiroshima. The roads heavily congested bore me a number of issues. Punctures today came like buses, I received two simultaneously. I would also notice that the rear tyre had some wobble to it. Finding an inch of shade, next to a stinking toilet block infested with droves of red ants, I patched up my inner tube only to discover that my rear rim had split. It was of no surprise really, considering the abuse it had undertaken over the past several months. It had traversed nearly 4,500 miles, with over 100kg bearing down upon it every day. Essentially, this would just mean that a little shopping binge was in order when I got to Hiroshima.

The roads became ever more clogged the closer that I got to the city, a city that largely imprints upon many a people's minds when they think of the final days of World War II.

On the 6th August 1945, the American B-29 Bomber "Enola Gay", would pass over the city of Hiroshima, from its crew of 12 men only 3 of them knew the real purpose of their mission. I cycled through the beating heart of the city, through a number of vibrant shopping districts, past okonomiyaki joints, karaoke bars and high-rise buildings. I sped along tree clustered boulevards, past a bustling train station and across a network of bridges that oversee many of the city's six rivers that flow through it – all the time wondering how such a place could have virtually been wiped off the map.

'My God, what have we done?' were the words of Robert A. Lewis, co-pilot of the Enola Gay. For the Enola Gay carried what was known as "The Little Boy", a weapon of mass destruction – an atomic bomb - the first of its kind to be used in warfare.

South-west of the train station I came face to face with a ghost from the past. People gathered around it in a morose silence, looking on reflectively as an eerie three-storied structure with a domed roof stood stoically before them; with a sort of dreary pride. Once known as the Hiroshima Prefectural Industrial Promotion Hall, an exhibition hall designed by Czech architect Jan Letze in 1915, it today stands for something quite different. The Japanese refer to it as the *Genbaku* Dome, but the International community knows it as the A-Bomb Dome. It acted as the hypocenter of the atomic bomb's mass destruction. The Little Boy fell for some 43 seconds before packing a punch equivalent to 12,500 tonnes of TNT, a force so powerful that surrounding temperatures would rise to well over a million degrees centigrade - before burning up the surrounding oxygen and creating a fireball that would spread over a 1.2 mile radius.

The bomb killed 80,000 people instantly, some becoming nothing more than a set of shadows singed into the ground.

69% of Hiroshima would be levelled, the A-Bomb Dome being just one of the few central buildings to withstand the blast. Structurally anyway, for the building today sits scarred with twisted metal, stripped brick work and caved in walls; a constant and haunting reminder of the evils of war. Today that is its exact purpose alongside the Peace Memorial Park and its historically important museum.

It was a sombre experience, one I would share with not only the Japanese but with people from all across the globe. It is vital that we all learn from the difficulties of our past, for it is the only way to head into a peaceful future.

Seeing the pictures and video footage of the aftermath of the bomb in the Peace Museum - and moving around in today's modern city of Hiroshima with its 1.5 million inhabitants - gave me a hearty feeling. A city once broken and condemned to tatters, and yet exactly 69 years and 1 day on, the city stands firm. Having defied the naysayers that said the ground would be wronged with radiation for years to come, the people of Hiroshima have created a very forward thinking, prosperous and cosmopolitan city. A city to be proud of and a city that I would come to know quite well.

Having visited a bike shop in regards to my split rim (not as painful as it sounds!) I was told that they would have to get one shipped down from Tokyo which could take a few days. With that in mind - and a typhoon still fannying about in the Pacific, refusing to make up its mind - I would end up staying in the city for the better part of a week.

Hiroshima – Shunan
74 miles

Typhoon Halong, which I had been bracing myself for, never made it to Hiroshima, a front of heavy rain passed, but a brunt of the storm passing up through Kyūshū and Shikoku, wound up heading east - colliding heavily with the Kii Peninsula where it would cause widespread damage to Wakayama Prefecture.

The typhoon, killer of 10 people - soon weakened as it made way towards Siberia, where it would eventually fizzle out. Hiroshima wouldn't fully escape the evil doings of Mother Nature however, as exactly 9 days after I'd left the city, heavy rainfall in the area would lead to a devastating series of landslides to the north, causing one of the biggest tragedies of the year - claiming 74 victims.

Today was dry and overcast; I was eager to finally get moving again, for tomorrow I planned to be on Kyūshū, Japan's fourth main island. And with my new sparkly rim job (not as gross as it sounds!), a new tyre and a slightly expensive 'Made in Japan' waterproof odometer - with accuracy down to the millimetre and enough unnecessary functions to baffle the most constipated of tech-savvy whiz kids - I'd say I was more than equipped to tackle Kyūshū. There would be just one more main stop though, before I left Western Honshū for the penultimate time.

Miyajima, a small island just off the coast across the Onoseto Strait is home to the 16 metre high torii gate of Itsukushima Shrine. The gateway that climbs up prominently out of the sea gives the impression that the inland shrine - set a couple of hundred metres back - is floating, yet it is not. It is considered one of the 'Three Most Scenic Views of Japan.'

Hopping on a ferry I travelled over with a heap of other tourists, cameras at the ready. Many of us had reason to be thankful, as it was once forbidden for commoners to even set foot upon the island. Despite that rule long ago being overturned, there are still a couple of others that stand defiant. No one can give birth or die on the island, both are deemed incredibly impure to the deities of the Itsukushima Shrine. Again thankfully, I had no plans to do either of these today.

Disembarking from the ferry terminal, revealed a rather unusual spectacle. Walking amongst the humans were deer, completely fearless. The residential deer with no natural predators were seemingly living the lives of emperors and empresses. They had lost their affinity to the natural world and appeared to be at home with mankind. The deer only neared those who possessed nibbles though. Although the commoners are encouraged not to feed the deer, I feel that the animals' overall cute factor more than outweighs any human's morals. Mischievously, they rifled through unsuspecting handbags to munch on used tissues and lipstick, chewed people's hair, pulled at loose fitting clothing and pestered pretty much anyone in their direct path.

One small boy was reduced to tears as a deer had eaten his ferry ticket back to the mainland - the boy's father told him that he would have to remain on the island forever! The boy, very upset, tried to kick out at the deer who made a hasty getaway. Many a commoner pointed at the small boy and laughed, it was great.

Muscling through the crowds, I got my all-important snaps, stroked a deer and then headed back to the mainland to saddle up.

For the remainder of the day I'd traverse a shoddy road westerly, towards the considerably undesirable city of Shunan in Yamaguchi Prefecture. A prefecture I would have to visit again properly at some point in the future - upon my return from Kyūshū. Alas for just one night I'd find a park in the city to set up camp, my first stint of camping since that humid and restless night some 2 weeks previously on Shikoku.

It was still as humid as hell, but I had developed a new technique. Smothering myself in DEET and lighting two mosquito coils at the entrance of my tent, allowed me to spend the night un-pestered by the spawn of Satan - with the added allowance of some modestly fresh air. A Tom cat however poked its head in my tent at one point to see what was going on, observing me with disgust I snarled back at him sending the pervert scarpering back off into the night.

Come morning and I'd be getting the ferry to Kyūshū, but, for the moment, laying back upon my musky sleeping bag, I thought of my overall progress. Then I fell asleep with a gloating smile imprinted heavily upon my face.

STATS

Dates: 4/08/2014 – 11/08/2014
Total miles traversed: 4,541 miles
Total time in the saddle: 459 hours and 38 minutes

29. OITA
大分県

Shunan – Beppu
57 miles

The early morning ferry across to Kyūshū was a bit of a bruiser: rustic, noisy and completely battered. Only myself and a small handful of other fellow humans would be risking passage to Oita Prefecture's Kunisaki Peninsula - a remote area of farmland stemming down from the foothills of Mt. Futago, towards the coast.

On a map, the peninsula looks a little like the ball-joint of Kyūshū's femur; somewhat detached from the fractured socket of neighbouring islands', Honshū and Shikoku. I followed the perimeter of the ball-joint esque peninsula south - around the coast along its quiet country roads - all the way towards the popular tourist city of Beppu.

Approaching Beppu, one could perhaps make the mistake of thinking that the place had just been shelled. Vast plumes of white gas drifted up into the sky from all over the city, a scene that would repeat itself all the way up into the distant mountains. This was in fact steam, Beppu's big crowd-puller. For the volcanic belt that runs directly through the area - known as the Kirishima Range - contributes to some 2,800 hot springs throughout the region… the most in all of Japan. And if there's one thing that the Japanese truly adore, it is most certainly a good bath. Yet not all springs are for human submersion, especially not 'The Nine Hells of Beppu.' These hells, known in Japanese as *Jigoku*, are a collection of hot springs spread mostly across the mountainside, each yielding a varying myriad of colours and features - accompanied by a curious depiction of names. For example: 'Monster Mountain Hell,' 'Sea Hell,' 'Cooking Pot Hell,' 'Spout Hell,' 'Shaven

Head Hell , 'Golden Dragon Hell' and, most disturbingly, 'Bloody Hell!' The latter being a sickly blood red colour induced from the surrounding clay soils with steaming hot waters as spicy as 78°C.

Writings from the Edo Period dictate that this was the place of a number of barbaric human roastings, hence the reason for the water's bloody appearance. It was surprising to see how many tourists were jokingly pretending to push one another in. Standing next to the water's boiling edge I gulped at the thought of tumbling into Bloody Hell, it would have probably been a bit like the equivalent of falling into a pool of Xenomorph blood. A fraction too toasty for my liking.

All bloody hell'd out, I'd scale the steep mountainside down into the hub of the eggy stench of central Beppu. Here I became inspired to have a bath. Amongst the city's old and winding back alleys, I found a launderette with an adjacent pay as you go bathhouse. I quickly chucked my stinking clothes into the washing machine, before they self-combusted, and then popped next door for a soak. Sticking 200 Yen into a slot in the wall, an electronic door slid open, presenting me with my very own bathhouse. Well, I assumed it was all for me - as it was completely devoid of life. Inside was an extremely barebones affair in a dingy cell of a room, yet the water was piping hot and that's all that really mattered. I plunged in, committing myself to my standard 3 minutes and 24 seconds. It was celestial.

With my bath and laundry out of the way, I went to meet up with my night's Couchsurfing host. Tetsuo was a student at Beppu University and upon my arrival at his apartment was having a little party amongst friends. They conceded that they'd need as much help as possible in consuming some alcoholic beverages. In turn I would confirm with them that they'd found the right man for the job. And with that we all clanged our beers together and had ourselves a party, 'Kanpai!'

Beppu – Kamae Oaza Kusumotoura
81 miles

It had rained during the night, the ground still wet, stripping the atmosphere of its humidity. A temporary affair however, as by lunchtime the climes had scaled back up into the 30's and I was beginning to feel quite sick.

The previous night's alcohol consumption clearly had not aided my cause. Reaching the city of Tsukumi via a wretched, potholed tunnel - with some deep and nasty open drains to the sides of the road - I would take a short break in order to try and resurrect myself. I sat under the cool shaded eaves of a supermarket, next to a yakisoba marquee, its owner blasting out some southern rhythm & blues via a ghetto blaster. I sat for some time, the music gradually lifting my spirits. Grateful I purchased some yakisoba, it was the least I could do.

Back on the road and the first signs of the rice harvest became evident. The plants now a rich and golden colour making the paddies look like an ocean of gold. After months of meticulous and intensive labour that all-important payday now finally beckoned.

Pulling myself up into the mountains, it was more physically demanding than usual. The sun beat down in its standard and unforgiving fashion, the accompanying inland air was also completely static and without favour. My current state of weakness made my rig feel as heavy as it had ever felt; a slow puncture stealthily beginning to ease air out of the rear tyre was also a far from welcome acquisition. From the forests, the cicadas sawed away raucously, *were they mocking me*?

Eventually winding my way back towards the coast would see joy envelop. With very few curvatures in the roads descent to slow me down, I could cruise at a leisurely 35mph. I progressed along Route 368 at sea level, flanking Kawachi Bay. The bay a picturesque fishing hamlet, situated alongside calm turquoise waters. An old fisherman stood at the end of a jetty casting out his spinney, in hope of that big catch. An elderly lady sat close by on a veranda, reading; seagulls cackled high above and crabs scuttled across the road towards the water. Local youths swam; racing one another to a remote wooden docking platform amongst the bay. In my mind's eye a romantic notion saw me returning to this spot, in order to write my memoirs in peace. Alas it was not to be, a stuffy attic in Cambridge would have to suffice.

Farther along the coast, I found a truck stop with a seating area. I sat and wrote for a while and had a couple of beers - before setting up camp next to a toilet block for a night of limited sleep.

Kamae Oaza Kusumotoura – Miyazaki
91 miles

A couple of trucks arrived late and left their noisy engines running, whilst a parade of drunk girls stumbled about in the car park, screaming and shouting, seemingly in search of some trucker cock. At around 4am, a man was outside my tent, chucking his guts up, it was then that I knew it was time to make a move.

I screamed like a frightened virgin whilst packing away my tent, after being taken completely by surprise by a spider the size of a clenched baby gorilla's fist. It had fallen from one of the tent poles and onto the back of my hand. Its big fat juicy abdomen it's most alarming trait, almost making me shit my pants directly off their hinges. I hate spiders, I've always hated them. Several years earlier, whilst working on a dairy farm in Tasmania, I'd pulled on my pants, early one morning, only to discover a huge huntsman spider. To this very day I can still feel it groping my junk.

I shuddered as I gingerly packed the rest of my gear away. Forgetting about breakfast entirely, I journeyed south on an empty stomach.

It wouldn't be long before a sinister zig-zagging ascent was in order and I began to burn up calories that my body could

275

barely acknowledge. My only saving grace was the early start, the air still relatively cool would be joined by a light and comforting drizzle.

In the mountains, the rice plants were still green – I watched a farmer open up a hand-crafted sluice gate that allowed some more water onto his crop. Another farmer looked at his watch. In time he would reap the benefits of the land, just like his sea level counterparts. But for now, as I descended down from the mountains in order to penetrate my 30th prefecture, the farmers' would bide their time with patience; as amongst other fine-tuned talents, patience was a virtue.

STATS

Dates: 12/08/2014 – 14/08/2014
Total miles traversed: 4,770 miles
Total time in the saddle: 481 hours and 39 minutes

30. MIYAZAKI
宮崎県

Route 10 into Miyazaki City was knackered, bumpy and torturous. Its inhabitants, ruthless. A gran at one point emerging from a supermarket intersection would decide that I was a ghost and attempt to drive directly through me. In order to prevent myself from becoming embedded into the bitumen, I waved my hands about manically. Eventually noticing me, she'd slam on the brakes within a mere fraction from taking my life. Delicately, I swallowed a small lump that had consequently formed at the base of my throat. I then offered her a gnarly frown as she slowly began to sink down behind her steering wheel and out of sight.

Minutes later, whilst held up at a red light, I witnessed a motorcyclist smash right up the arse of a motionless minivan. The biker flew up and onto the roof of the van, before sliding back down again into a crumpled heap next to his bike. It looked bad, but both vehicles appeared to be unscathed and, within milliseconds, the motorcyclist was back on his feet again and picking up his bike.

There must have been something in the air in Miyazaki, giving its citizens the portentous ability to drive like crazies. And as I veered into the city, I keenly opted for the sidewalk, preferring my chances with the *mamachari* and pissed up and stuttering salarymen, to losing my spleen on Route 10.

Before the Americans gave the Japanese back Okinawa in 1972, Miyazaki was once the go-to place for Japanese holidaymakers and honeymooners. A pleasant climate with eye catching beaches in close proximity to a selection of scenic mountain ranges that would wow the masses for decades. Yet this string of success slowly began to deteriorate in the 80's - Its city centre slightly frayed around the edges, as it tries its best to wobble on gallantly from a drip feeding of summer migrants.

My Couchsurfing hosts lived to the west of the city and were incredibly difficult to find, with an address of multiple numbers and confusing Kanji that saw me navigate through a concrete jungle of identical looking apartment blocks, whilst I frantically scratched my head in frustration - until it bled.

It was only when I overheard the words 'Pokémon Yellow' disperse from over a balcony in an American accent, that I knew I'd found my hosts. Knocking on the door to their fourth floor apartment, I'd meet Pete and Beatrix, two American English teachers from Virginia. Pete was really excited, as the young couple had only just moved into their apartment and its previous tenant had left a heap of his belongings behind. Amongst them, the classic Game Boy game 'Pokémon Yellow'.

'Good find,' I commended. 'Didn't by chance happen across any tentacle porn, did you?' I queried.

'Not yet man, but one can only hope!' replied Pete, good willingly.

Beatrix poured us all some green tea, as we filled each other in on our respective lives. The couple had married some two years previously and had spent the majority of their married lives teaching in China. After deciding that China was not their cup of green tea, they decided to try their chances in Japan instead. And here they were. Having only been in the country a week or so, I could tell that they were both still buzzing with excitement about the road ahead of them. Watching a weather bulletin on TV, I wished I could have felt the same. For tomorrow saw heavy rain and thunderstorms across the region. I tutted drolly to myself as Beatrix proceeded to pour me out a refill.

'Good luck, man,' offered Pete, 'I'll be thinking of ya whilst I'm inside playing Pokémon Yellow!'

'Fuck you Pete, fuck you!'

Miyazaki – Miyakonojo
53 miles

Regardless of the Japanese public's diminishing attraction to Miyazaki, it's most famed prize of past and present, is Aoshima to the city's south. A small island measuring no more than 11 acres, it is surrounded in a delicate white sandy beach and interior jungle, which attracts a bulk of the prefecture's summer catchment of tourists. The island's central shrine is said to bring good luck to married couples and those desperate souls looking for a spouse.

Walking the perimeter. I dared not venture into the thick of the jungle; visions of marriage putting about as much fear in me as a huntsman spider in my pants copping a squeeze of my priceless crown jewels. *No thanks fella, not today.*

And in not paying my respects to the shrine, I would become instantaneously cursed. Less than a mile away from the island, I received a puncture to my rear tyre. Under the shade of an overpass, I patched up the hole and then proceeded west into the mountains. Another puncture happened, 6 miles later! In the car park of a 7-Eleven, I would again fix up another hole in the rear tyre before continuing.

Just 3 Miles later - whilst ascending a steep mountain - puncture number 3 struck. In general disbelief, I began to unload my rig in order to get to the rear tyre once again. On the hilly incline, by the side of a busy road, with a complete lack of shade, the sun beat down upon me maliciously. I became saturated in sweat, making the task in hand all the more difficult. I angrily ripped off my wet-rag of a t-shirt, and threw it to the ground in an act of provoked frustration. A car pulled up whilst I was in the process of assessing my inner tube, and a man reached out and gifted me two ice cold bottles of *pocari sweat* - a popular nationwide isotonic drink. This act of kindness soothed me somewhat.

Returning to the inner tube, I came to the conclusion that it was completely fucked, so I whipped in a new one and ventured onwards with caution. Yet this was to no avail, as 4 miles later another puncture decided to join the party, this time at the front.

'Un-fucking-believable!' I yelled, jumping off my bike and lobbing my crash helmet across the road in a strop.

I felt truly cursed, finding it bizarre that I'd managed to cycle for some three months at the beginning of my journey - receiving just the one puncture - and yet today I had traversed little over 15 miles and received four! Rotating the tyre, I noticed a big fat drawing pin embedded into it, a true classic. I wondered if I should have gone to visit the shrine on Aoshima, after all. Alas it was all too late to turn back now, the only way forward being westward in the direction of Miyakonojo.

The rest of the day's journeying would go without incident and by the time I'd pulled into Miyakonojo, my puncture grief was behind me; a distant memory from a questionable curse. My arrival in this border city (with Kagoshima Prefecture) was somewhat fluky, as the heavy rain and thunderstorms that had been due all day, were now just about gearing up to play their part.

I tracked down a Californian by the name of Seth and would become his first Couchsurfing victim in Miyakonojo, a city famed mostly for producing traditional archery bows from the area's abundant resources of bamboo.

Our greeting was short and sweet, for Seth had big plans for us. After I'd showered, we headed over to a local izakaya, there I would meet a vast contingent of his international English teaching counterparts. It being a Friday night - and the end of the schooling week - it seemed only natural that they should all get bladdered and talk utter smack, and that I too should become part of that said process.

Outside, an indignant yet fantastical storm unfolded, as thunder shuddered through the very foundations of our surrounds. A vast congregation of lightning bolts blitzed the skies; one bolt cracking off so loud and so close that it would make everyone inside the izakaya scream out like a bunch of end of day's mentalists. The rain soon flooded the streets, as, like my new found friends, I drank deep into the night.

I awoke with little memory of the night before. A notion that I'm led to believe is how any good solid drinking session should be orchestrated. It was nice to be part of these relatively normal transactions from time to time; the pressures of the road being eased somewhat by partaking in the traditional art of going down the boozer for a skinful and talking a pile of absolute dross. Even if the time spent was with complete strangers - it just didn't matter. That night we had a distinct narrative and purpose, and what better place to exploit that than down the pub.

STATS

Dates: 14/08/2014 – 15/08/2014
Total miles traversed: 4,823 miles
Total time in the saddle: 486 hours and 47 minutes

31. KAGOSHIMA
鹿児島県

Miyakonojo – Kagoshima
52 miles

It was a steady rise up into the Kirishima mountain range, away from Miyakonojo, where I would shortly cross into Kagoshima Prefecture.

Gliding down toward Kagoshima Bay, which nuzzles itself in between the prefecture's two peninsulas of Satsuma and Ōsumi – I saw the symbol of Kagoshima filling a triumphant void between the surface of the bay and all the way up some 1,117 metres into the troposphere.

I'd seen a number of volcanoes on my travels now, but the sight of Sakurajima was a striking one; an image that somehow I hadn't quite prepared myself for. As from the exact moment that the gigantic mass of rock hit my line of sight, it would give me something of a mental jolt. 'Woooaaaah!' I'd proclaim, doing my best Bill & Ted impression.

Sakurajima is considered one of Japan's most active volcanoes, averaging some 500 or so eruptions every year; in fact my previous night's Couchsurfing host, Seth, said that he could often hear and feel it rumbling away some 40 miles away, in Miyakonojo.

The last major eruption though was back in 1914 and it was so big that it ejected enough molten material to connect it from its locale as an island in the middle of Kagoshima Bay to the eastern peninsula of Ōsumi. Deaths are rare from the eruptions of Sakurajima, but throughout the year, the locals of Kagoshima City will have to contend with the vast quantities of falling ash emitted from its vibrant crater. The ash blocks out the sun and turns the skies grey, as it falls down upon the streets like a nuclear winter. The surrounding streets often have to be ploughed as the citizens don umbrellas to protect their skin and clothing from the hot ash. Yet, for the local farmers, this comes as a prized gift, for the ash makes their lands extremely fertile - enabling the production of some freakishly huge, radishes. I picture the farmers walking around the countryside stroking their prized veg like beloved pets and mocking neighbouring prefecture's for their ridiculously insignificant sized radishes. *You call that a radish? Now – this… is a radish!*

Today however, Sakurajima was on its best behaviour. Cycling from the north around the glistening bay - towards the city of Kagoshima - ensured that the great beast would never leave my sights. A sick part of me wanted it to blow its molten load, just so that I could boast about it to my friends on the booze-scene back home down the pub. *Shit!* To witness something as raucous as that may well have just seen me well on my way to a free packet of pork scratchings, or better still, a rimjob in the pub car park from a human! Alas, Sakurajima would contain itself, there would be no full English rim-jobs on my return to Blighty. What a shame.

With its prominent volcano and enchanting bay-side setting, the city of Kagoshima is often referred to as the "Naples of the East", being largely similar to the famous Italian city with its prolific Mt. Vesuvius. In fact, the two cities joined forces in 1960 to become sister cities.

Upon my arrival, the wide city streets were bustling with activity, serving up a positively flamboyant vibe. I had arrived during the *Obon* festival period, where families gather across the country to pay respects to the spirits of the dead. Amongst the festivities, lanterns are lit to help guide ancestral spirits in the afterlife. Graves are scrubbed clean, dances danced, food gormandized, alcohol guzzled and massive wads of fireworks are simultaneously spunked into the night skies. Because of the festival, I'd had trouble securing any accommodation, so opted for an Internet café - in the city's outer suburbs. This would set me in a good stance for progressing along the inner thigh of Satusuma Peninsula, the following day. From there I planned to take a short ferry ride across Kagoshima Bay to the neighbouring Ōsumi Peninsula - as I advanced ever closer to Cape Sata, the southernmost point of Japan's four main islands.

Kagoshima – Minamiosumi
35 miles

I trailed southerly alongside the shores of Kagoshima Bay, its lilac blue waters as calm as a grave. Reaching the tourist resort of Ibusuki, I would round Mt. Uomidake, its cliffs rising abruptly from the road side. The sun shone so brightly that I could barely look up towards its summit without wincing. Farther inland a wilderness of greenery spread itself across the mountains and far beyond the natural sight of any man.

Many flock to Ibusuki for its famed sand baths, where natural steams rise up through the volcanic soils, warming the surrounding sands and offering up an alternative therapeutic option. People here will be buried up to their necks in the sand, leading them to perspire excessively, the act said to enable good blood circulation. Yet, in the current climate of 33°C it seemed about as necessary as a kick in the bollocks before bedtime.

Veering on towards the Yamagawa ferry terminal, I made the crossing over to Minamiosumi on the Ōsumi Peninsula. The crossing gave me scope of the land that lay between myself and Kyūshū's most southern limit. A jagged backbone of mostly uninhabited mountains sprawled for just over 20 miles; resembling the spine of a sleeping dragon. Reports online invariably dictate that the ride from Minamiosumi to Cape Sata is a testing one, and from the middle of the bay it most certainly looked it.

I wouldn't have enough time to tackle the 40 mile round trip to Cape Sata upon my arrival in Minamiosumi, and so decided to spend the night in town. The only hostel was fully booked, so I opted for a small coastal park close by. Under the shade of a concrete veranda, I washed down with some wet wipes and then proceeded to set up camp for the night. The plan the next day was to rise early, in an attempt to beat the heat, which as always would try it's very best to dampen my spirits. But only if I let it, as with my heart still beating, I knew that it would take a lot more than just weather to stop me now.

Minamiosumi – Kagoshima
88 miles

A storm passed through during the night, bringing with it a heavy bout of rain, yet come morning there was little evidence left; the sun casually baked and dried up all traces of damp within its sight.

Leaving camp at around 6:30 I convinced myself that I was getting used to the heat – but, even so, I mumbled and cursed my way up into the mountains along a jaunty rollercoaster of a road. The route was quiet and traffic free; the deep impenetrable jungles to the sides of the road saw macaques clinging to palm trees and eyeing me wearily as I passed. Cicadas occasionally burst into chorus: *'die, die, die...,'* as ample numbers of dragonflies darted past en masse, looking for a mate.

In just over 2 hours I made it to the car park of Cape Sata, from here it was just a short walk to the Cape itself. A lonesome lighthouse about 500 metres off shore sat perched atop a rugged islet, beyond it a vast blue void. I'd made it. And in doing so I'd set myself a new milestone. It had been just a little over 2 months by this point since I'd left the country's northern most point of Cape Sōya, in Hokkaidō. The 3,050 miles felt like a very, very distant memory. So much had happened in the time since Hokkaidō. The adventure I'd always dreamed of, had become a priceless reality, one that I wouldn't have changed for anything. But it was all still far from being over. For many this would be the end of a long and successful journey from the country's distant northern reaches, yet for me I still had 16 more prefectures to conquer in order to fulfil my goal. Feeling like a pint was in order, I turned my back on the Pacific and began the journey back to Kagoshima City, where it would most certainly be beer '0' clock upon my arrival.

Descending away from the Cape, I'd traversed merely 300 metres, before I noticed the tops of the palm trees that towered up around me swaying precariously. Cloud cover had also increased, as loose vegetation began to flitter across the surface of the road. As I rounded a bend, I was offered a view out to sea, an overly uninviting view. The skies were grey, merging into black and I could see a band of white spray at the forefront that was heading ashore in my direction. There would be nowhere to run and nowhere to hide.

I continued to peddle, hoping that the oncoming weather front might just skirt around me. Sadly, I was headed uphill on at least an 8% gradient and thus escape was futile. In mere moments, a gust of wind groped me from behind as a front of hard hitting rain succeeded it, lashing down furiously around me. It was freak and unexpected, considering how roasting hot it had been just a few moments previously.

The polarities of the Japanese weather were a constant. Whilst traversing the country, I had heard people comment on the fact that the weather had been behaving very strangely this year - and they most certainly weren't wrong.

Pulling over to the side of the road, I was able to take up some minimalist cover from an overhanging tree branch. The rain continued to gush down violently for a further 4 minutes, before suddenly petering out like someone had just quickly turned off a tap. The sun then appeared from out of the grey as if nothing had ever happened! Steam in turn rose up from the asphalt surface, as the water upon the road began to burn up instantly. *Welcome to the sub-tropics.*

To get back to Kagoshima, I again made passage alongside Kagoshima Bay, this time upon the opposite peninsula which would lead me all the way up to the southern base of Sakurajima. En route, I was pulled over by a pair of very serious looking plain clothes police officers. They showed me their badges and asked to see my passport. I did as I was asked. One of the officers spoke in pitch perfect English, with an American twang; much to the awe of his non-English speaking partner, who studied me up and down very carefully. The English speaking officer asked me what I was doing and where I was headed. He seemed quite impressed with my answer, as he translated this to his partner, who smiled. I was overjoyed to see them both smiling, as I had been wondering what it was that I might have done wrong. I asked the officer if everything was okay, and he confirmed that they just wanted to let me know that there are a lot of crazy drivers in Kagoshima Prefecture. It was then that I realised that I wasn't wearing my crash helmet. Quickly, I reached around to the rear of my bike and unclipped it from my baggage and proceeded to place it upon my head. Both officers found this act side-splittingly hilarious as they laughed directly at me, before wishing me a safe journey, in Japanese.

I was thankful for the concern from the officers, even if it was a case of one cop showing off his English skills to the other cop. I had actually noticed an increase in stunt driver wannabes within the area. On at least eight separate occasions I would nearly find myself maimed by victims of bicycle blindness. A majority of the incidents, like the incident back in Miyazaki, stemmed from people pulling out of junctions and looking directly through me - as if I was nothing more than an apparition. Being *Obon* weekend, I wondered if the locals thought that I was the spirit of a *gaijin* cyclist, but I doubted it. Regardless, I felt as if I needed a new approach to these drivers to make them more aware of their bicycle blindness condition.

Through the power of eye to eye contact surely it would be possible to relay a psychic message between cyclist and automobilist, thus making them completely aware of my presence. As it happened, it wouldn't take me long before I got to try out my new experiment. An aged lady, driving a purple monstrosity, approached an upcoming T-junction onto a section of road that I was about to pass. I began to look directly at her. Correctly slowing down for the junction, she looked to the right, in the direction that I was coming from, and appeared to look directly through me. It was only when I branched my neck out a little further, converting my stare into something a little more in line with an obvious glare - that we were then able to lock eyes. A connection was thus made. And as we stared into one another's eyes, I felt a mutual bond of recognition formulate between us. Almost spiritual. I smiled as she smiled back, surely sealing the deal.

For her, I was in existence in real time, and this was exactly what I wanted her to think. The very idea of her pulling out on me now would surely defy logic, in every possible sense. However, she pulled right out on me, regardless, nearly killing me. Miraculously, my split second swerving into oncoming traffic and then bumping up onto the sidewalk on the opposite side of the road would save me from the jaws of death. Eye contact obviously wasn't the answer to this beefy conundrum.

As I approached the foothills of Sakurajima, rain began to set in; the volcano's summit was swathed in gloom. The ground around the mountain's 30 mile base was strewn with dispensed ash that, under the rain, was turning into black, gooey sludge. My lack of mud guards saw to it that I was getting rampantly caked in the stuff, and by the time I'd reached the ferry (that would take me across the bay, back to Kagoshima) I looked like I'd just crawled out of an old bonfire.

The crossing back to Kagoshima took a mere 15 minutes. And as the rain got heavier, I was relieved to have found myself a hostel for the night. Settling under a sheltered balcony, with a pack of beer, I watched the rain crash down in torrents over the city. I found myself devoid of thought, with very little worrying me, and that felt good.

Yakushima
28 miles

As my ferry from Kagoshima approached the Miyanoura harbour, I was greeted by some unusually clear skies, for in this part of the world - the locals will often joke - it rains 35 days of the month. The island's topography consists of a wild and rugged interior, dominated by a number of mountains that rise up close to some 2,000 metres, boasting some of the most beautiful primeval forests on the planet. The island of Yakushima is almost completely circular in shape, with a circumference of 84 miles and was the basis of Miyazaki's 1997 animated fantasy feature 'Princess Mononoke'. This film was based on a story about the Gods of the forest and the plight of man hell-bent on destroying their home.

Today, the bulk of the island's forests are protected and for two days I would have the great honour of trekking amongst them; discovering a small portion of this beautiful island's rogue interior. Under the cool, dense forest canopy a mystical world unfolds, the intense summer sun is filtered out, allowing one to really get lost amongst the dramatically aged cedars. Deer trample fearlessly on a forest floor littered in fungi and moss, fresh water drips from overhanging rocks as the bulbous tree roots run the forest floor like an aged wooden cabling system; appearing to bond the lifeblood of the forest together. It was clear to see where Miyazaki got his inspiration from.

The prize of the forest however is grand master *Jōmon Sugi;* a cedar tree so aged and grandiose that it can't even be dated properly with modern 21st Century technology, not even in Japan! From its size alone though, scientists believe it to be about 7,200 years old. And with a height of 25.3 metres and a girth of 16.4 metres, it is a true behemoth of a tree.

With a lack of cycling during my time spent on Yakushima, it had almost felt like a holiday. As usual that feeling made me feel a little uneasy, but then I thought of my next destination, Okinawa. And having now cycled some 5000 miles, the sudden thought of a sun, sea and sand holiday didn't seem like such a bad idea after all. If anything it would be wholesomely rewarding, a chance to relax in a tropical paradise and recuperate, to drink cold beer and swim in crystal clear waters, to eat fine Okinawan tucker and learn the secrets of a long and fruitful life. Yes, actually Okinawa would be just the ticket.

STATS

Dates: 16/08/2014 – 23/08/2014
Total miles traversed: 5,026 miles
Total time in the saddle: 506 hours and 20 minutes

32. OKINAWA
沖縄県

Okinawa entailed the longest ferry ride of them all. Situated some 475 miles south-west of Kagoshima, I would have to endure a 25 hour journey to Naha, the prefecture's capital.

After buying my ticket at the Kagoshima ferry terminal, I stood and lingered next to my bicycle by the loading bay, watching the giant forklift trucks load various freighter crates onto the humongous A-line cruiser. With at least 2 hours from disembarkation, I was surprised when a guy came running over to me, to ask if he could see my ticket. I showed him and then was ushered aboard. Just like that. The rest of the other ~~suckers~~ passengers were still sat in their cars or in the ferry terminal, playing the meticulous waiting game. I was to be one of the lucky first on board.

Leaving my bicycle with the lads on the car deck, I proceeded up the escalators like a guest of honour. Now let me tell you, it's exciting times when one happens to be the first to board a ferry, you really want to get to know the vessel in a lay of the land sort of way, without all the added interruptions of tripping over someone's luggage or getting stuck in a conversation about the weather. I immediately found my room on the 5th floor; the carpet was snot green with 21 futons in rows of 7, and not a millimetre to spare between them.

I then scouted the deck looking for the usual amenities: toilets, restaurant, Street Fighter II and a bunch of vending machines containing food, drink and a plethora of mysteries. Next would see me do a quick and meaningless safety check of the outer deck, although I didn't really know what I was looking for. But as far as I could tell, the vessel was a mostly solid steel affair with a hull that appeared to float well, this essentially made the boat feel all the more boaty. Satisfied I

291

returned to my futon and abused the ship's electricity supply something wicked.

My room would eventually become a full house as the other passengers began to pile on board. The room contained everything one would need to muster a successful sausage party. 21 males were packed tightly like sardines in a can; and an hour or so out to sea, all of my roomies were sleeping like babies. When the snoring started up, someone would close the cabin door, in an effort to contain one of the most persistently obnoxious noises known to man. And, of course, with the door being closed, the farts would also begin... got to keep those farts contained so that everyone can have a good old sniff. For the majority of the night, I'd stay awake having a Game of Thrones marathon on my laptop whilst sniffing 3rd party farts in the lacklustre confidence that I might just somehow nod off. I didn't, but with a new dawn, a new hope would arise and an abundance of vending machine coffee would be quaffed.

I spent the morning on the outer deck ocean, gazing and island spotting. The sea was a measureless void of turquoise, calm yet treacherous, breaching into the horizon and seemingly feathering up into the skies, before offering up a more translucent shade of blue. As the A-line surged forth, it passed a number of the 160 Ryūkyū Islands that dot a stretch of the Pacific for some 620 miles, from the borders of Kyūshū all the way down to Taiwan. Islands both inhabited and uninhabited, appearing as mere specs in any atlas. Thick jungle terrain hugged coastal hillocks as steep cliffs dived down abruptly and into the ocean.

Occasionally, civilisation crept out of the vegetation; as a cluster of homes with farming plots decorated with a life of self-sufficiency emerged. Life remote in the outer islands, being able to sustain a livelihood and also keep one's health intact, was key. Not that health was a huge issue for the Okinawan's - it is a well-known fact that these hardy islanders yield the largest number of centenarians of anywhere in the world. Five times as many Okinawan's live to over 100 years than compared to the rest of the mainland. A fact no doubt accredited to the Okinawan's graceful diet of fresh fish and tofu, along with local delicacies specific to the islands such as the bitter melon known as *gōyā* and the sweet purple yam. A diet low in fat and sugar and high in vitamin D... a longevity recipe for success. For me personally, I was still happy that I'd somehow managed to make it into my thirties, a fact that baffles me every day when I awake from the nightmares of my teens.

At dinner time, I headed down to the canteen on the lower deck to dine on some lukewarm Japanese curry. I planned to stay and read for a while, but was surrounded by a bunch of excitably noisy drunks that wouldn't leave me be, screaming and shouting for no reason. I was by this stage finding myself becoming increasingly irritable about the smallest of things: bicycle punctures, the humidity, a mucky camera lens, missing socks, a bogey on the wall next to me, being told *'Nai'* constantly... shitty drivers determined to send me to my maker. I felt that all these definitive issues were somehow having a detrimental effect upon my general well-being and my mental health. *Would Okinawa act as my cure?* It was true I needed time out, a breather, I needed beer, to read a book, to do some normal things that weren't cycling up and down mountains all day long and making myself feel sick from exhaustion. This much was certain. And so I urged Okinawa to be my refuge and place of sanctity, I hoped sincerely that it would fulfil my expectations.

Naha
66 miles

My hostel in Naha was run down and grubby, carrying with it the feel of a random backpacker's hostel plucked straight out of the back streets of somewhere in South East Asia. In fact, the city itself had a very different vibe to the Japanese mainland. Being one of the country's poorest prefectures, it had buckled and sand swept sidewalks, ramshackle buildings and city parks that resembled nothing more than small pockets of wild, mosquito infested jungle. But this by no means detracts from this outgoing city, if anything it gives it an underlying quality.

The Okinawan's themselves have quite a different ethos to that of the mainlanders, with their bronzed skin and tattooed bodies; they are a people that throughout the course of history have been noted for being extremely accommodating. This was clear to see when the receptionist at my hostel offered me a beer upon arrival, something that would soon become a problem.

With beer in hand I took a leisurely stroll into the city centre, along *Kokusai dori,* International Street. For just over a mile the road stretches: buzzing and vibrant with cafes, bars, night clubs, restaurants, souvenir shops and department stores. A number of sheltered shopping arcades also trailed off from the main strip, meandering around the capital's backstreets. Here I made a new friend; on a small market stall a dear old lady served me some home-made *bento* for the meagre price of just ¥200, about a quid.

I paid her a visit most days and every time she would chuckle joyously upon my approach to her stall. I would tell her how good her cooking was, in my worst Japanese, and she in turn would burst into further hysterics and tell me to stop.

Settling some place for just the briefest of time allowed me to familiarise myself with my surrounds and develop a new pattern. I got to meet local people and eat and drink where the locals would dine themselves – and I was always welcomed. It felt very humbling to be in this situation – even if it was just for a short while.

On this beery evening, I took in some more beers and walked the streets at random, soaking in as much as I could before I forgot which way my hostel was, and when such a time came… I just drunk some more.

I woke face down in a sweat drenched dorm bed, wondering how many others had sweated out their alcohol juices into the very fabrics of my mattress. Sitting up, my head consequently began to throb. Food would have been an appropriate resource, but as I wondered out into the open furnace-like streets, I instinctively walked in the direction of the coast instead. Just some 200 metres away from my hostel sat Naminoue Beach. Situated in a small cove, it was far from the island's most attractive beach; its view obscured by a vulgar high-rise bypass rammed with noisy, trucks whipping back and forth from the nearby docks. Yet the beach appeared clean and tidy and its waters were clear and inviting. Submerging myself into the cool relief of the ocean, considerably numbed the pain of my hangover.

Feeling better I noticed a vendor sat in a deckchair close to the shorefront who happened to be selling cold beer, *hair of the dog* I thought. My empty stomach condemned the idea, but I refused to listen to it, and after a few more beers I wouldn't feel the pain any more anyway… so what did it matter?

The older I get, the worse my hangovers get, the August heat was unforgiving too. Instead of lingering about feeling sorry for myself and dripping sweat all over the hostel furniture, I thought I'd let my sweat roll all over the island's roads instead. Filling up my water bottles, I grabbed my bike and went for a little excursion around Southern Okinawa.

As the biggest island of the chain of Ryūkyū Islands at only 70 miles long and 7 miles wide, it wouldn't take me long to explore the southern reaches of the island. Sadly, this would be about the full extent of what I would be able to achieve during my time on Okinawa. As romantic as the notion was to visit further islands, time and money restraints just wouldn't allow. And in the 100% humidity I was also quite relieved as just a few short miles to the east of Naha I'd find myself getting vaporised by the sun's relentless rays.

Yet, had I been here between April and June 1945, the intense climes would have been the least of my worries. The horrors of the last ground-based battle of World War II on Japanese soil became more than apparent as my day progressed. I visited a number of sites across the island's south. The Battle of Okinawa or the 'War of Attrition' as the Japanese would call it, was one of the bloodiest battles of World War II; one that would scar these islands for years to follow. At the time, surrender was not an option for the Japanese, for if the Americans took Okinawa, then they would be only one small step away from the mainland. Capture wasn't even considered for the heavily outnumbered Japanese troops, and in such an instance it was common for the Japanese to either die martyrs or to commit the ancient samurai ritual of *seppuku*. And in no place would this be more evident than my first port of call at the 'Former Japanese Navy Underground Headquarters' - in the outer suburbs of Naha. Here, by foot, I descended down a gloomy flight of stairs into a network of doom-clad tunnels that stretched claustrophobically for about 450 metres.

The atmosphere sombre and the air stale, this was a site initially used as a command bunker for the Japanese Navy – eventually becoming a tomb for over 4,000 soldiers.

In early June 1945, Admiral Ōta, along with his men, found themselves cornered by the American advances. Ōta, knowing that all was lost, would sign off by sending one last telegram to headquarters, 'There are no trees, no grass; everything is burnt to the ground. The food supply will be gone by the end of June.' He then turned a gun on himself, many of his men following suit, some using hand grenades instead of bullets - this was evident by the shrapnel-splintered walls of the tunnels.

Exiting the tunnels back into the light of day, I suddenly felt very sober. I continued south in a heat unparalleled to anything I'd experienced back on the mainland, all the time thinking about the war, thinking about how lucky I was to be able to be doing what I was doing.

By the coast, I found Heiwakinen Park, home to the Peace Memorial Museum. Here an even more sobering account of the grim realities of the Battle of Okinawa are remembered, in the shape of an informative museum – its timeline of events leading up to and after those grim months of 1945.

The park and grounds were immaculately kept, as expected, with a cenotaph listing the names of the fallen soldiers and civilians from all sides. The Japanese military lost some 70,000 men and the allied forces 12,000, yet the greatest casualties were those of the Okinawan's, where it is thought that over 100,000 citizens perished - almost a third of the island's population at that time. It was thought that the Okinawans would welcome the American's as liberators, but anti-American propaganda from the Japanese military soon saw to it that the Okinawan's would not side with them. They were told that if they fell into the hands of the enemy that they would be raped and tortured, many stories speak of fathers killing their wives and children through fear of what the enemy would do to them if they were captured.

Just a short ride away from the Peace Museum was a much smaller memorial dedicated to *Hime-yuri no to*, The Princess Lilly Girls. The Japanese under heavy attack had little in the way of medical assistance and so 222 local high school girls were selected from local schools - to aid the wounded and crippled infantry. They would do so with little or no experience in dire conditions, amongst caves and uninhabitable swathes of jungle, whilst a relentless shower of mortar shells rained down around them. It isn't possible to enter one of these caves, but you can peer down into one. It was dark, dank and craggy, a nightmarish, foreboding sort of place. Here, girls were forced prematurely into becoming women - women of war. I'd like to say that there was a happy ending for all the girls, but of course for many there wasn't, it was war, and war will always be spiteful. During the actual 3-month-long conflict, it was thought that there were just 19 student fatalities, it was only when the Japanese had officially surrendered the islands that the death toll would raise to 123 student deaths. The girls had been told by their superiors not to surrender to the Americans... and so many students in a state of panic would jump off cliffs to their deaths, whilst others pulled the pins of hand grenades issued to them by broken bodied soldiers.

These museums, cenotaphs and memorial sites are a constant and important reminder of the horrors of war that once plagued these islands; horror stories that I hope, first hand, that you and I will never get to experience. Yet, despite all I'd seen and learned today, as I cycled around the island's southern tip - amongst the most idyllic of tropical paradises - I still found it hard to believe that such atrocities ever took place here. But they did, they really did.

I awoke the following morning without a hangover, this would be the first and only such instance during my entire stay on Okinawa. The previous days' sombre outing destroyed that sensual holiday vibe. Today, however, I planned to get back on track, but not before exploring a little more of the south.

Cycling south-easterly out of Naha, I hit Mibaru Beach. There a quiet and secluded portion of coast greeted me, its waters calm and its beach pristine. I slung down my bike, peeled off my sweat-soaked backpack and hastily immersed myself into the wet stuff as if my life depended upon it.

Coming from England it will always be a surprise to me when I look down into crystal clear waters and see my own feet planted firmly upon the sea floor; a complete polar opposite to the shivering cold, murky depths of the North Sea. Casting my mind back to Skegness 1992, I'll always recall two red-headed children playing catch in the sea with a used condom; a truly tragic day for gingers.

My fun would be spoilt when a series of rain clouds began to encircle me, the weather in Okinawa not to be trifled with, as multiple tropical storms and typhoons often play havoc with the island's annually. It just so happened that through my own supreme timing, I'd arrived during the middle of typhoon season.

Exiting the sea, I jumped straight onto my bike wet and journeyed back west towards Naha. With the searing heat, I'd be dry in minutes. Weaving in and out of the rush hour traffic, along a selection of horrifically destroyed roads, I'd just about make it back to my hostel before a ferocious rain storm broke. Relieved, I plucked a cold beer from the fridge and pitched a seat on the *tatami* floor, next to a passed out drunk. *A man after my own heart.* Pulling back the ring-pull of my beer let forth that unmistakable and expected hiss, a noise that for me would also signal the beginning of an unwarranted 12-day binge.

Once the beer started to flow, I knew it would be difficult to wean myself away. For when it comes to alcohol, my genes are extremely susceptible to its poisonous wrath. On a nightly basis, I would meet up with an eclectic contingent of characters, some strange, some beautiful, some dangerous. And where each consecutive night would lead I felt that not even the god's could have fathomed. From the night clubs, to the karaoke bars, to the house parties, to the back streets - each morning, afternoon or evening that I awoke, my head would be a scrambled and dreary mess. Some of it I remembered, some I didn't, and what I did remember I mostly just wished that I didn't. Why did I chose to drink to complete and utter excess each night? I really don't know. It was only when I woke up in the foetal position on Naminoue Beach early one morning, feeling a series of abnormal heart palpitations, that I realised I was beginning to lose sight of my actual goal. For each day I wasted on the piss, was a day that both punctured my health and crippled my chances of making it back to Tokyo in an able-bodied state. I stumbled to my feet with difficulty and brushed myself down, my body pouring with sweat. Reaching into my pocket, I pulled out my iPhone to check the time. Steve Job's little brother was shattered and dysfunctional, I sighed before instinctively skimming the phone into the Pacific Ocean. I sighed again. *Now, why did I just do that?*

It was time to leave these shores.

Returning to my hostel, I vomited a little and then gathered my belongings, before taking a brief cycle ride to the ferry terminal. I'd enjoyed the buzz of Okinawa, worlds apart from the mainland, it had a completely separate country-feel to it. A little like Hokkaidō, but with a slight edge. I felt I'd merely scratched the surface however, and not completely done my break here justice, for obvious alcoholic driven reasons. However, I had reached and just about survived my 32nd prefecture. Grabbing a bottle of water, I toasted to just 15 more, and then vomited on my arm.

The 25-hour ferry ride back to the mainland was a choppy one that certainly did no wonders for my dicky stomach. I shook and sweated out like a junkie, as the mother of all hangovers took a grapple hold on me. *I'll never drink again.*

STATS

Dates: 24/08/2014 – 9/09/2014
Total miles traversed: 5,092 miles
Total time in the saddle: 512 hours and 29 minutes

33. KUMAMOTO
熊本県

Kagoshima – Minamata
76 miles

The alcohol shakes had just about subsided upon disembarkation at the Kagoshima ferry terminal. It was now time for a more straight edge approach as I headed north-westerly out of the city and along the lugubrious Route 3, towards Kumamoto Prefecture. The drivers of Kyūshū back to their old tricks of trying to turn me into mincemeat, I would cling to the sides of the roads like a squirrel clings to his prized nuts, but even then I wasn't safe. At one point in the afternoon I met a Scottish cyclist coming from the opposite direction, both of us stopped for a quick chinwag. He'd only been cycling around Kyūshū for a few days, but couldn't quite believe that he wasn't dead yet. I confirmed that I often wondered myself whether or not I was invisible, judging by how many near misses I'd had on the island. But the fact that my fellow Brit had noticed my very presence and was talking to me just about cleared up any anxieties that I might have been having at the time. We wished each other God-speed before both going our separate ways.

After two weeks of pissing my life savings up the wall in Okinawa, there was some small hope that as I started back out on the road again - it being September - that the climes would have simmered somewhat, yet at a baking 30°C there was no such luck. Not only would I continue sweating from where I last left off but my pace had also slowed considerably, making me feel lethargic; my weaker right knee beginning to ache again just as it did when I first started out cycling at the beginning of my tour. And to top it off, my weird heart palpitations continued to worry me. All a bad omen. Yet, despite these physical setbacks, I did still manage to make my mark by reaching Minamata by early evening.

Minamata Bay is a place with a grim past. During the 1950's and '60's a series of residents from the local fishing community began to fall mysteriously ill, their nervous system's breaking down. They began to lose their sight, their hearing would become impaired, their speech and movement would degrade as chronic fatigue and severe headaches would also set in - before ultimately leading to death. The cause was mercury poisoning. Mercury was being deposited into the surrounding bay by a local chemical factory; a factory that despite being aware of the damage it was causing, didn't actually stop releasing harmful metals into the waters until 1968. By this time, Minamata Disease affected the lives of some 2,265 people - 1,784 of which would lose their lives. Chisso, the company behind the disaster, is still in operation but has long since fessed up to the damages caused, compensating thousands of local residents.

A vast section of the bay was dredged of its contaminants at great expense to Chisso and the national government. And then on an area of reclaimed land, a substantial eco-park was built. The park's grounds are beautified with a collection of ornate gardens, memorial sculptures, a museum, a scientific research centre, a playground, an athletics field and a splendid bayside esplanade. I sat on a bench along the esplanade with a box of wet wipes, removing layers of thick black gunk from my legs.

The sun looked like a giant enflamed peach as it slowly sunk behind a set of islands dotted unevenly across the bay. People happily walked their dogs and did laps of the esplanade. It was unquestionably a beautiful park, it's just a shame that it was born out of the death and misery of others. *Shame on you Chisso, shame on you.*

Minamata – Kumamoto
63 miles

It was a crimson dawn, just as beautiful as the previous night's sunset. Layers of heat were already beginning to ripple off the surrounding mountains, as I ventured over to a 7-Eleven to carry out my morning ritual of causing absolute anarchy in the toilets. Without my iPhone now, I could no longer get casual GPS updates at convenience stores, my route was becoming holistically devised around hand written notes and my untrustworthy 'Made in China' map book of Japan - complete with incomplete pages. Today though there would be no qualms, Kumamoto City, being the prefectural capital would be well sign-posted and easy to find.

It is a city that in recent years has seen a spike in tourism; largely associated with the prefecture's cutesy mascot 'Kumamon'. In 2011 Kumamon won the mascot equivalent of 'Pop Idol' or 'The X-Factor' by being voted the country's most favourite mascot. And he certainly is a rather infectious character, a big, well-rounded and clunky black bear with big red dimples, that would make the most ardent of badasses go 'Awww, *kawaii!*'(Awww, so cute!) One can't go far around the bustling city of some 700,000 inhabitants without spotting an image of him with teenage girls, and fully grown hairy men alike, posing by his side whilst throwing out the V's.

He's got the masses under a spell, that much I'm certain of. But what his true underlying intentions were, I just couldn't pinpoint - I suspect it to be something baleful and untoward. Citizens of Japan, don't say I haven't warned you.

I'd find little in the way of parks or covert places in which to camp, so found myself heading easterly into the city's outer suburbs to a Manga Café. In the dim and seedy glow of the Café, I filled up a bowl with ice cream and sauntered off to my private booth to infiltrate the world of the Internet, or as my Nan would call it, 'The Interwebs.' I love Nans, they're great.

Kumamoto – Aso
28 miles

I didn't quite get as much sleep as I'd intended. My heart palpitations were bothering me, so I ended up surfing the Internet deep into the night.

After which, I headed off into the mountains of the Aso Kujū National Park.

I'd start out in the dark just before dawn, the air cool and crisp. And even as the sun broke upon the horizon directly ahead of me from the east, the climes would reach an accommodating 18°C. The ascent along Route 57 however was far less accommodating and more borderline frightening with vast stretches of road undergoing maintenance, allowing for meagre gaps between myself and the hefty deluge of passing traffic. Occasionally, I'd get held up by traffic lights, that were allowing the flow of a one-way traffic system along some tight sections of road. A safe and precautionary measure for motorised vehicles no doubt, yet for the budding cyclist not so much. When one starts out on an ascent through a green light and doesn't quite make it out at the other end - before the lights go green for the oncoming traffic - this will always lead to an assortment of capers.

It was all very ugly to say the least and I could tell that the construction workers clearly hadn't thought that there might be a halfwit with a bicycle ascending the mountains. This was more than noticeable as I passed through one such section, much to the bewilderment of a construction worker who began to rapidly scratch his head in confusion, before commenting to me '*Abunai yo!*' It's dangerous!

'No shit,' I confirmed.

By late morning, I'd made it to the city of Aso, where I'd pre-booked a night's accommodation in a backpacker's hostel. There, I dumped my bags and tied up my steed in the stables - before jumping on the next bus to Mt. Aso.

Mt. Aso looms grandly over the city, the largest of Japan's active volcanoes with its highest peak at 1,592m above sea level and a caldera with a circumference of some 75 miles. It has five actual peaks, of which only one is active, Naka-dake. The land unravels into a natural spectacle the closer one draws to the summit. It has a mixture of rolling green hills and rich fertile plains that are grazed by both cattle and horses. Random clumps of rock lay dispersed across the park from eruptions that date back as far as 300,000 years ago. The giant mountains are claimed to be one of the most ancient and active bad boys in the land.

Looking up toward the baron and craggy crater of Naka-dake, would reveal that it was almost excessively rampant with life as smoke bellowed up furiously into the atmosphere. This however led to disappointment upon reaching the Aso-Nishi base station, as it meant that both the walkway and cable car ropeway to the summit were currently off limits. Just 2 months after my visit, the volcano would spew its guts up for the first time in 22 years, projecting lava, smoke, debris and plumes of ash up to half a mile high. The ash reaching as far away as Kumamoto City - some 25 miles to the west - this in turn also led to significant crop damage in the area and the cancellation of flights.

I was though in need of a trekking fix, and so walked back in the direction of Aso City to scale the summit of the inactive Mt. Kishima. Its cylindrical crater was paved over by a lush coating of grass and would've been the perfect locale for an exotic baseball pitch. Views in the direction of Naka-dake were now limited by a smoky haze, it was like trying to look at something incredibly sexy through steamed up spectacles. Even so, it was still incredibly sexy.

Aso – Isahaya
68 miles

The descent from Aso was dangerously dicey, and because I'm a ridiculous person, exciting. I blazed along the heaving Route 57, mere inches from self-destruction; the accelerating speed only adding to the intensity as I shot past trucks and slower road vehicles like a man possessed. Coming down from the mountains with the aid of speed, allowed me to make my mark at a greater rate, making it down to the flats of Kumamoto in a little over 2 hours - almost halving the time it took me to ascend. From the city I rode further west towards Kumamoto Port. There, a ferry to Shimbara, Nagasaki Prefecture would await me.

As I reached the ferry terminal at 13:32, I saw a notice board indicating that the next ferry would be departing at 13:40. Once again, I was cutting it fine as I raced into the terminal and over to the ticket counter. Initially, there were no queues, but then suddenly a man appeared from nowhere. We both ended up awkwardly approaching the ticket counter at the exact same time. We then had a silent stand-off, glaring into one another's eyes, my determination to go first rife, as I knew that I was about to miss my ferry and I'd have to wait another 2 hours for the next one. And so for a solid 3.2 seconds we eyeballed one another intently, before the man no doubt sensed my desperation and urged me ahead of him. I nodded a thanks and stepped quickly forward, only to find that I'd completely forgotten how to speak Japanese. The lady at the counter asked me what I wanted and as my jumbled brain failed to recollect any words of relevance, I simply pursed my lips together and made a weird, mostly sad sounding noise. I needed to take a few moments to collect my thoughts and question whether or not I'd just had some sort of stroke.

I took a step away from the counter and ushered in the man who had kindly let me go ahead of him. He nodded in kind and asked for one ticket to Shimbara. 'Shimabara *made ichi-mai kudasai.'* He was served his ticket immediately and left the premises with his dignity intact. Mine in tatters and smeared all over the waiting room floor, I stepped up to the counter for another shot.

'Shimabara *made ichi-mai kudasai,'* I said, like a boss. And, like the previous customer, I was served a ticket within seconds, yet when the lady behind the counter handed me my ticket she tapped her finger upon her watch to express that I didn't have much time left. Then she grabbed a walkie talkie and shouted into it something about an alien wanting to come aboard.

I dashed outside and into the car park where one of the ferry crew would greet me. He also tapped his watch. I hastily jumped onto my bike and as the crew member raced ahead of me, I followed him all the way up and into the glum hull of the ferry. Within seconds, the drawbridge was raised and the hull secured, and at 13:40 - on the dot - we were off to Nagasaki.

STATS

Dates: 10/09/2014 – 13/09/2014
Total miles traversed: 5,327 miles
Total time in the saddle: 535 hours and 2 minutes

34. NAGASAKI
長崎県

The ferry across the Ariake Sea to Shimbara took about an hour, by design I was the last man on and the last man off the vessel. Mt. Unzen leered dauntingly over the city upon my arrival, as I prepped my bike for the road.

I headed through the busy town's high street and out into rural Nagasaki prefecture. The rice crops - a mixture of greens and yellows - illuminated the surrounding landscape as the background was eaten up by the dark and menacing outline of a fearsome set of mountains.

Straddling the coast, I avoided these harbingers of doom as I made for Isahaya in the centre of the prefecture.

Arriving just before nightfall I was in a good position to make it to Nagasaki City in the morning - just some 20 miles away to the south-west.

For a Saturday night, Isahaya was about as lively as a morgue. Cycling through its uneventful streets in the darkness, I stopped off at a supermarket to get some late night deli counter deals, and in doing so, I happened across some much needed light entertainment. Propping my bike up against the supermarket window, I noticed an elderly gent who was practising an imaginary golf swing. On a nearby bench sat an open jar of sake. He wobbled as he sliced the invisible ball into the night sky. I quickly snuck past him and into the supermarket, just as he was looking to the skies to see where his invisible ball was going to land. Throughout my life, I've always had this massively talented ability to attract the eccentric… and the drunk. So as I escaped the drunken night golfer - on this occasion - I knew deep down that it wouldn't be long before he inevitably caught up with me, for it was fate, plain and simple.

At the deli counter, I grabbed a couple of discount boxes of sashimi and went to exit the store. Just as I was about to leave, I felt the sudden urge to make small talk with the urinals, so I headed over to the toilets - an instantly regrettable idea. Inside was the aged drunken golfer extraordinaire. The problem was there was only one urinal and it was in use by the said drunk. Upon noticing my presence, he instantly turned towards me. Now I didn't look directly at 'it' per se, but I was more than aware of a certain fleshy item peeking out from between his legs that appeared to be leaking fluids. I jumped instinctively backwards into the wall, to escape its dribbly wrath.

'Oh, so sorry,' said the golfer.

'Err... err... that's okay... I guess,' I uttered, meekly.

'My...my power swing,' he continued, as he began to demonstrate his technique.

It was then that it dawned on me that he wasn't actually apologising for nearly pissing on my shoes, but more so for his lacklustre imaginary golf swing. I mean he had every right to be concerned, as he wasn't arching his back enough for my liking - but considering the circumstances that wasn't really the point.

'Ok, well err...*ganbatte ne!*' I left sharpishly, nearly tripping over his bottle of sake on the way out, suddenly not needing the toilet so much after all.

It was a bizarre incident, just when I thought I'd seen it all. I cycled round the corner - laughing it off - before finding a set of swings in a dark and weed infested playground. I sat on one of the swings and scoffed my sashimi, looking over my shoulder from time to time to make sure that there weren't any drunks around, practising their slice or any imaginary golf balls heading in my general direction. Thankfully there wasn't and I was very much alone.

After my late night dinner, I set up my tent atop a disused skate ramp. And as I lay in the black of night, the tree tops around me began to rustle and creak as a steady wind set in. When I closed my eyes, I saw drunken Japanese penises everywhere and they were coming straight for me. I slept uneasily.

Isahaya – Nagasaki
23 miles

The ride into Nagasaki from Isahaya was short; climbing over the mountains to the east I would descend down into the heart of the city for breakfast. It's a city that rarely needs an introduction, being only the second ever city in history to face nuclear demolition. At 11:02 local time on 9th August 1945 - just 3 days after the bombing of Hiroshima, the American B-29 Bomber Bockscar released the 'Fat Man,' a plutonium bomb with the critical impact of 20,000 tonnes of high explosives. The bomb would incinerate 40,000 people instantly, another 40,000 would follow in due course from the side effects. These ranged from severe burns, radiation sickness, leukaemia, malnutrition and a whole array of varying other chronic and debilitating injuries.

The bomb, although more powerful than the 'Little Boy' dropped on Hiroshima, did less damage, due to the area's uneven terrain. Locked in amongst the mountains - visibility from the skies at the time of the bombing were poor and the actual bomb itself missed its mark by some two miles. Yet the bomb would still cause damage on an unprecedented scale, flattening whole neighbourhoods, torching crops, blitzing the dock yards and destroying many remnants of the city's once cosmopolitan past.

Six days later, on August 15th - Japan surrendered; marking the end of World War II.

Cycling through the city in the glorious sunshine and around its affluent port area, with its scenic backdrop of Mt. Inasa, I again struggled to come to terms with the fact that this vibrant city - like Hiroshima - was once turned inside out.

311

Heading over to the Peace Memorial Park, the site of the hypocenter of the bomb, would spell things out a little more clearly. Here one can find remnants of Urakami Cathedral, a solid stone structure that, at the time of the bombing, must have been tossed around like a child's teddy bear, in the jaws of a rabid Rottweiler. The cathedral was also a link to Nagasaki's longstanding relationship with the West that dates back to the 16th Century, when Portuguese Jesuits first came to its shores, to spread the word of Christ. They also traded produce, thus making Nagasaki one of the first cosmopolitan cities of Japan.

To see the city flourish like it clearly once did - walking hand-in-hand with the West, signifies the epiphany of peace and reconciliation that was and still is so important to Japan and the rest of the world post 1945. The past cannot be erased but the future can be altered, so that we never have to see a repeat of that fateful day, back in 1945, for rest of eternity.

Just off the coast of Nagasaki was a place of great intrigue to me. Gunkanjima, a.k.a. Battleship Island. It is a small rock just 10 miles from the port of Nagasaki that was once heavily mined for its coal reserves. In its heyday it was home to some 5000 inhabitants, it housed apartment blocks, schools, bathhouses, shops, restaurants and a hospital. The island measured just 480 meters long by 150 meters wide and was so built up that from the sea it looked like a gigantic, fortified battleship. In 1974, however, the mining operations ceased and the island was abandoned, leaving it to the ruinous wrath of both time and Nature.

For over 35 years the island and its decaying buildings have sat as ghostly relics in the East China Sea. But, in 2009, tour operators began to run tours to the island and I was more than interested in paying a visit.

After securing my bike at the ferry terminal and stuffing all of my belongings into a coffin-sized locker, I was joyfully whisked away on the 50-minute ferry ride to the island.

Gunkanjima also featured in the bond movie 'Skyfall,' to where many like myself would also associate the island. I expected no Bond-esque shenanigans today though as the ferry waded docilely through the calm ocean waters toward the island. On the approach, the first thing that strikes one is the high-rise almost communist style era apartment blocks, an eyesore upon the horizon. Dull and weathered looking buildings with blown out windows that looked as if they'd felt the full force of a thousand typhoons.

When the ferry docked, a number of tour guides split people up into groups, before leading them around the island. Unfortunately, you can't roam at will, as many of the structures are considered unsafe. Most of the scenes in Skyfall were filmed in the special effects green room back at Pinewood Studios, England. But just from walking along the stable sections of the island, it was enough to soak in this edificial graveyard of former habitation. Rubble lay strewn across the ground, whilst rustic steel framework protruded out of the decaying buildings. Vegetation grew out of the cracks in the ground and smothered everything in its path. It was an eerie place, a place where one definitely wouldn't want to find oneself stranded for too long. It was most definitely the perfect Bond villain hideout. I happily snapped photographs for an hour or so, amongst fellow tourists and Bond fans alike - before taking the ferry back to Nagasaki.

On the way back, everyone on the boat seemed to have had their energy zapped from them, myself included. After a couple of mild days, the weather had now chirped up again and the temperature was pushing back up into the thirties. In these sorts of climes, it doesn't take long for one to lose energy. I looked around the boat and saw a contingent of people with their heads down, or nuzzled upon a partner's shoulder, throwing out a merciless supply of 'zzzzzz's.'

I tried my hardest to fight the curse, but before I knew it, the ferry had docked back at Nagasaki harbour as I found myself jutting awake suddenly - as a group of passengers piled past me, each one of them looking at me like I was some sort of bleary-eyed smack addict.

It was early evening when I met up with Couchsurfer, Richie, a Kiwi teaching English in Nagasaki. Richie and his Japanese friend, Jin, took me out for some sushi, before we headed up 333 meters to the summit of Mt. Inasa. The city below was a hive of activity, glistening with a flurry of lights, all the way up into the darkness of the mountains on the opposite side of the valley.

From the ashes, this great city had risen again, to prove the worth of existence through belief, courage - and some seriously hard fucking labour. Nagasaki was back on the map; here to stay.

Nagasaki – Tosu
96 miles

Leaving Nagasaki, I cycled back on myself for a short time, as I headed north-easterly - returning to Isahaya momentarily before branching away toward the coast of the Ariake Sea. There, I etched around the hazy foothills of Mt. Tara, passing through a number of laid back rural villages before slipping into the incredibly sleepy Saga Prefecture.

STATS

Dates: 13/09/2014 – 16/09/2014
Total miles traversed: 5,446 miles
Total time in the saddle: 550 hours and 55 minutes

35. SAGA
佐賀県

In my fleeting visit to this quaint prefecture - that plays the part of the middle man between Nagasaki and Fukuoka - I would spend the afternoon cycling amongst its charming and picturesque countryside.

The pace of life here seemed relaxed, its drivers even willing to pass me by with an etiquette of grace. My pace however was rapid, as I made good ground amongst the prefecture's abundant low-lying agricultural plains and reached Saga City by nightfall. A city about as exciting as a wet sock, where I struggled to find anywhere to bum camp for the night. And so I continued to cycle further and deeper into the night along Route 34, in the direction of Fukuoka.

The entire 40 mile stretch from Saga to Fukuoka, appeared to build up with more highways, industrial factories and residential dwellings, the closer I got to Kyūshū's biggest city. It would be close to midnight before I'd find some suitable habitat in which to camp.

On the cuff of the prefectural border - in the city of Tosu - I found a patch of parkland in which to throw up a tent for a few hours; knowing that tomorrow morning the overall quiet and sleepy grace of Saga would be a thing of the past.

STATS

Dates: 16/09/2014
Total miles traversed: 5,446 miles
Total time in the saddle: 550 hours and 55 minutes

36. FUKUOKA
福岡県

Tosu – Fukuoka
30 miles

With a population of close to 1.5 million people, Fukuoka City is some 5 times larger than Saga City, making it not only the biggest city in Kyūshū but the 6th largest in the country. From Tosu it would take me just over an hour to reach downtown Fukuoka. The city's streets were choked with traffic whilst its sidewalks took a pummelling from the hoards of shopaholics milling from one shopping mall to the next. I'd booked a night in a hostel close to the city centre and upon arrival found myself taking a little siesta. I'd hammered it from Nagasaki yesterday and the wear and tear on my body was more than evident as from the moment I lay my head down, I was out like a light.

Awaking around dusk I put on my best soy sauce stained t-shirt and took a walk over to Nakasu Island. The inner city island surrounded by the Naka and Hakata Rivers is one of the busiest red light districts in Western Japan after Osaka. Huge neon billboards were perched atop a row of high-rise buildings advertising various alcoholic beverages, hostess clubs and love hotels. Yet on the deck I couldn't see anything that resembled the seedy world of a red light district, just a few convenience stores, a Mister Donut and a couple of 100 Yen shops. All seemed very innocent and inoffensive. My main draw for being here however was not to experience an expensive and meaningless chat with an attractive Japanese girl, whilst she lights cigarettes that I don't even know how to smoke properly, but more to sample one of Fukuoka's *yatai*, an open air food stand. Across the city one might find some 150 *yatai* stands which generally sit around 6 to 8 people, and if you can find a seat, it's yours. The air lingered richly with the fine smells of Japanese cuisine as I took a seat at one such stand and ordered some Hakata Ramen, one of the local favourites. Served with ultra-thin noodles it was a thick bleached white looking broth made from the boiling of pork bones, collagen and fat. It was scorching hot and would take me nearly 30 minutes to nurse, but it was delicious and made a welcome change from 7-Eleven noodles. I washed the ramen down with my first beer since Okinawa. Yes, yes, I know I said I was never going to drink again, but my strange heart palpitations had since ceased and so one could only assume that I was fixed and therefore ready to enter back into the sordid realms of the booze industry.

By the time I'd left the *yatai* stand it was gone 10pm, there were now reams of drunken salarymen parading up and down the banks of the river, one drunk was giving another a piggy back, whilst a colleague chased after them, kicking them both up the arse. Suddenly, the innocence of the pre-10pm watershed was lost. Scantily clad girls began to loiter the neighbourhood, many wielding signboards that detailed some information that I couldn't understand along with how long one gets and how much money it will cost them. Many of the girls seemed upbeat putting on brave smiles as they screeched out their wares and invited passers-by into their clubs, others looked miserable as sin as their mind played on the night ahead. I watched one young girl lead a happy bunch of middle aged salarymen into a shady looking building, the men would enter happy and no doubt leave happy. Sadly, I felt the same perhaps couldn't be said for the bulk of girls working in this industry. The thought depressed me a little and I called it a night.

Fukuoka - Shimonoseki
75 miles

Leaving central Fukuoka, was slow and tedious. Traffic lights, busy three lane highways, clustered and bumpy sidewalks and of course a cutthroat contingent of guileless *mamachari*. The weather was overcast, yet extremely humid, the vast throngs of heavy traffic and exhaust fumes only adding fuel to the surrounding stickiness. Eventually, when the traffic finally thinned out, and I'd left the last of the high-rise apartment blocks behind me, I secured myself a scenic route through a procession of lonely hills and rice paddies. This would lead me on to the scruffy industrial sprawl of Kitakyūshū.

Kitakyūshū is the northern most city of Kyūshū with over a million inhabitants and it serves as one of the largest industrial hubs in the country. It is also a gateway to the neighbouring island, Honshū. Cycling along the north of the Dokai Bay, I saw nothing but dull looking factories and an expanse of power plants.

In the 1960's, the bay was referred to as the 'Sea of Death,' due in part to the amount of wastewater and pollutants that were being evacuated into the bay on a daily basis. Yet amid protests that started with housewives complaining that they couldn't dry their laundry on washing lines - because when they took it in, it was black with soot... the city council began to feel the pressure. Over the years the city's industrial sector would learn to grind out the country's needs in a more environmentally friendly manner. Of course, that doesn't stop the place looking like a complete shit hole... But then, industrial zones are not meant to be pretty, their job is to produce product and by any means produce it well. And, considering the amount of trucks whizzing past me every 5 seconds, that was exactly what Kitakyūshū must have been doing.

I hit a stumbling block upon reaching the suburb of Wakamatsu, where I found a bridge and a tunnel that could lead me across the bay and further into central Kitakyūshū. Unfortunately, both bridge and tunnel happened to be toll roads, and as the traffic steadily flowed I would be greeted by a no cycling sign. I was though feeling somewhat crafty. Halting near the bridge entrance, I took a sneaky look around. *Go on Dan, you know you want to, it's probably only about 400 metres across, it'll be fine, nobody will probably even notice…probably, and if they do just play the dumb foreigner card…*

My eyes narrowed as I set about pedalling, and the very moment that I did, I heard a whistle blow. *Shit!* Through some mesh fencing, a uniformed man appeared from a little bunker with a cigarette in his mouth, he wagged his finger at me like an angry headmaster. *Double shit!*

I smiled cheekily and swiftly did a 180° turn, darting off in the opposite direction blushing slightly. I was too embarrassed to look back over my shoulder because I'd been a naughty boy.

For some five miles or so I backtracked around the bay, until I found a bicycle friendly bridge. But here my frustrations would mount as I hit the rush hour traffic and a number of other no cycling signs that forced me to find alternate routes. Lacking any maps or notes in which to aid me through this urban nightmare, I would try my best to orienteer my way through the city via compass, but unfortunately it had no way of detecting dead ends.

Heading up a steep, almost vertical hill, for about 20 minutes in a residential area, I found a dead end. Coming back down the hill the same way, I found another dead end that I swore wasn't there earlier. The layout of the city was preposterous. An absolute mindfuck. After further milling about, I found Dokai Bay again and the other side of the toll bridge from Wakamatsu. I'd just wasted the best part of 2 hours!

I looked around for something dainty and soft to kick, yet there was nothing but concrete, so I just pushed onwards into the brewing dusk, my rage haphazardly piling up in the process.

From the Oseto Strait I trailed the coast through Kokura, considered the heart of Kitakyūshū and once home to one of the biggest armament factories in the country. This had been the primary target for the second atomic bomb during World War II.

On the cloudy morning of 6th August 1945, Major General Charles Sweeney piloted the Bockscar to Kokura, yet due to climatic conditions was unable to find the target, thus Kokura was spared. Instead, turning the plane around, Sweeney would guide the weapon of mass destruction to its secondary target of Nagasaki, where fate was not so kind.

Continuing farther afield, I cycled parallel to the Kanmon Strait, across from which I could now see the bright lights of Shimonoseki. A multi-coloured Ferris wheel lit up the night sky, along with an ambient glow cast from the Kaikyō Yume Tower - a structure that standing at 153 metres tall was the tallest building in Western Japan. Reaching the old trading port of Moji, I found a lift that took me deep down into the ground. There a sweaty 780 metre long pedestrian tunnel led me directly under the Kanmon Strait and back onto the island of Honshū.

The final stages of my trip were now drawing ever closer, and suddenly the stresses of the manic streets of Kitakyūshū were relieved.

STATS

Dates: 17/09/2014 – 18/09/2014
Total miles traversed: 5,551 miles
Total time in the saddle: 559 hours and 54 minutes

37. YAMAGUCHI
山口県

Shimonseki – Hagi
67 miles

I'd spent the night on a promenade overlooking the Kanmon Strait. Over a convenience store breakfast, I watched a selection of ships sail its busy waters. It is a strait that has seen hundreds of vessels ply its waters on a daily basis, for many hundreds of years. From the surrounding ocean, many a fisherman will return with their prized catches, namely *Fugu*, a.k.a. the pufferfish. Shimonoseki is considered the *"Fugu* Capital" of Japan, where specially licensed chefs will precariously prepare the fish, so that they are palatable for human consumption. If prepared incorrectly, the fish contains enough neurotoxins to paralyse every muscle in the human body... which in turn can lead to death. Knowing this, and knowing that I still had over 1500 miles to cover, I decided that for breakfast I'd stick to a 7-Eleven ham and cheese toasty.

A cold front reaching out off of the strait saw me don my fleece for the first time in months; a coldness that would trail north with me up into the highlands of the rather majestic Akiyoshidai Plateau. This is a 50-square-mile area that some 300 million years ago was actually a coral reef, yet through time geological processes have shaped the limestone karst topography into an ocean of weather beaten rocks that dot a landscape of abundantly rolling green hills - making it look like a giant monolithic creature, bathing in an ocean of grass. Underneath these hills run a network of some 400 or so limestone caverns, the biggest of which - the Akiyoshidō Cave - can be explored on foot. The cave is said to span some 5 miles and it is one of the longest in Asia. Walking down a flight of steps, 100 metres into the earth - amongst a permanently cool 16°C - a dark and mysterious world unfolds. A world of stalagmites and stalactites, with waterfalls that run a dazzling cobalt blue and iridescent limestone pools that sit stacked up like rice paddies of the underworld. A world just as beautiful and imaginative underground as it is above; yet here inside the earth, Nature's artistry seemed at its most drug fuelled and zaniest.

Emerging back into the daylight, I descended from the scenic plateau into the freshly harvested paddy fields of northern Yamaguchi. By late afternoon, I reached the coast and the old samurai town of Hagi. A town that has been relatively untouched since the beginnings of the 17th Century Edo Period. Here a number of old residential and merchant properties still stand amongst the town's narrow streets. I explored them before dusk set in, then found a small copse close to Kikugahama Beach, where I set up camp.

I sat on the beach and watched the sun go down. I was beginning to lose light earlier in the day now, and more than the mileage represented upon my odometer, the seasons had dictated the length of time that I had been on the road. From the bleak and freezing sleepless nights of winter, through to the wet and dreary sleepless nights of the rainy season - and then on into the hot and sweaty sleepless nights of summer. I had seasonally gone full circle as the climes finally became agreeable for my cycling trip around Japan.

Hagi – Yunotsu
92 miles

I don't know what to do about my stupidity sometimes; it is hard to shake off. Heading north out of Hagi along the cracked asphalt road – that was sufficiently spurned by vegetation - spiders floated weightlessly on the breeze, annoyingly entwining themselves across my face and handlebars.

As I tackled a repetitive procession of hills and tunnels, I switched off somewhat, my mind so numb that I couldn't even be bothered to think of the voluptuousness of breasts. Whilst slowly scaling a coastal mountain road, I passed an extremely odd looking rock. Odd not by the fact that it was grey, like many a rock that I'd seen in my life, but because it was hairy. It was a hairy, grey rock - something which I'd never seen before. Without hesitation, I felt I had no choice but to reach out and touch it, as I cycled past. It was at this point that something completely unexpected happened, the rock suddenly darted directly up the cliff face, before turning around to reveal the angry red face of a Japanese macaque. I'd just figuratively groped a monkey on the side of the road and he wasn't happy about it in the slightest. The monkey then went into a tirade of verbal monkey abuse, aimed directly at my person, which I found to be very offensive. Not only had he deceived me, but he also called me rude words with his sharp monkey tongue. I offered my sincerest apologies, but he was having none of it; he was disgusted with my sickening human behaviour. Feeling I had little to offer the angry little fellow, I pressed on through another lonely tunnel, deeply embarrassed by my sheer idiocy and slightly fearful of what the monkey police might make of it all.

Something told me that I wouldn't be welcome back in Yamaguchi anytime soon.

STATS

Dates: 19/09/2014 – 20/09/2014
Total miles traversed: 5,710 miles
Total time in the saddle: 574 hours and 19 minutes

38. SHIMANE
島根県

As nightfall approached, any preconceptions about being stuck in the mountains after dark, were countered by finding the remote, backwater *onsen* town of Yunotsu. Up until the 17th Century, Yunotsu was used as a port to transfer silver, harvested from one of the country's biggest mines, the Iwami Ginzan. The tradies used the town as a place to rest up and recoup as they went about their working lives. Today, mining has long since ceased in the area, yet the town's quaint streets are a testament to time; remaining somewhat untouched by the onslaught of the 21st Century. There you'll find a number of old-fashioned ryokans and bathhouses.

I brought my bike to a halt outside one such bathhouse; a building dating back to the Meiji-era, known as Yakushiyu. I could hear the splashing of water inside, which made me exceedingly happy; my body really needed this. It had been a long few days in the saddle with nothing but wet wipes for comfort; my body odour becoming so intense that I would have no doubt been able to scare a corpse back to life. A middle-aged Japanese lady came rushing out to greet me, as I went about securing my bike. She probably regretted coming over to me, upon catching a whiff of my putridness. She smiled though, before giving me her business card and, in excellent English, invited me into her bathhouse.

The *onsen* was a small yet cosy affair. As I submerged myself in its scolding hot, mineral rich waters, not only was I cleansed of the filth of everyday life on the road, but I was also pretty certain that the hot spring had eradicated some past sins too. After bathing for 3 minutes and 24 seconds, I rested on the building's third floor, where I helped myself to tea, before nearly falling asleep in an overly comfortable arm chair.

Feeling drained, I begrudgingly scooped myself up and ventured back out on to the far from mean streets of Yunotsu, to look for somewhere secretive to camp my clean white ass. As I was cycling along the chillingly quiet streets, an elderly lady emerged from the shadows on her squeaky *mamachari*. She stopped to talk to me, as we drew closer to one another, then she asked me where I was headed. I said some place close to the nearby lake - to camp. Instinctively, she offered me a bed at her home, but I felt it would be too much to invade her home at such short notice; also my head was completely dead... so, to converse in Japanese at such a late hour would have probably killed me.

I confirmed that I'd be all right, as I had my camping gear with me. She then pointed in the direction of a tourist information centre - which was now closed for the night – but it had toilets and a small yard. These facilities were right next to the lake's harbour, where I'd be able to camp for the night. I thanked her kindly for her information as she cycled off into the darkness; the eerie creaking sound of her aged bicycle slowly dissipating into the night.

Upon finding the tourist information centre, I discovered that I wasn't alone. Another tour bike was propped up against the outhouse. Poking my nose inside the toilet area, I saw a man lying down, snoring away to himself contentedly. I tiptoed around him and brushed my teeth, did a couple of secret farts and then went back outside to set up camp for the night.

Yunotsu – Yonago
82 miles

The temperature was dropping now, little by little, on a nightly basis, yet at 12°C it was still more than comfortable. Rising at 05:30am, I was packed up and ready to go by 05:45am, I had this tour cycling lark down to a T now...

325

The other cyclist was still dreaming of bike pump porn as I began to peddle away from the tourist information centre. And, barely had my day's cycling begun, before I was halted by the kind old lady from the previous night.

'*Ohayou gozaimasu,*' she said, smiling generously.

'*Ohayou gozaimasu,*' I replied, in turn.

'*Asagohan?*' she said, before pointing over to a little building which I presumed to be her home. Breakfast? I'd already refused her futon, so couldn't possibly refuse her food and so kindly accepted her offer.

I walked into an open plan room with *tatami* flooring, cluttered with hundreds of piles of newspapers. Behind one pile, a greying man appeared with a pair of spectacles perched precariously on the tip of his nose. The man squinted a little and looked a little confused by what he was seeing, before then looking towards his wife with caution. I quickly intervened and got to talking about the weather, this broke the silence and upon hearing me speak some Japanese, the man smiled broadly. I then went on to tell them both about my journey, after which I was truly accepted and invited to the breakfast table. For breakfast, I was served up a mean feast of marmalade on toast and a host of locally picked fruits and uber strong filter coffee – I ate until I was fit to burst. The couple told me that they ran a local newspaper printing business... hence the piles of papers. I was charmed by their kindness, so much so that we exchanged business cards, before shaking hands and getting on with our respective lives.

I traversed easterly toward Matsue, the capital of Shimane Prefecture. Farmers continued to harvest their golden rice crop as eagles soared high, in eager anticipation of exposed prey.

The temperature would raise steadily through the day, making it nearly uncomfortable again. The last remnants of summer stubbornly refused to let go. Along the coast, the beaches were immaculate, yet empty. The roads towards the prefectural capital were also quiet.

Just west of the city, sits Lake Shinji, Japan's seventh largest. Still this didn't appear to be drawing the crowds and neither did Matsue Castle - the country's second largest. But this is nothing new, as the prefecture of Shimane has long been hailed as the country's least visited prefecture. No one goes to Shimane, a place by no means horrible, but at the same time by no means particularly awe-inspiring. The prefecture's mascot is also the most miserable mascot of them all! Sprinkled across the prefecture, you might find various posters and souvenirs featuring the scowling Yoshida-Kun - with his oddly reddish tuft of hair. He's a stroppy teenager with nothing to prove and with no intentions of making friends with the general public, anytime soon. He is a far flung character from the lovable, if not quite sickly, Kumamon mascot of Kumamoto.

One poster of Yoshida-Kun with his arms crossed and a face full of hate, reads "Welcome to Shimane, the 47th most famous prefecture." Not a bad claim, if it wasn't for the fact that Japan only has 47 prefectures. I liked the cut of his jib though, and found his irony appealing. However, irony was thin on the ground in Japan – and judging by the low numbers of tourists moseying through the streets of Matsue, no one here cared for it too much either.

STATS

Dates: 20/09/2014 – 21/09/2014
Total miles traversed: 5,792 miles
Total time in the saddle: 582 hours and 41 minutes

39. TOTTORI
鳥取県

I would settle some 20 miles to the east of Matsue, just across the prefectural border in Yonago. The city - of an evening - had a much more appeasing vibe to it than Matsue, as I cycled its streets in search of a place to camp. A group of youths formed outside a public hall and sang along with a guy sporting a mullet; he was banging out the tunes on his semi-acoustic guitar. Many gathered around to clap and jiggle. A number of aged shopping arcades were placed around the backstreets, and quirky cafes provided the late evening revellers with their caffeine fixes.

I found what looked like some sort of castle ruin with walls that rose up 10ft high, forming a protective cove that shielded me from a busy main road. Fifteen minutes down the line and I would be playing the part of a happy camper.

Yonago – Iwai
81 miles

A cackle of crows woke me from my slumber. It was barely light outside as I exited my tent to see an old man doing some stretches, just five metres away from me. We acknowledged one another with a mutual nod. Once I'd packed up, he came over to me and gave me an energy drink for the day ahead. I thanked him, as two older ladies then arrived and they all in sync walked off into some scrubland together. I asked no questions.

On my way again, I trailed Route 9 easterly, buzzing off the ecstasy of the energy drink; riding almost blindly into the rising morning sun. The road lay sandwiched between an assortment of agricultural dazzle; rice being hung and dried in the fields, alongside other crops such as: watermelon, scallion, yam, persimmon and an abundance of pear, the prefecture's showcase product.

I would go on to lose a bulk of heavy traffic to a nearby expressway, as Route 9 became a more reclusive and habitable ride. The route eventually branching out towards a scenic coastline that rose and fell, very much like Shimane's coastline – as it offered up a plenitude of pristine and scantily clad beaches.

Tottori had an excuse for its complete lack of humans though, as with just a little over 580,000 heads, it is the least populated prefecture in all of Japan. Its capital city was a low-key affair; the only mild entertainment that I would stumble across was a collection of nattering local drunks, sat on a park bench; hands clasped firmly around their sake jars. What they were talking about I couldn't have possibly of fathomed, but it couldn't have been about anything that had actually happened in Tottori.

The prefecture does however have a big hitter that sits just north of Tottori City; its sand dunes. Despite their being formed over 100,000 years ago, it does feel like the Japanese had somehow copy/pasted a vast section of the Sahara desert onto their very own doorstep. The dunes are quite surreal and span some 10 miles of coast; some dunes reaching up as high as 50 metres. It's the only dune system of its kind in the entire country. I walked up the biggest one I could find, as a steady wind rolled off the Sea of Japan, casting tiny sand particles into the air that delicately bit the skin upon impact.

From afar, legions of tourists were trudging up distant dunes; they looked like an army of ants returning to the nest. The area receives about two million tourists every year and not only can one paraglide and board down the dunes, but one can also ride a camel. I actually once rode a camel called 'Dave' in Mongolia - and he ate an entire tree, it was weird. Camels are weird. I made tracks.

Heading inland towards the mountains of the Tajima Sangaku Prefectural Natural Park - Hyōgo Prefecture - I stopped off in the quiet *onsen* village of Iwami. It's the kind of place where people's jaws drop upon seeing a foreigner; they being extremely rare in these parts.

My clothes were stuck to my body by sweat and so I swiftly found the local bathhouse. It was a nice and spacious *onsen*, with only a few other locals about to look directly at my penis. Generally speaking, the ogling came from the older generation, as they like most old people didn't really give a shit. I'm looking forward to this era I must say, not just for looking at penises from a distant land without remorse, but just so that I don't have to give a shit about anything in general. It seems like something morally productive to aspire to.

Afterwards, I found a park right next to an old people's home that ran alongside a narrow and gentle flowing river. Amongst the darkness, I set up camp, before inserting my newly clean body into my fetid sleeping bag. By dawn, I would be a filthy stinker again.

STATS

Dates: 21/09/2014 – 22/09/2014
Total miles traversed: 5,873 miles
Total time in the saddle: 591 hours and 11 minutes

22.2 HYOGO & 21.2 KYOTO
兵庫県　京都府

Iwai – Miyazu
79 miles

Passing through the mountains, I revisited both Hyogo and Kyoto Prefecture's. The sun sat low in the sky first thing; advantageously out of my eyes and guarded by the towering mountain chain before me.

I passed several tunnels, some nearly 4,000 metres in length and, like all things tunnel-orientated, some were more fit for the taking than others. One truck passed so close that a strong vacuum of air tried to suck me under its wheels. Regardless of the danger, I kept pedalling towards that magnificent ray of light at the end of the tunnel, which bought with it an element of safety and refuge, until the next gruelling tunnel that was.

I'd eventually end up in the Kannabe Highlands, observing panoramic views of the final stages of the rice harvest; today not only would I witness the rice still being hung and dried, but the paddy stubble was now beginning to get burnt off in places. Reams of smoke poured out of an array of paddies - that made the area look like the set of a Francis Ford Coppola movie. It was dramatic. The golden crop would soon be feeding a nation.

Descending the highlands, I ventured back into the north of Kyoto Prefecture and ended up in Miyazu, where I found the third and final of Mr Hayashi's three most scenic sights in Japan. Amanohashidate is a narrow 3km long pine forested spit that worms its way out into the Miyazu Bay, connecting a section of land from north to south. From the southern end of the spit I took a cable car to the summit of a stunted mountain; at the top of which I found a theme park with rollercoasters, a crazy golf course and a Ferris wheel. Amanohashidate means

"Bridge to Heaven", as it is meant to resemble a pathway between heaven and Earth, something that I'm largely unable to comment upon as I'd only ever witnessed Hell on Earth.

Many tourists were bending over backwards and looking out across the bay through between their legs - the spit from upside down apparently creating that Bridge to Heaven feel. I didn't join in with such tomfoolery; instead I took a photograph and turned my camera screen upside down afterwards. As I suspected, the view was of a bay turned upside down. It was a nice view all the same, splendid enough, but one of the top three in the country? Never. My top three you ask? Well alright then, here you go:

1. Mt. Fuji, from every angle,
2. Hakodate, at night, and
3. Tokyo, from the Metropolitan Building.
   And now you know.

Miyazu – Kyoto
80 miles

I'd spend the night in an official and free camping ground alongside Miyazu Bay. I slept well, which was important as I knew from looking at the map that the journey south towards Osaka was going to be a mountainous trudge. In fact, my day began vertically, as no sooner had I ventured from the outer confides of suburban Miyazu, would I find myself staggering up Mt. Ōe in a light drizzle. It was a satisfying enough ascent though, with little traffic to share the road with. The peak of Ōe is meant to offer stunning vistas across the prefecture. Yet on this day, it was a wet, windy and dreary place, and due to the slippery road surface, I descended with caution. I'd nearly done 6000 miles by this point, without any hiccups, and I wasn't about to start breaking any limbs now.

Reaching the city of Fukuchiyama (*easy now!*) I would rekindle my affinity with Route 9, which happened to be on

332

fine hell-raising form. I wouldn't expect anything less as I strayed back towards the Keihanshin area; one the busiest regions in Japan. I branched away from the mayhem at one point with the idea that I might find a more docile country road, but was swiftly turned back by a road maintenance crew. I ended up being re-routed back in the direction of Kyoto. Buried amongst the mountains, Kyoto has to be one of the most difficult cities to reach via bicycle. Being shrouded the way it is historically gave the city its strategic advantage, as all passes could be monitored for enemies. And that's exactly how I felt every time I cycled into this ancient city - like the enemy. It was a monotonously steep and sweaty climb, just as it had been some two months previously - when I'd entered the city from Shiga to the east.

Rain started to fall heavily as I descended down into the city. Being rush hour, the roads were heaving with traffic. I'd decide to spend the night in a hotel in Kyoto and head over to Osaka the following morning; the mountains and the rain had done me in for one day.

I rocketed down the mountainside at 30mph, swerving in, out and around some tediously slow moving traffic; it was mad yet thrilling. I would've though been more than willing to put my hands up and admit stupidity, should I have ploughed straight into the back of a Nissan Micra and shattered a testicle. I was being cocky and letting the 6000 miles unbroken factor undoubtedly go to my head; I was feeling somewhat invincible. I was of course no superhero - and my approach thus far, although very successful, was a trifle haphazard. So, I guess what I'm trying to say is, 'Kids, don't try this at home!'

By the time I'd found a hotel in central Kyoto, it was absolutely lashing it down. The bags under my eyes felt heavy and upon looking at my reflection, I appeared destroyed. As well as darkened eyes, my hair was bedraggled and I had chain oil smeared across one of my cheeks. Also, my beard was horrifically unkempt and made me look like a sex offender. I felt that somehow during the course of one day, I'd managed to age at least nine years.

To rectify this, I had a long hot shower followed by a shave which let me claim a few years back. I then bought a couple of beers and waded over a map book that I'd found at the hotel. I tried to decipher my best route to Osaka for the following day. It seemed that it was almost entirely possible to cut out a bulk of traffic and traverse alongside the Yodo River for some 30 miles or so and all the way into downtown Osaka. I took a big hit of beer and then, finally content, I closed my eyes.

STATS

Dates: 23/09/2014 – 24/09/2014
Total miles traversed: 6,032 miles
Total time in the saddle: 606 hours and 55 minutes

40. OSAKA
大阪府

Kyoto – Osaka
38 miles

I awoke with the map book on my face and half a can of muggy beer by my side. I sat up and cracked my head-on the ceiling, forgetting that I was in a capsule bunk. Capsule hotels are commonplace in Japan, especially in the bigger cities where during the week employees may have to commute from rural areas to work in the city. With the long hours of work expected of the Japanese, returning home is not always an option. The capsules are a simplistic and cost effective commodity; roughly the size of a coffin and often with a TV featuring pay-as-you-go pornography, a reading light and a compulsory shelf in which to store bogeys.

I'd stayed in a few in my time, they are quite soulless really and if I had to stay in one every night like many a commuter, I'd soon get depressed. It probably stands to reason why most salarymen and women spend their evenings getting wankered before going back to their shitty capsule to watch 'Tug Hard 9.'

The shift towards Osaka was a painless one, as I avoided the densely packed roads to straddle alongside the Yodo River for a vast swathe of the journey. If it was pre-1994, I would've been entering the country's smallest prefecture; yet since the building of the Kansai International Airport - on an artificial island constructed in Osaka Bay - the prefecture had created just enough land space to beat titchy Kagawa Prefecture.

Inevitably, I soon branched away from the river and into the metropolitan madness of downtown Osaka. Having now cycled through some of the most bustling cities in the country, tackling the country's third largest with a population of some

335

2.5 million and the biggest economic powerhouse in the Kansai region, appeared to me now as nothing more than an unintimidating marvel.

The city housed an explosion of life, with the roads and sidewalks choked respectively with vehicles and pedestrians. I did my usual combining of both road and sidewalk, in an attempt to try and take full advantage of the army of red traffic lights.

The owner of my hostel - a smiley, middle-aged lady - was surprised to hear that I was cycling around the country and she instantly informed me that I would make a good husband! Now ordinarily that might have made me blush, but by this point in my journey I'd become rather accustomed, if not neutralised, by the completely and utterly random expressions that I would become subjected to. I thanked her sheepishly for her nice comment, before checking in.

For the following few days, I traipsed the distinctively vibrant purr of Osaka. As with Tokyo, a new adventure waited around every corner, along streets you could spend an eternity investigating. From the city's central districts that can be divided up into *kita* and *minami* (north and south) - one can't miss the 173-metre tall Umeda Sky building, with its floating garden observatory that gives one scope of the cities sheer size. In the southern district, is the rambunctious Namba, featuring Dontonburi, a place that feels like the esoteric hub of the city. By night, the area is soaked in an orgy of neon with a procession of bars, restaurants and shopping outlets that rarely close their doors.

Osakans pride themselves on their regional cuisine and one is never far away from a culinary treat. *Takoyaki* (Octopus dumplings), *Okonomiyaki* (savoury pancake), *Teppanyaki* (grilled food) and *Kushikatsu* (deep fried meat and veg) are all staple local dishes - or their own variations of other regional dishes which more than fulfil the most engaging of appetites. I beered and dined for three nights, in this amazingly diverse city. Yet, Osaka like Tokyo - with a plethora of attractions – rapidly allows one to be relieved of vast sums of cash. Things were getting tight and so was my time. I had to press on.

Osaka - Nara
29 miles

The day saw me needing to traverse just 30 miles east to Nara City; a piece of piss I'd initially imagined. I couldn't have been more naïve. Now don't get me wrong, I would have rathered the day's physical self-destruction, as opposed to the likes of what happened on the Norikura Skyline, or say cycling through Tropical Storm Nakri again. Yet regardless, the day's demands were still nothing short of ridiculous. I knew I had a mountain to climb and along the national Route 308 - a busy stretch of road in downtown Osaka - I'd expected a pretty standard no thrills day of cycling. But, as the mountains began to spring up around me, and I breached the last of the outer suburbs of Osaka, the road suddenly narrowed and rose steeply. As I hit a treeline, the road narrowed some more, and further steepened, until the point of sheer obscenity. It felt like I was cycling up the side of an alpine riddled skyscraper.

For the first time in 40 prefectures, I had to admit failure. Being forced to dismount from my bike, I would have to push my 50kg's of kit up into the mountains instead. The road narrowed some more in the process, until it became just about fit for smaller vehicles, i.e. Micro Machines.

Every time a vehicle approached, I'd have to pull my rig over into the undergrowth, to allow it to pass. One saving grace however, was that I was under a canopy of trees, shaded from the sun. Pushing its way back into the 30's, summer obstinately refused to fully let go.

Unfortunately, I was walking at about 2.8mph, in prime mosquito territory; I trudged on cursing and complaining with every step I took. Pushing my rig would also get all sorts of muscles pumping and working overtime, until I was shaking like a nervous wreck. My child-like biceps - which for the best part of this journey had only directed my bike and participated in the occasional 5-finger shuffle - were beginning to burn up. My pedals, with their serrated edges like piranha teeth, bit into my shins and drew blood. I cursed some more as the road steepened ever further to my disadvantage; my hamstrings becoming taut, feeling like they needed to give birth to something hideous.

A car passed, its owner revving the guts out of its engine in a high gear, as a young boy with his face pressed up against the passenger-side window, turned and said something to the driver. They both burst into laughter. I knew the drill by now and the boy was right... I did look like a wanker.

Intermittent breaks were key, and it was whilst having one such break and shouting at a moss-laden rock, that an elderly couple approached me on foot from the opposite direction. *'Taihen ne?'* Isn't it a bit difficult? Asked the elderly man, pointing at my bike and gear.

'Hai, chotto tanoshi ja nai yo,' Yes, it's a little bit no fun.

They both chuckled before telling me that I wasn't far from the summit. And with that there was one last, cruel slog before reaching the peak of the dastardly Route 308. Here the streets were cobbled and there were a few old farm houses and a restaurant. The view down across Nara City revealed that the old city didn't appear to be anywhere near as big as I'd expected. This principally being due to the fact that it was Ikoma, a completely different city altogether. To get to Nara City, I still distressingly had one more mountain to scale. But I had however made it to my 41st prefecture, so that at least accounted for something. I trudged on.

STATS

Dates: 25/09/2014 – 29/09/2014
Total miles traversed: 6,099 miles
Total time in the saddle: 614 hours and 10 minutes

41. NARA
奈良県

My second mountain along Route 308 offered up the same steep aggressiveness as its predecessor, but thankfully wasn't as big. The layout of Nara City, coming down from its summit, also seemed more to scale; I was definitely in the right place.

Tucked down a narrow side street in the Naramachi district, amongst a procession of Edo Period merchant houses, was my guesthouse. The friendly owner greeted me in English, and even offered me a safe place to store my wheels. I had arrived at the guesthouse shortly before dusk and was somewhat shattered. The building was quaint, traditional and full of character; with its creaky wooden floor boards, sliding *shoji* screens and a chilled out and welcoming vibe.

Legend has it that David Bowie once owned a property in this very neighbourhood, but upon enquiring about this, I received a series of puzzled looks. End of conversation.

I chatted on though with various travellers at the guesthouse, whilst still trying to get to grips with one of the most unexpected and arduous day's graft of my entire trip. And when I started to nod off, mid-conversation, I and my fellow travellers all knew that it was time for me to retire for the night.

Nara

As an ancient capital, the city of Nara is far from an intimidating place; with a population of little over 360,000, the city is relatively small by Japanese standards. It was designed in a similar fashion to many a Chinese city; in a grid layout making it easily navigable by foot or bicycle. Naturally, I'd choose the latter way to explore.

The city was crowned capital of Japan from 710 to 784, bringing about the Nara Period that would become heavily influenced by Buddhism. This era paved the way for many temples, shrines, statues and books - which today remain well preserved. In fact, Nara has more UNESCO World Heritage listings than any other prefecture in the country.

I started out with a short cycle ride over to Nara Park; a huge inner city green space which hosts a bulk of the city's national treasures - inclusive of its 1200 resident shika deer. Just as with Miyajima in Hiroshima, or the wilds of Yakushima, the deer have no natural predators and are completely fearless of humans. The story goes that when Nara was originally built, the mythological God of Thunder and Swords - Takemikazuchi - arrived at the Kasuga Shrine in Nara Park on a white deer, to protect the newly established capital. From this time, the deer were seen as some sort of messengers for the Gods and have long since been protected. Despite the usual signs advising visitors not to feed the deer, there are vendors selling deer crackers to the public; the crackers sending some of the animals into a bit of frenzy.

Throughout the day, I saw various deer galloping after humans like packs of hooligans, before mugging them blind of crackers. Yet, whilst some behaved like yobbos, others were more gracious, often bowing their heads to their guests, before accepting their treat. Something I thought I'd never see, but then such is the magic of Nara Park.

Amongst the varying temples and shrines in the Park, the highlight is the Tōdai-ji Temple; one of the largest wooden structures in the world. First completed in 752, it had at the time so much influence that some 32 years later, the government was forced to move the country's capital from Nara to Nagoaka - in order to try and dumb down the impact the temple was having on governmental bureaucracy.

Despite now being 33% smaller than its original incarnation, due to subsequent fires, the temple is still a grand sight to behold, inside as well as out. It also holds the biggest bronze statue of a Vairocana Buddha in the country, measuring in at around 15-metres in height. One isn't meant to take photographs of the grand Buddha, but that didn't stop the Chinese tourists... because they do what they want.

Towards the afternoon, the park and temple grounds had become too heavily crowded with camera-toting tourists and screaming school children, and so I went in search of something a little more off the tourist trail. Just slightly north of Nara Park - jutting up into the skyline - was what appeared to be the relic of a rollercoaster. Opened in 1961, it was heavily inspired by Mr Disney's popular Californian theme park, but just not quite as popular. To prove this point, in 2006 it went bust and closed its doors to the outside world forever. Yet, instead of being bulldozed and turned into a vulgar series of apartment blocks, it was just simply left to the winds of time; and in that there is an inner beauty that has attracted many an urban explorer or *haikyo* - as they are known in Japan. This place was Nara Dreamland.

The parking lot was running wild with vegetation as lamp posts and signboards stood bent, rusted and strewn with graffiti. A lacklustre chain blocked the entrance, yet just several metres away another chain was down. I cycled inside to investigate. A couple of vandalised toll booths dictated the parking rates and read 'Welcome to Dreamland.'

Heading to the ticket office, and the main entrance to the park a little further afield, I felt like I'd stumbled across the set of 'The Walking Dead.' In the eight years since its closure, the Park had truly lost its fight with time, giving it a spooky sort of post-apocalyptic edginess; it was a surreal place. At the ticket counter, the blinds were down, the Dreamland sign above it was faded and dismal looking. To the right of the ticket office was a dark and dingy tunnel that led further into the confides of the Park; the tunnel boarded-up with 12ft high plywood. I could have climbed it, if it wasn't for the fact that I didn't want to leave my bicycle behind.

I'd heard rumours of huge fines and people getting kicked out of the country for getting caught inside this place. Whether or not this was just all Internet propaganda or fear-mongering, to aid an adrenaline rush, I couldn't be too sure – so, I decided to explore a series of boarded-up souvenir shops and buildings just to the side of the entrance instead.

Cycling slowly into the ground floor of a murky and doomed looking multi-storey car park, I happened across a plastic bag curiously positioned in the centre of the floor. Coming to a stop, my natural inquisitiveness led me to poke my nose inside to reveal some rolled-up clothing with a wallet on top. As soon as I saw the wallet I knew that I wasn't alone and quickly looked around into the surrounding gloom. I saw nothing for a few short moments as I slowly began to peddle away from the scene with the feeling that I might have been being watched. I need not have really worried, as cycling a little further, my curiosity was met in the purest form by a completely naked Japanese man prancing about with headphones on, listening to his iPod. He was loving life as he bopped back and forth with his eyes closed, completely in his element. I was a little shocked and nearly crashed my bike into a concrete bollard. Startled by my presence, the naked man of whom I swear was just about gearing up for a slut-drop opened his eyes and quickly guarded his limited manhood…

'*Konnichiwa*,' I offered kindly, trying my hardest not to burst out into laughter. For a chubby fellow, he certainly moved fast as he scuttled off into the shadows, completely abandoning his plastic bag. I cycled out of his seedy lair and back into the safety of daylight. I wondered what kicks he got from being naked in a car park on the outskirts of town… *had I completely ruined his day by invading his naughty time*? Or did he secretly want to get discovered?

I appreciate the fact that fantasies and fetishes exist, but strutting about starkers in an abandoned parking lot… how is that ever sexy? I guess you could say don't knock it until you've tried it. I'll probably never try it though… probably.

Several moments later, I saw the nudist running up a hillside and into the undergrowth. He now donned a flannel shirt but his bare behind was still exposed. In his hand was his plastic bag. Yes, I had definitely ruined naughty time. I felt bad.

Any temptations I was initially having in regards to investigating the amusement park any further were now redundant. If there was just as many naked Japanese men prancing about on the inside of the Park as there were on the outside, then I would declare it all a little bit too rich for me. Things would be much more novel if I were back in the quaint little Naramachi district, drinking green tea and talking about the weather - as if nothing weird had ever happened today, nothing weird at all.

Nara – Hashimoto
39 miles

Moving on from the fetish scene of Nara, I traversed southerly into the Kii Peninsula - the largest peninsula in Japan. There I ventured on the fringes of the foothills of Koyasan.

Arriving late in the day - in the rather unimpressionable city of Hashimoto - I bunkered down for the night alongside the Kinokawa River.

An early start the following morning would see me tackle the most sacred mountain range in Japan.

STATS

Dates: 29/09/2014 – 1/10/2014
Total miles traversed: 6,138 miles
Total time in the saddle: 617 hours and 38 minutes

42. WAKAYAMA
和歌山県

Hashimoto – Koyasan
16 miles

"To be enlightened is simply to understand fully the true nature of your own mind. Understanding fully the true nature of your own mind is equal to understanding everything."
Sutra from the 7th Century Dainichi-Kyo

Throughout his 62-year tenure on Earth, Kōbō-Daishi travelled far and wide across Japan - and as far as China - in a quest for religious knowledge of Shingon, the Japanese Buddhist Sect. In 826, with the vital knowledge gathered, he constructed a temple complex amongst the arresting mountains of Koyasan. The mountain range has eight peaks and is said to resemble that of a lotus flower; the Buddhist symbol for enlightenment. His teachings and symbolic edifices remain to this day as the holiest of the holy across the Japanese archipelago.

The ride up into the 800-metre mountain range was modestly steep, along a narrow and winding road clustered with pines. The cool mountain air was fresh upon my cheeks and, as I climbed, I felt almost weightless amongst the mountains mystical silence. At about 600-metres, the surrounding tree foliage began to lose its vivid summer colouring, as the clutches of autumn drew ever closer.

With my pragmatically early start, I took myself to the summit within a few hours and checked myself into the Kokuu Guesthouse, a newish establishment with clean spacious capsules.

Arriving early enough allowed me to enjoy the entirety of the day exploring the Koyasan complex on foot. The main draw was Okunoin, a graveyard set in an aged cedar

345

woodland where some 200,000 tombstones surround the resting place of Kōbō-Daishi. Buried here one might find feudal lords, monks, locals, celebrities, royalty and strangely commercial companies - such as electrical giants Sharp, the car manufacturer Nissan, as well as a pest control company that has a memorial for all the termites that they have snuffed out over the years.

Towards the back-end of the cemetery is the Torodo Lantern Hall: a worship hall with over 10,000 lanterns kept eternally lit. Behind the Hall is the Kōbō-Daishi Gobyo Mausoleum; inside of which, the Grand Master rests in an eternal state of meditation. An elderly woman was reciting a mantra as I passed. Though not a religious person, I appreciate the significance of beliefs; they can truly guide us when we need clarification the most.

The site receives over a million visitors every year, some to pay their respects to Kōbō-Daishi and Shingon and others, like myself, that wish to observe respectfully an almost ageless series of rituals.

I'd walked most of the temples by the afternoon, finishing at Kongōbu-ji; the official headquarters of Shingon's 3,600 nationwide temples. By this stage, I was quite naturally 'all templed out,' and thus returned to my guesthouse for a siesta.

At night I returned to the graveyard of Okunoin. Even though it was pitch black, with only the dim glow from a few lanterns, the graveyard was once again welcoming.

At the Torodo Lantern Hall, the monks held a prayer service. A number of tourists and locals poured into the hall, squeezing themselves onto the *tatami* floor to observe a procession of twenty monks as they chanted mantras for an hour. Even though I had no idea what the monks were saying, there was something soothing about their repetitiveness and tone. In fact, I felt compelled to stay, even though others piled out after only minutes. Unfortunately, I'd picked a crumby position in which to sit, as an invisible walkway appeared to develop between myself and the performing monks. A contingent of elderly couples kept flooding past me; every now and then the traffic stopped and I'd get a face full of senior-arse. I had to draw the line however, when one hefty tourist stumbled, thrusting her nether regions into my face; it smelt like she was in the process of smuggling koi carp out of one of the sacred ornamental ponds. I left, gagging.

And the OAP assault wouldn't end there… whilst trying to sleep in my capsule, back at the guesthouse, a lady returning from the crap house opened up my capsule and tried to get into bed with me - presumably not realising that she'd returned to the wrong capsule.

'Oi!' I said, slightly alarmed, not being able to think of anything else to say through general fear of getting touched up.

'OHHHHH!' hollered the unbeknown intruder equally alarmed, *'sumiemasen, sumiemasen,'* she offered, whilst retreating backwards and bowing four times in the process.

After that, I locked the door firmly, and was forced to sleep with one eye open for the remainder of the night. *What was wrong with these Japanese grandmothers*? Maybe it was the fresh mountain air. I'd be ashamed of my Nan if she behaved like this on holiday!

Koyasan – Wakayama
49 miles

Descending the ropey road down from Koyasan was a bit of a trial, as I headed west along a heavily populated route towards Wakayama City. A procession of road works and tourist-filled buses caused me to slam on the brakes on numerous occasions; one oncoming bus swerving wide around a blind corner just inches from erasing me only added to the thrill.

Back down at sea level, I joined up with a soulless highway that served me all the way to the prefecture's capital. Any spiritual notions that I may have been harbouring from my time in Kōbō-Daishi's playground, were soon levelled out by the highway's monotony.

In Wakayama, I met my Couchsurfing sponsor Zangief; a short framed and spritely Belarusian student studying at the local university. Zangief spoke five languages, he didn't drink booze and he didn't take drugs, he just studied and, by all accounts, he studied hard... in Japanese! This fact made my brain ache just thinking about it. He told me that he loved his country, but enjoyed life in Japan more, in fact, he wanted to stay on and open a business. After a cup of tea and a Tom Cruise movie, we dined on some exorbitantly flavoured home-made sweets that his mother had sent him over from his homeland.

Later that night, I learnt that the season's 8th typhoon - Typhoon Phanfone - was approaching from the southwest and was on collision course with Wakayama. I would have no choice but to hole myself up at the seaside retreat of Shirahama for a bit, whilst it blew over. I just hoped that I could get there before the burly Phanfone did.

Wakayama – Shirahama
74 miles

It was overcast as I left Wakayama, with a wind that grew steadily to the point of intimidation as the day went on. Zangeif had shown me a cycle path on a map, that would lead me all the way out of the city and into rural Wakayama - without my having to touch the roads.

Oranges decorated the mountain sides on the city's periphery; with orchards being carved into the mountain's very slopes. The prefecture prides itself on its fruit with its oranges - known locally as *mikan* - being its showcase yield. Painted on the side of a cliff face was a giant friendly orange with facial features, he was tilting his little red hat gaily to passers-by. In the essence of things to come, Mr Mikan was putting on an incredibly endearing face.

The day was all about the mountains; inland wasn't an issue as I was shielded from the wind, which allowed for some more than capable climbing. However, upon reaching the coast, towards the final third of the way to Shirahama, my progress would become severely stunted. It hadn't rained though; that much I was thankful for.

Shirahama is one of Japan's premiere *onsen* towns, alongside Beppu in Kyūshū and Atami in the Izu Peninsula; but in October and with a strong typhoon heading in, tourist numbers had plummeted – its pure white sand beaches lay all but empty. So it was no surprise that when I checked into my guesthouse, there wasn't a soul insight. In fact, it wouldn't be until early evening that someone would arrive to take my money and then depart again, effectively leaving me in charge of the entire house. But then there was a really big fuck-off typhoon on its way and the last place anybody really wanted to be was by the coast, myself included, but what choice did I have? Still, at least I wasn't camping.

The typhoon didn't hit during the night but was still looming out in the Pacific as the wind intensified throughout the following day. I sent the guesthouse owner an e-mail and said I'd stay another night until the storm had passed. He never replied.

After breakfast, to avoid the onset of cabin fever, I cycled a short way to the nearby Sandanbeki Cliffs. The steep weather-worn cliffs looked dramatic as a procession of truly ferocious waves battered up against them, sending ocean spray high up into the skies. The sea was massively unsettled as Phanfone inevitably made leeway towards the mainland; Mother Nature would again soon be strutting her vengeful stuff; all I could do now was look on uselessly and marvel at her illustriousness.

The storm by this point had already taken the lives of three U.S servicemen in Okinawa, all of who were no doubt doing something very similar to myself before they got caught out. When the rain set in, I backed away from the cliffs, bought some rations from 7-Eleven and returned to my abandoned guesthouse.

By nightfall, the storm hit the shores of Shirahama and my food rations were exhausted. I praised having a roof over my head though as outside the rain lashed down and the wind raged. I could hear metal objects clanging about, the smashing of glass and the rustle of tarpaulin. The fixtures of the guesthouse were rocking as the windows rattled violently and the electricity went out. Several times, the entire building shuddered, as if it were about to give way under the storm's wicked wrath. Lightning lit up my darkened dorm room, as I lay in bed perilously trying to read James Clavell's Shogun, on my Kindle.

At 9pm, 11pm and again at 3am, there were a series of muffled public service announcements - across the public tannoy system. I failed to understand them, but hoped that the messages were just cautioning residents of the potential dangers spawning from the Pacific... and weren't an immediate evacuation order.

The wind and rain continued on relentlessly, proceeding through until dawn and throughout most of the next day. I ventured outside briefly to check the scale of the damage: my bicycle had been toppled over and there were a few broken plant pots scattered about the place - and a piece of tarp was wrapped around some electricity wires. But failing that, the daunting sounds that I'd heard throughout the night seemed to have more or less exacerbated the scale of damage actually caused. Although that being said, throughout its 15-day cycle, the storm caused over £60 million worth of damage and was responsible for at least 12 deaths, inclusive of the French

Formula One driver Jules Bianchi, who lost control of his vehicle in wet conditions at the Japanese Grand Prix.

Beginning to feel somewhat marooned, I e-mailed the guesthouse owner again to let him know that I'd be staying one more night in his lonesome guesthouse. Again he never replied.

Shirahama – Shingū
71 miles

With blue skies and a steady cool breeze, I was fit to return to the road again. Whilst I gave my bike the once over, the guesthouse owner decided to show his face. He seemed surprised that I was still there. I told him that I'd e-mailed him, but he said that he never received anything. Regardless, I paid my dues and hit the road.

The ocean sat calm, like a stagnant pond. It was a shame the same couldn't have been said for Route 42, around the tip of the Kii Peninsula. The road was chock-a-block with construction vehicles; the most I'd witnessed since traversing the disaster-struck Sanriku coastline. A new expressway was in the works. There was also a road littered with fallen trees and rubble that, during the typhoon, had been bought down from the surrounding mountains. I regretfully lined myself up for another shifty day in the saddle.

Rounding the peninsula, I journeyed north towards the border of Mie Prefecture; winding up in the city of Shingū. This small and diffident city was about as vibrant as a breeze block. It was home though to the Kumano Hayatama Taisha Grand Shrine. It looked brand new, like they'd just pieced it together yesterday from a 'Build your own Shrine kit' that they'd purchased from the local Asian branch of IKEA. A nice enough shrine. But let it be said, by this point in my travels, I'd quite frankly seen enough similar looking temples, shrines and castles to keep me going for the next couple of decades.

The buzz of finding somewhere to camp though would never bore me; there was always something exciting and challenging about this part of the day. I scoped out a couple of potential parks, before finding the ideal locale alongside a small cut of water that edged away from the Shingū River. There, amongst a perfectly habitable patch of grass, I nestled my being. And, as night breached - for the first time in many months - I shivered a little as I slept.

STATS

Dates: 2/10/2014 – 7/10/2014
Total miles traversed: 6,348 miles
Total time in the saddle: 637 hours and 8 minutes

43. MIE
三重県

Shingū - Ise
94 miles

Crossing the Shingū River into Mie, I trailed along the coast and up into the mountains; and from there back down to the coast. The far reaching alpine-clustered terrain seemed to blend into a horizon of faultless infinity, as a collection of freshwater rivers raucously poured out to sea. Tea plantations divided harmonious villages, as I worked my way north-easterly with nothing but my compass and a keen eye for signposts. At a cool 18°C the cycling was all too easy and the thought of getting lost amongst the prefecture's beautiful scenery was almost enticing.

Upon arrival in Ise, I was starving hungry. I treated myself to a bowl of ramen, six gyōza, a Japanese curry, a croissant, a mystery flavoured yoghurt, three iced-ring donuts and two cans of beer. I certainly know how to party! I'd earned my feast... but I definitely needed a lay down afterwards.

The skies grew ominous as night drew in. I set up a camp along a vast stretch of parkland next to the Miya River. From my tent I watched the lightning scorch the mountaintops to the west. Gradually, as the storm worked its way towards me and the air got damp, I retreated into the lurid depths of Sir Leaksalot. The white noise of the rain beat on the nylon; easing my body and mind into an wonderful world of nothingness.

Ise – Nagoya
72 miles

Just as the rain eased me to sleep, it would ease me back awake; by about 6am it was just as heavy as it had been all through the night. I chanced a cheeky peak outside. Things were looking morbid, yet I hated hanging around, so I packed up camp.

At a nearby convenience store I had some coffee and donuts and pulled out a notepad full of scribbled notes of what there was on offer for the budding tourist in Ise. The notes read a little like this:

- The Grand Shrines of Ise Jingu (Yay! More temples)
- Nothing

The rain wasn't ceasing and looked as if it would continue to flex its muscles for a vast majority of the day. I'd obviously had enough of shrines by now, but heard that the two Grand Shrines of Ise Jingu were the most sacred in the Shintō religion, and this fact would make me feel bad, if I didn't at least show my face for a few a measly minutes.

In Ise there are 125 shrines - inclusive of the two Grand Shrines that are separated by a few miles from one another. The Naiku Inner Shrine is said to house Amaterasu Omikami - the Sun Goddess. The Geku Outer Shrine, houses Toyouke Omikami: the God of food, clothing and housing. This second God was basically Amaterasu's slave, because she needed someone to feed and clothe her - as she couldn't be bothered to do it herself. But, then, she had been hanging around since about the 3rd century AD; so I guess we'd all probably need somebody to feed and clothe us by this point.

The closest shrine to where I stood, was the Geku Outer Shrine. As I parked my bike up in the bicycle lot, there was a foreboding rumble of thunder as the rain continued to penetrate my surrounds. I huffed as I walked into the shrine complex that was gravel-lined and surrounded by Japanese Cypress trees. A few other keen tourists were also stomping about in their brightly coloured anoraks. I approached a huge fortified fence with a gateway, where a security guard stood; resplendent in a wide-brimmed hat that gushed water from its peak. He reminded me not to take photos because of the shrine's sacredness.

Passing through the gateway revealed a very modern and relatively bare shrine with a thatched roof. A shrine so plain, in fact, that even now I can barely even remember it. But there was definitely a bit of thatch, some wood and a barrier preventing me from getting any closer to the hut-like building. I also learnt that the shrine being as sacred as it was, gets smashed up every twenty years, and a new one built directly next to it. But that in reality wasn't as half balmy as it sounded – as it was a tradition that dates back to the late 7th Century; allowing the skills and knowledge of temple building to be passed down from one generation to the next.

I still wasn't over impressed, not that I was expecting to actually see a god of course, that naturally would've been asking way too much. Plus, as I was about as religious as a potato, I'd surely never be worthy enough of a god's divine presence.

I looked at another tourist who approached the wooden barrier next to me; his hair soaked and plastered to his forehead as water pissed out of the sleeves of his snazzy lilac anorak. His face was deadpan, he just wanted to go home and look at some boobs on the Interwebs; he looked thoroughly sad.

I didn't bother going to see the Sun Goddess afterwards, as I doubted that she would've warmed me up on a day such as this, the only thing that was going to make my day now was a nice cosy hotel room in Nagoya. I fetched my bike from the parking lot and headed north, my damp panties chafing me every stride of the way.

Traversing along the heavily trafficked Route 23, I was sprayed by copious amounts of liquid from all angles. The fresh water from the skies above was far from a deterrent from the passing vehicles that caked me in all kinds of unmentionable squalor.

From Ise, all the way to the Aichi Prefectural border, lays the Ise Plain; an area of dense industrial might with ship yards, car manufacturers, chemical plants and oil refineries. Passing through the city of Yokkaichi was like passing through the nation's scrap yard amongst some subliminal layer of hell. The sides of the roads were littered with high volumes of busted up televisions, patio chairs, underpants, odd socks, mannequin heads, scrap metal, knackered tyres, rusted bicycles, beer bottles, jazz mags, Big Mac wrappers and decaying animals. I also spotted what looked like the Japanese equivalent of a box set of Jethro DVD's, *perhaps the world's most unwanted Christmas present since Cornwall started brewing comedians back in the early twentieth century.*

Yokkaichi had always had problems though, in the 1960's through to the 70's many of the city's residents suffered from what was known as Yokkaichi Asthma. The localised burning of petroleum and crude oil released vast quantities of sulphur oxide into the atmosphere, causing some incredibly thick smog which created a series of health issues across the city. The local government eventually used flue-gas desulfurization to blanket the amount of sulphur oxide emissions that were reaching its city's citizens. Today the city still comes across as vulgar and uninviting, however, a puncture would cause me to linger for far longer than was necessary.

Farther north, I crossed - via bridge - the monstrous Kiso River. From its source in Nagano - some 142 miles north-easterly – it gushes wildly with its two gaping mouths into the Pacific. And out there somewhere another typhoon dawdled. The biggest of the year - Category 5 Super Typhoon Vongfong

- approached deviously with a fistful of malice. It would be passing through the region within the next few days. And so, for the next week, I would have no choice but to call Nagoya my home.

STATS

Dates: 8/10/2014 –9/10/2014
Total miles traversed: 6,514 miles
Total time in the saddle: 653 hours and 31 minutes

44. AICHI
愛知県

Nagoya

It was dark as I surged fourth towards Sakae, the city's central hub. The roads some five lanes deep were heavily congested. Lights twinkled around every corner and a taxi cut me up to refuel with passengers; the driver paying me no heed. During this transaction, my rear tyre burst. A businessman close by, eating a late night ice cream, saw the incident and quickly looked away when I caught his eye. A stranger eyes a stranger, but just for a moment. A city of strangers, just like any other vast metropolis that surges with millions, each with their own intricately woven lives that are all but a mystery to the causal passerby.

Nagoya is Japan's 4th largest city with an urban population of over 2.2 million. It is a prosperous, economical powerhouse of a city and, due to its geographical locale in the centre of the country - sandwiched between Tokyo and Osaka - it forms the country's third largest metropolitan area; sprawling close to 4,400 square miles, housing just over 9 million people. One such stranger was a Couchsurfer from Canada. But upon learning that the Couchsurfing Canadian had been living in Nagoya teaching English for the past five years and that his name was Dudley, he was no longer a stranger to me. I wheeled my bike the remaining couple of miles into Sakae, to meet Dudley.

At this late stage in the day I just didn't have the willpower to fix a puncture. I'd do it in the morning when my rig was empty.

It was the weekend and Sakae was positively bustling with life. If you happen to be in Nagoya, then Sakae is not to be missed, as there's not a great deal else to see in the city apart from its quirky planetarium and fancy pants castle with an elevator. Any display of deep cultural roots in the city being severely limited, as most of it was erased by widespread firebombing during the Second World War. Yet in Sakae the lights never go out and the beer never stops flowing; there are more shops, bars and eateries than your old uncle Herbert can shake his fully loaded catheter bag at.

After dropping my gear off at Dudley's house, we set off deep into downtown Sakae to set a damnable trend for the weekend. Having been living in the city for some time now, Dudley was quite the connoisseur around town, shaking hands and greeting a wide range of faces as we strolled the district's lively streets. Like myself, Dudley was in his early thirties but drank like he was still in his early 20's, fast and heavy. Together we formed a mutual bond of drunkenness that can only be bestowed to other like-minded Englishmen and Canadian-men out on the rip together... in Sakae. Neither of us were fazed by our reckless drinking, perhaps because neither of us could recall much from the weekend, apart from the critically burdensome hangovers that would inevitably follow at around Sunday lunchtime... when Dudley informed me quite bluntly that I had to leave.

'Oh,' was my first response. Nothing else faintly intelligible springing to mind.

'Yeah you gotta go man, I just got a Couchsurfing request from some hot French chick, look.' Dudley passed me his laptop with some profile pictures of a scantily clad French girl. I saw his angle.

'Sex sells, huh?' I quipped.

'It certainly does my friend, it certainly does, now get the fuck out!'

And with that I was back out on my arse again. I thought about my Couchsurfing profile picture; a sweaty looking guy with a grisly beard. It was little wonder most of my Couchsurfing requests were turned down, I obviously needed to start showing more flesh. I wondered if I should head down to the beach with my mankini and try to sex things up a bit

359

with a racy photo shoot. But then I recalled the imminent danger that Typhoon VongFong still posed, as it steadily surged closer to the city. My Playgirl shoot would have to wait. I patched up my puncture and tracked down a hostel on the other side of town.

The hostel wasn't the kind of place that one goes to make friends. In a dim and windowless room that lingered with the prevalent stench of farts and unwashed pants, the bulk of the room's inhabitants slept all through the day. Most would snore nonchalantly, another would fiercely grind his teeth, and one frustrated individual would tussle about behind a drawn curtain, cursing to himself and sighing pathetically, before falling silent for hours at a time.

Addressing a hangover, I endorsed the hostel's anti-social aura as I climbed up to my top bunk bed and went into hibernation mode.

I awoke to the sound of beating rain on the rooftop, accompanied by a wind that whipped and hissed. Vongfong had arrived. I'd slept for far too long and my stomach was now begging for food. I'd have to venture out. Naturally it is ill-advised to go outdoors during a typhoon… due to risk of general all-round death. But needs must, my belly required a feed, and anyway, who are we if we don't take a little risk here and there?

The streets were saturated and there were now fewer cars on the road; as they passed they sent piles of cascading water across the sidewalks. Neon lights reflected off of every wet surface as I honed in on a convenience store. In just short of two minutes I was soaked to the bone, but no longer hungry.

When I got back to my decaying hostel, I fired up my laptop to find that I'd received a Couchsurfing message from a stranger. Clicking on the message revealed that it was from Asami, a local Nagoyan girl who, like Dudley, was now no longer a stranger. She asked if I wanted to meet up tomorrow for a drink, so that she could practice her English. I clicked on her ambiguous looking profile picture in the hope that there might be some bikini pictures. No such luck, her only picture showed a silhouette standing upon a cliff edge, somewhere in Northern India. So, I had no idea what she looked like.

The following day I would still be in Nagoya - as the leftovers of the typhoon passed through - and so I accepted her invitation. I'd only be sat in my dorm bed all day giggling at my own farts if I didn't go, and thus it all made sense... I would go on a sort-of-date.

We agreed to meet by the big Ferris wheel in Sakae at 4pm. I was bang on time and she was 20 minutes late. But it was worth it. A young woman approached me gingerly and asked if I was Daniel.

'*Hai, watashi desu!*' Yes, that's me! I countered.

She responded with an infectious giggle, brushed aside a strand of hair, revealing to me that she was an absolute stunner. She was 22 and had a stylish, elegant look about her, with her short-cropped bob hairstyle, white short-shorts and a tank top that hugged her slender body with confidence.

'So, what do you want to do?' She asked smiling, as I placed my eyeballs back into their respective sockets.

'Errr...' I replied like a dumbass.

She laughed again. I'm pretty sure that she was already aware of the effect that she was having on me. I looked around quickly and saw that we were outside a pachinko parlour.

'Pachinko?' I offered.

'Ok sure, do you know how to play?' She asked.

'Not a clue!'

'*Watashi mo!*' Me too!

As we approached the parlour, the automatic doors slid open and we were almost blown away by the decibels being flung from out of them. It was so loud it was almost a little bit scary. Standing side by side, the pachinko machines formed alleys and trailed off deep into the parlour. Men and women sat on little stools with cigarettes hanging from their lips, directing some sort of handle in front of them that steered a bunch of ball bearings all over the place. I really didn't understand as I sat down and placed 1,000 Yen into the slot. Before I knew it, I had balls pissing out all over the place.

'What do I do with my balls?' I shrieked to Asami, as she buckled over with laughter. 'Don't laugh, this is serious,' I said.

She confirmed that she had no idea and went to fetch some assistance. A man on a machine to my left looked over my shoulder and sniggered to himself, gleefully. Asami brought over one of the pachinko parlour assistants who was dressed as a sexy maid. I didn't see how this was going to help me. The assistant started to reel off the rules to me in Japanese and I didn't understand a word, but she then took my hand and directed it over a button that stemmed the flow of ball bearings... or directed them. She then wished me luck and disappeared.

I turned to Asami who returned to my side. 'What was that all about?' I asked.

She shrugged her shoulders.

'Shall we just go and play Mario Kart instead?' I suggested.

'*Hai,*' Yes, she confirmed.

God bless Nintendo's Mario Kart; bringing the world together since 1992. We would each pick out our own kart to sit in and a respective colourful character to reflect our own personalities: I Bowser, King of the Koopa and she, Princess Toadstool of the Mushroom Kingdom. In two thrilling matches we went on to win one game apiece, a best of three - although a consideration was argued against on grounds of defamation of our own budding Mario Karting egos. And, so we retreated from our Karts and called it a draw. Even though, deep down, I knew that I would've destroyed her, should it have gone to that all-important third and final deciding match, but alas I was playing the part of a gentleman, an English gentleman no less.

Pachinko and Mario Kart had made me work up a thirst and so we agreed to find an izakaya to get some food and drink. Walking along the windswept Nagoyan streets, Asami spoke fluently in English of her travels, having spent many months travelling overseas - and her affinity to India. She dreamed of working there, after finishing her degree in International Relations. I told her that it's always good to have dreams, especially real dreams, ones that you know you can attain.

As well as being beautiful, she was incredibly intelligent and I could see no reason why she couldn't follow her dream. Take me, for example, I would follow one of mine by cycling around Japan and I'm a bloody idiot! Everyone knows that!

'Ah, we're here,' said Asami, stopping suddenly in front of an ominous looking wooden door. 'Are you ready?' she asked.

'Err...yeaahhh,' I replied hesitantly.

Asami giggled and pushed the door open, leading me inside. After walking down a flight of stairs, until we were underground, we were greeted by a guy with half of his face hanging off. The monster held up two fingers and Asami nodded, before it took us into the horror-themed izakaya that was set inside a barely lit dungeon. Monsters of all kinds paraded about, serving customers rudely - as Asami and I were shown into a prison cell. The candle-fashioned electrical lights flicked on and off - and cobwebs dangled from the rafters. The attention to detail was incredible, as our rather ill looking monster gave us a menu and then closed the cell door behind, as it left.

'Scared?' asked Asami.

'No, I'm fine, seems nice,' I replied. 'You?'

'*Chotto...*' She was a little scared.

'Ah you'll be fine, let's get some beer and nibbles.'

We ordered and chatted away. My heart strings tweaking a little when she made me an origami love heart. Things were going well, too well in fact. And then the lights went out, completely, the whole building lit up with the screams of the izakaya's clientele. Asami groped my calf, presumably in fear.

There was a knocking noise, some rattling of chains and an odd shifting sound amplified through a loud speaker. There were moments of silence that became sequentially broken by the screams from various parts of the izakaya. Suddenly our cell door burst open and a neon masked zombie appeared, Asami yelped and pressed her head into my chest. *Nice!* I coolly placed a protective arm around her, as the face of the zombie approached our table, in what was to become an incredibly freaky ordeal. The zombie pushed his face directly into mine and stared me out for a lengthy space of time; as Asami dug her talons into my leg almost causing me to yelp. Then there was a banging noise from afar as the zombie instinctively turned and ran away, leaving us alone together in the darkness. I could feel that Asami was trembling and through her breast pressed up tight against me, her heart was pounding. Lowering my head, I could feel her warm breath on my lips - which now were just millimetres away. If I was to ever strike then this would've been the moment, but my mind was struggling with itself as it always generally did.

Maybe kissing her was a bit rapey and she was just plain scared and that would then seem like you are trying to take advantage of her?

Or is that what she wants? Was that her plan?

But what if I'm wrong?

But she made you a love heart you fool?

Yeah, that's true, that probably stands for something? Yeah I guess. Then kiss her you dickhead, do it, DO IT!

Then, suddenly, the lights flickered back on, and my opportunity became squandered forever.

'There we go, all better now,' I said as I withdrew my arm unromantically and took a massive chug of beer. *Loser.* 'Yup!'

'Err... who are you talking too?'

'Oh, err...never mind, *kanpai!*'

As we toasted another round of 'cheers' we continued to get on well, but I'd definitely blown it. A fascinating girl, perhaps a little naïve, but adventurous and outgoing, and that for me was a massive turn on. As we left the izakaya, we discussed meeting up again the following day, she said she would let me know. I gave her a gentleman's handshake as we then both went our separate ways. I would never see her again.

Nagoya – Hamamatsu
69 miles

Emerging early from my crummy hostel bed, I sighed as I had failed to get any sleep. Deciding that I didn't want to get besotted by any feelings; I left Nagoya. My heart wanted me to stay, but my willpower urged me forward; a task still lay in hand and any such emotional feelings had no part to play in it. I pressed on north-easterly, merely days now from the borders of Tokyo.

The skies continued to be dreary and I got wet on and off. I'd be treated to a puncture and a broken spoke alongside the scruffy and mind-numbing Route 1; this further dampening my spirits. My mother always said that there would be days like this, well actually she didn't, I just read that somewhere. But she was definitely right, mums are always right - even when they're wrong.

I kept cycling, barely stopping to eat and by evening wound down for the night at a Manga Café, damp and angry at the world. I should have gone for the kiss.

STATS

Dates: 9/10/2014 –15/10/2014
Total miles traversed: 6,583 miles
Total time in the saddle: 660 hours and 41 minutes

45. SHIZUOKA
静岡県

Hamamatsu - Shizuoka
57 miles

It was a cold start; my breath clinging to the air. It would be good to wrap things up during the coming week, before the temperature dropped any further. I'd traverse along Route 1 until it converted into an inaccessible expressway, from that point on I followed the quieter mountain roads up amongst one of many of Shizukoka's tea plantations; it is there that 40% of the country's entire green tea crop is produced. Not only will the leaf be used to produce the most popular beverage in the country, but it will also make appearances in a varying array of food products like chocolate, ice cream, salt, cookies, donuts and noodles.

The mountain roads steepened, and as they did, the climes gradually warmed. I was eventually led to the city of Shimada, where I would not only rekindle with Route 1 but I would also come across my first sign for Tokyo in what felt like a long, long six months. A non-jizz commencing buzz of excitement jolted through me. I stopped to stare at the blandest of blue signboards and took a picture of it in the process. To the passers-by that eyed me more strangely than usual, I was certain that most would've had no idea of the ordeal's that I'd been through in order to get this far. Tokyo just seemed like such a lifetime ago for me; I couldn't wait to be back there. Yet I still had one more big hurdle to pounce upon before I returned to the big smoke. And an exciting one at that.

Mid-afternoon I arrived in Shizuoka City with its likable centre of cobbled streets and parks. I treated myself to a Burger King, like a filthy bastard, and sat on the curb to dine;

366

next to my pushbike. Just then, a great booming southern-American accent exploded from over my shoulder.

'It's 'dat cha home, brudda?' I nearly lost my gherkin as I turned to see a man dressed conservatively in black, he had the look of a preacher about him as he gestured towards my bike and its contents.

'Err… yeah… yeah I guess it is.' I replied.

'Huh, well would cha look at 'dat, well good day to ya sir.'

'Thank you, you too mate.' And with that he was gone.

The encounter made me think some more. This bike had carried me and all my worldly possessions for thousands of miles; in unison we'd worked together to get us this far. Was I, for the first time, seeing my bike as more than an inanimate object? No, I wasn't, that would be silly. But the mechanics of my beast of burden had barely faltered; just the wear and tear one would expect after so many miles. Although, despite knowing that the vessel was lifeless and that I was its main drive, I couldn't help but feel that I owed it one. My initial plan upon return to Tokyo was to sell it for some quick cash; I couldn't do that now, we'd been through too much together, it would've been like selling a limb. I decided to keep it, forever. That fact asserted, I finished off my burger and climbed up off of the curb. Looking around to make sure that nobody was watching me, I non-sexually patted the saddle of my steed. 'You've done me proud… brudda!'

I met Couchsurfer, Takeshi, towards the evening; a student of Shizuoka University. He'd just recently come back from a 4-month backpacking stint in south-east Asia and wasn't offended by my Couchsurfer's profile picture, so invited me to spend the night. He would also take me to a bike mechanic he knew to get my broken spoke replaced, after which we would retreat to his apartment in the suburbs.

Squeezing my home into his small apartment was a tight one. His apartment was cluttered with books about computer science and random components. He picked up a few and tossed them to one side. 'Sorry,' he apologised, 'I put books everywhere, because sometimes my landlord comes to make sure I study; books everywhere make me look busy.'

I laughed. 'But you're not busy?

'Hmm... not so much. You hungry?'

'Always.'

'Ok, I make Oden for us.'

Takeshi was the last Couchsurfer of my trip and I'm glad of that fact. He was laid back and had a good sense of humour; understanding some of my predicaments of being on the road, as he too had done some cycling trips around Japan. Stuffing our faces with boiled eggs and fishcakes, our conversation soon after petered as we fell asleep sprawled out across the floor of his apartment, bloated.

Shizuoka – Fujinomiya
37 miles

Takeshi cycled with me for a while up until the city's borders. Crossing a bridge over an expanse of rail yard the skies were as clear as glass, apart from one distant and pure white puff of cloud. *That's not a cloud you idiot!!* My mind bellowed. I pointed it out to Takeshi and he shrugged his shoulders in a bit of a *yeah so what* gesture before telling me that the snow had only appeared over the past couple of days. With the shift in seasons, it would now remain until the following summer. I wanted to get closer. I needed to get closer. I would get closer.

I said my farewells to Takeshi and proceeded in the direction of the sleeping giant; and for the next few days, the nation's jewel would barely leave my sights. At 3,776 metres and with a circumference of 78 miles it is the largest active volcano in Japan. Well documented throughout time by works of art and writing, its geological history dates back well over 100,000 years, and for a millennia its huge slopes have been a pilgrimage for the Japanese.

Stopping off at Shimizu Port, I would be spoilt with one of the most grandiose of views of my entire trip. In its presence I felt unworthy, its scale and might glorious in every way, making me feel like nothing more than a piece of chewing gum tiresomely attached to its heel. Mt. Fuji was magnificent.

I cycled all day, staring almost rudely into the face of what the Japanese call Fujisan. With its most sublime of conical peaks, it carried with it the allure of that picture-perfect postcard look, that it was synonymous with, the world over. I couldn't think of a time that I'd been more constantly in awe; I felt star struck. The volcano, although considered active, hasn't actually erupted since 1707 when the streets of Tokyo were showered in ash some 60 miles away and the surrounding area plummeted into a 10-year blight of famine and social upheaval. And so, having plans to cycle closer to its peak the following day, I hoped that old Fujisan would stay dormant for me just a little bit longer. But then if I was to ever die, having 'Murdered by Mt. Fuji' etched upon my gravestone would certainly have quite the ring to it. More so than getting bludgeoned to death by a broken beer bottle in some south London back alley - as my unkindly dreams often like to dictate.

By mid-afternoon I arrived at Fuji's southern base in Fujinomiya and there I'd spend the night in a hostel… in preparation for scaling one of the greatest and most famous mountains in the world.

Fujinomiya – Fujiyoshida
40 miles

*"A wise man will climb Mt. Fuji once; a fool
will climb Mt. Fuji twice."*

A familiar saying amongst the Japanese; and they see
thousands scale its crowded slopes every year. Although, in
my case, I was not strictly climbing to its summit, as climbing
season was now over - but I would however cycle the
circumference of the mountain and ascend closer to its
northern base in Fujiyoshida at around 900 metres.

One would have thought that after all the miles traversed, I
wouldn't be able to get myself lost, especially in the shadow of
one of the biggest mountains on the planet. Yet traversing
Route 139 around the base of Mt. Fuji – which I was led to
believe would lead me all the way to Fujiyoshida - would
soon take me to another one of Japan's annoyingly
'inaccessible to cyclists' expressways.

'Oh dear,' I said, a rough translation of a very nasty
explosion of vocabulary that was initially delivered.

Pulling out my crumby map book revealed no answers, as
again the pages I needed were missing. It would now be a trial
and error scenario, but knowing that I needed to be to the
north of Mt. Fuji meant that the mountain should always be
on my right if I was approaching it in a clockwise fashion.
Unfortunately, there was no telling where the mountain roads
might swanny off too and I didn't have it in mind to add
another decade onto my journey. I picked a random mountain
road which appeared to run along in close proximity to the
expressway. After about 10 minutes the road branched away
and ascended abruptly, before coming to a dead end in some
sort of mountainside industrial estate or possible contender of
a home for a doomsday cult. One man exited from a side
building of a warehouse, eyeing me skeptically.

'*Konnichiwa,*' I offered, and before I could ask him any further questions, he waved his hands at me and told me to go back down the mountain.

'Boo!' I replied childishly before cycling back from whence I came.

Back at the start of the expressway I would thankfully happen across life; a man walking his dog across a bridge. Catching up with him, I asked him how to get to Fujiyoshida and glumly he pointed to the expressway. *Another route perhaps?* I tried to suggest in terrible Japanese.

He then pointed to a road running west from the expressway, before proceeding to make a collection of shapes and arches with his hands that suggested that the alternative route would entail a cumbersome amount of twists and turns along the way... accompanied by a fuck load of climbing. I thanked the man and his dog and went on my way. Soon finding a sign for Fujiyoshida, I relaxed a little.

It was a steady ascent, climbing up through a procession of alpine forests and rugged pastures. The smell of cow shit lingered in the air, reminding me once again of home and a distant life so very far away. Fuji's iconic peak was out of sight today, shrouded in a thick and gloomy murk. But I knew that the giant was watching its minions; it would always be watching.

The higher I ascended, the cooler the mountain air became. The climb however was hot and sweaty and it was only when descending the occasional slope that the cold layer of sweat that had built upon my back felt like it was freezing solid, as a fierce and cutting wind attacked my flesh, chilling me to the bone. These chills though would never compare to what came next.

STATS

Dates: 16/10/2014 –18/10/2014
Total miles traversed: 6,717 miles
Total time in the saddle: 674 hours and 34 minutes

46. YAMANASHI
山梨県

I had to stop, for nature called. Leaving my bike by the roadside, I walked into the woods. A sign told me to think twice, to console with loved ones and that my life is a precious gift from my parents. Inside the wood, not one creature stirred, they daren't. Trees were packed so tightly together that the midday sun was a useless accompaniment to the hour. It actually felt like the witching hour had approached from the very moment that I'd stepped inside this eerie secluded spot at the foot of Mt. Fuji. A place riddled with folklore with the most wretched of pasts. It is known as Aokigahara, The Sea of Trees, The Demon Forest... or The Suicide Forest. It's a place not to be taken lightly. But a good enough place no less to relieve one's self after many hours in the saddle.

Various sources link the woodlands to the inner recesses of evil. An unproven myth tells of how this dark ancient forest was once a place of *ubasute*, a 19th century practice whereby the frail and the elderly - deemed a burden upon their families - were taken by their loved ones far out into the wilderness and left to die. They say that the forest is haunted by these angry lost spirits, known as *yūrei*. It's also Japan's number one suicide spot. Every year police and local volunteers sweep the forest for the dead, in some years over 100 victims were found. The site is so synonymous with suicide that the police had to stop releasing statistics, in an effort to try and dumb down the morbid attraction. Why so many people choose to end their lives in this forest is still a bit of mystery, but a disturbing book released in 1993 entitled 'The Complete Manual of Suicide' wasn't helping an already escalating problem. The book not only informed its victims of the more convenient ways in which to ease themselves off of the mortal coil, but also the best places in which to do it; including certain areas of

Aokigahara, situated far from any tourist trail. I read one Amazon review of the book, by user, 'yagov':

> *'This book is a very effective guide to suicide.*
> *I have tried most of the methods myself, and I*
> *personally enjoyed burning myself to death*
> *the most. Many of my friends have tried*
> *falling to their deaths out of a window, and*
> *they said that it was rather painless.'*

Obviously yagov's words are to be taken with a pinch of salt, but, on a serious note, it is no secret that the Japanese work long and stressful hours and this stress can lead to unhealthy thoughts. But Japan is also a country whereby suicide - out of shame for one's honour - was the norm. So, is the problem ethnically rooted? I really wouldn't like to say. Suicide of course, is not exclusive to the Japanese, it's a global issue that reaches far and wide. I felt uneasy being in the forest; it's eeriness almost beyond words and it's silence unsettling. Although that being said, it was in parts quite beautiful and alluring.

After relieving myself, I zipped up and took a step back, stumbling slightly on the uneven ground. The branches of a nearby tree entwined with another and seemed to reach out towards me in a gesture. I stood as still as I could in an attempt to try and absorb my surroundings. There was a temptation to go further, a temptation that I decided not to comply with. So gingerly retreated back to the roadside, feeling cold and weird.

After a short descent I'd pass Kawaguchi Lake, one of the 'Fuji Five Lakes' located at the lowest elevation of the five, at about 800 metres. Just a little farther east and 100 metres higher I would ascend to the town of Fujiyoshida: a battered old town at the foot of Mt. Fuji, with that same element of deterioration that many a rural town in Hokkaidō and to the country's north suffer. I cycled slowly along its fractured roads, along an aged boulevard full of crumbly looking buildings; downtrodden by the countless years of long hard winters. An agreeably clean and warm hostel though awaited me in town. A good thing, as the temperature was dropping fast. I thought of what it might have been like to spend the night camping in Aokigahara Forest. I shuddered and then instinctively flicked the kettle on. *No thanks.*

Fujiyoshida – Kamakura
75 miles

Fujisan was in hiding as I left town. It appeared that our first encounter would've been our greatest; this wondrous and impressionable mountain though will always be etched clearly in my mind.

Trailing east, I passed Lake Yamanaka, the largest and highest of the Fuji Five and the only one to have a natural outflow in the form of the Sagami River, which meanders deviously out towards Sagami Bay in the Pacific. Turning my back on Mt. Fuji, I too would descend and leave the landlocked prefecture of Yamanashi behind, returning to the coast and entering Kanagawa, the 47th and final prefecture of my journey.

STATS

Dates: 18/10/2014 –19/10/2014
Total miles traversed: 6,792 miles
Total time in the saddle: 680 hours and 58 minutes

47. KANAGAWA
神奈川県

Well I'd done it. I'd officially cycled to every prefecture in the country. It had taken me the best part of six months, with the odd elongated stop-off here and there. I'd seen much and I'd met many. But before I could get too sentimental, the journey wasn't quite over, for the name of the game was 'Tokyo to Tokyo.' Just a little further now.

Some 40 miles south of Tokyo I would reach the coast in the popular and ancient capital of Kamakura. In the summer months, the beach would be crammed with visitors from all over the Kantō region. Makeshift bars and restaurants would be set up along the beach as varying activities such as: raves, barbecues, surfing, volleyball and football tournaments figured on a near daily basis. Being the wrong end of October however, many such attractions had now been packed up for the year. The day had that lazy Sunday afternoon feel to it; and it was *actually* a Sunday. People were walking their dogs, some were jogging and others, in the moderate 18°C, were having a picnic. I grabbed a couple of beers and sat on the beach, watching the world go by, knowing that tonight would be my last night on the road.

As the sun dropped out of sight and the chills set in, I had the choice to keep warm and attend a local hostel in Kamakura or to stealth camp for one last time. For old time's sake, I felt I had no real choice but the latter. I cycled north for a way, before finding a rough patch of grass in the suburbs. Pulling out Sir Leaksalot from his holster, I gagged instantly. It suddenly dawned on me that since its soaking back in Mie Prefecture - some 10 days previously - I hadn't aired it out or allowed it to dry. This fact had allowed Sir Leaksalot to ferment somewhat. Tonight would definitely be the old boy's last innings. I mopped up the inside of the tent with an old rag and lay down in the damp, amongst the smell of musk and decay. Beautiful.

Kamakura – Tokyo
45 miles

I awoke to what I thought was the sound of sabotage as my bicycle tyre exploded. It would've been all so very typical that on my last night I'd finally meet a disgruntled local that would slash my tyres in protest of my presence. But, upon quickly popping my head out of my tent, there was no one, I was alone, just as I always had been. The inner tube valve had exploded and so I passed the blame to the mechanic back in Shizuoka who may have put slightly too much air pressure into the tyre when he fixed my spoke and rebalanced the rim. But then I never bothered to check the pressure afterwards, as at this late stage in the game, complacency was very much becoming common place.

However, there was some small form of sabotage that took place, in the name of mans' best friend. Whilst changing my inner tube, I noticed that my tyre was laced with a substance that was thick, curdy and incredibly stinky, i.e. dog shit. The smell, just as grimacing as the hum of Sir Leaksalot, who still stood erect by my side, looking rather pleased with life. Well, about as pleased as a knackered old tent could look anyway. It was a grim start to the day, but having before this great journey started, experienced the extremes of a face full of dog excrement, I wouldn't be letting this faze me now. The world could throw whatever it wanted at me today as I was confident enough now to know that I would most definitely be making it back to Tokyo today, no matter what.

After breakfast, I cycled north-easterly. As the roads began to widen and pulsate more prominently with life, I'd breach Yokohama, Japan's second largest city. In 1853, Commodore Matthew Perry and his fleet of warships arrived along the shores of Tokyo Bay and here, for the first time in over 200 years, Japan opened up its doors to trade with the west. Yokohama would become one of the most international cities in the country and within two years of trading with the West would be manufacturing its own beer and ice cream; the staple diet of any real foolhardy sailor. The city would continue to trade and flourish and today houses over 3.7 million inhabitants. A city so large in part that its borders have long since merged with its monstrously proportioned neighbour Tokyo - to form part of the far reaching Greater Tokyo Area.

I paced alongside the consistent drawl of traffic, dwarfed by skyscrapers of varying and intricate architectural detail, stopping for a coffee around mid-morning at a convenience store. Sitting on a bench just outside the store, I watched nonchalantly as the traffic buzzed past. Soon a heavily bearded Kiwi donning an 'All Blacks' baseball cap approached me and sparked up a conversation.

'Cycled far?'

'You could say that,' I mustered.

Still, at the time, not quite being able to absorb the miles which I'd actually conquered. I filled him in on the particulars of my trip and he kindly bought me another coffee to congratulate me. Rufus was a professor from Dunedin and was doing some work at Yokohama University, he too was a budding cyclist, having only just finished a cycling trip with some university students. He asked me what I planned to do with my bike and I said I was going to box it up and fly it back home to England with me - as I didn't have the heart to sell it.

'I've got a bike bag, you can have it!'

Moments later and we were making our way to his hotel where he would surprise me with virtually a brand-new bike bag. Which certainly made more sense than the plastic bag which I'd flown my vessel over in, but then a plastic bag I could throw away upon arrival to save weight, as opposed to a proper bag like this new one. This bag was a keeper. I told

Rufus that I'd send him a free copy of my book - if I ever wrote one.

'Of course you'll write one bro, I'll look forward to it,' he said, before we shook hands and said our farewells. What a bloody nice bloke.

Whilst chatting to Rufus, I'd had about four coffees and was getting a bit hyper, so I couldn't wait to hit the finish line. I surged on with my new bike bag strapped firmly to my rig. It felt a little heavier, but that didn't matter anymore, not much did.

As I crossed a bridge over the Tama River, I met a sign half way, 'Ota Ward, Tokyo.' I bulldozed across the invisible finish line and fist-bumped the air jubilantly, to the attention of a few strangers that chose to ignore the weird *gaijin*. The streets were as vibrant as I'd left them, each one undoubtedly with a thousand more stories to tell since our last meeting. It would take me another couple of hours to penetrate this vast, sweeping and extraordinary metropolis, before pulling up alongside the banks of the Sumida River in Asakusa, where it had all began.

Close by the Tokyo Skytree pricked the heavens above, as the Asahi Brewery's golden flame sat boldly atop its premises - looking like a massive Godzilla spermatozoa. An old boat chugged past almost idly, a flock of gulls chasing it. A smile would soon beam across my face and I'd be unable to prise it off for some days to come.

I'd just cycled from Tokyo to Tokyo. Now what?

STATS

Dates: 19/10/2014 –20/10/2014
Total miles traversed: 6,837 miles
Total time in the saddle: 685 hours and 10 minutes

EPILOGUE

As it all came to a close, I felt a little lost leaving the life that I had become accustomed to over the past several months on the road.

Apart from setting myself free from the womb back in the early 80's, this journey had been one of the most epic life challenges I have had to face. There had been an abundance of ups and downs, quite literally in every sense of the word. At times a bullet to the shin would have seemed far more appetising than cycling through the likes of the Japanese Alps; especially in: tropical storms, gale force winds, typhoons, rainy seasons, snow, freezing conditions, extreme humidity - and whatever other nasties the elements decided to throw my way. Mother Nature had been far from kind and She would often lead me to impolitely question my being, my purpose... my mind set. But it was in the mountains that I often found myself. They had been crafted by cantankerous fault lines which through the centuries have enabled an amazingly beautiful set of islands to be forged. A set of islands not only intrinsically clustered with natural beauty but also embedded deep with one of the most appealing and concrete of histories and cultures.

The Japanese are a people whose hospitality towards me had been second to none, as I made many new friends along the way. On a plethora of occasions I was touched by the kindness of a people who I am barely able to communicate with. Being the stranger at the dinner table was a frequent occurrence, but I was treated as if I were one of their own; like one of the family. I was inquisitively eyed by many, but rarely was it with contempt, merely curiosity; I guess it's not every day you witness somebody resembling that of a soliloquizing mental patient riding a bike with 30kg of absolute tripe attached to it - cycling directly up the side of a mountain. I'd feel inclined to throw rotten tomatoes at such a fool, but hey, that's just me!

I bore witness to the devastation caused by the 2011 Tōhoku Earthquake and its consequential tsunami. A scary, depressing post-apocalyptic landscape broken by Nature's wrath. Yet, I met local residents and survivors of the terrors of the sea that have suffered the ill fate of losing loved ones and had their own lives reduced to nothingness. But I also saw the strength and spirit it has taken them to pull together and rebuild their lives after the destruction and carnage which has blighted so many coastal towns for hundreds of miles.

How I managed to survive the roads without getting absolutely mullered by traffic or at least tumbling from my steed I shall never know. Fate? Karma? Blind luck? Fuck knows. Whichever it is I am thankful all the same, considering I half expected myself to be dead in a Fen ditch by 27.

The road was long and at times invariably hard, both physically and mentally. Yet there are no doubts that my journey along the way was littered with an almost limitless supply of experiences, ones which I hope will remain with me into my final days. I hold the warmest of memories when I think of my time in Japan. Going back through the notes in my diary - in order to write this book - allowed me to rekindle some great moments in my life of a truly beautiful and unforgettable country.

Sharing my story with you has been a huge privilege, thank you.

ACKNOWLEDGEMENTS

The road at times became an accommodating place to be, largely in thanks to its good-natured and charitable inhabitants: from the nameless strangers who bought me a coffee or gave me a carton of eggs, to the Couchsurfers that offered me a place to rest my nagging muscles and a refuge from the inclement climes. Your generosities will never be forgotten.

And, beyond Japan, the road to the completion of this book has been just as long and arduous as my days in the saddle. To the people and the drugs that have helped shape this literary journey: the Family, the TC, the Duncan's, the Rye's, the Smith, the Zingy-Twister, the Ricketts, the Hibbs, the Iida, the coffee, the beer and the donuts. Your encouragement, feedback, patience, advice, deliciousness and expertise in all shapes and forms have been immeasurable.

The next round's on me.

Printed in Poland
by Amazon Fulfillment
Poland Sp. z o.o., Wrocław